PRAISE FOR
Lives of American Women

"Finally! The majority of students—by which I mean women—will have the opportunity to read biographies of women from our nation's past. (Men can read them too, of course!) The Lives of American Women series features an eclectic collection of books, readily accessible to students who will be able to see the contributions of women in many fields over the course of our history. Long overdue, these books will be a valuable resource for teachers, students, and the public at large."

—COKIE ROBERTS,
author of *Founding Mothers* and *Ladies of Liberty*

"Just what any professor wants: books that will intrigue, inform, and fascinate students! These short, readable biographies of American women—specifically designed for classroom use—give instructors an appealing new option to assign to their history students."

—MARY BETH NORTON,
Mary Donlon Alger Professor of
American History, Cornell University

"For educators keen to include women in the American story, but hampered by the lack of thoughtful, concise scholarship, here comes Lives of American Women, embracing Abigail Adams's counsel to John—'remember the ladies.' And high time, too!"

—LESLEY S. HERRMANN,
Executive Director, The Gilder Lehrman
Institute of American History

"Students both in the general survey course and in specialized offerings like my course on U.S. women's history can get a great understanding of an era from a short biography. Learning a lot about a single but complex character really helps to deepen appreciation of what women's lives were like in the past."

—PATRICIA CLINE COHEN,
University of California, Santa Barbara

"Biographies are, indeed, back. Not only will students read them, biographies provide an easy way to demonstrate particularly important historical themes or ideas. . . . Undergraduate readers will be challenged to think more deeply about what it means to be a woman, citizen, and political actor. . . . I am eager to use this in my undergraduate survey and specialty course."

—JENNIFER THIGPEN,
Washington State University, Pullman

"These books are, above all, fascinating stories that will engage and inspire readers. They offer a glimpse into the lives of key women in history who either defied tradition or who successfully maneuvered in a man's world to make an impact. The stories of these vital contributors to American history deliver just the right formula for instructors looking to provide a more complicated and nuanced view of history."

—ROSANNE LICHATIN,
2005 Gilder Lehrman Preserve American
History Teacher of the Year

"The Lives of American Women authors raise all of the big issues I want my classes to confront—and deftly fold their arguments into riveting narratives that maintain students' excitement."

—WOODY HOLTON,
author of *Abigail Adams*

Lives of American Women

Carol Berkin, Series Editor

Westview Press is pleased to launch Lives of American Women. Selected and edited by renowned women's historian Carol Berkin, these brief, affordably priced biographies are designed for use in undergraduate courses. Rather than a comprehensive approach, each biography focuses instead on a particular aspect of a woman's life that is emblematic of her time or made her a pivotal figure in the era. The emphasis is on a "good read," featuring accessible writing and compelling narratives without sacrificing sound scholarship and academic integrity. Primary sources at the end of each biography reveal the subject's perspective in her own words. Study Questions and an Annotated Bibliography support the student reader.

Julia Lathrop

Social Service and Progressive Government

MIRIAM COHEN

Vassar College

LIVES OF AMERICAN WOMEN
Carol Berkin, Series Editor

WESTVIEW
PRESS

Westview Press was founded in 1975 in Boulder, Colorado, by notable publisher and intellectual Fred Praeger. Westview Press continues to publish scholarly titles and high-quality undergraduate- and graduate-level textbooks in core social science disciplines. With books developed, written, and edited with the needs of serious nonfiction readers, professors, and students in mind, Westview Press honors its long history of publishing books that matter.

Published by Westview Press,
An imprint of Perseus Books, LLC,
A subsidiary of Hachette Book Group, Inc.
2465 Central Avenue
Boulder, CO 80301
www.westviewpress.com

Every effort has been made to secure required permissions for all text, images, maps, and other art reprinted in this volume.

Westview Press books are available at special discounts for bulk purchases in the United States by corporations, institutions, and other organizations. For more information, please contact the Special Markets Department at 2300 Chestnut Street, Suite 200, Philadelphia, PA 19103, or call (800) 810-4145, ext. 5000, or e-mail special .markets@perseusbooks.com.

A CIP catalog record for the print version of this book is available from the Library of Congress

PB ISBN: 978-0-8133-4803-2
EBOOK ISBN: 978-0-8133-4804-9

10 9 8 7 6 5 4 3 2 1

This book is dedicated to my daughters, Julia Hanagan and Nora Hanagan. Their work on behalf of social justice inspires me every day.

CONTENTS

SERIES EDITOR'S FOREWORD

Beginning in the 1890s a group of determined Americans began to search for solutions to the problems of their newly industrialized nation. Rather than give in to pessimism, they decided to face the issues raised by mass immigration, urban poverty, shocking labor conditions, and the dangers to consumers caused by unregulated industries. These women and men were true activists; they did not simply protest—they proposed programs and policies that would improve the conditions they found unacceptable. No one more fully embodied the spirit of these reformers during the Progressive Era than Julia Lathrop. Lathrop devoted her life to child welfare, women's rights, educational reform, the creation of a juvenile justice system, the professionalization of social work, and the rights of immigrants—and in the process she became the first woman appointed to the Illinois State Board of Charities and the first woman to head a federal agency. Small wonder that when she died in 1932 she was remembered as "one of the most useful women in the whole country."

In telling the story of Lathrop's life and accomplishments, Miriam Cohen draws a vivid portrait of the Progressive Era and of the challenges female reformers faced as they entered the public sphere. Women like Lathrop, Jane Addams, Florence Kelley, and Lillian Wald were harshly criticized for undermining the traditional role of woman as wife and mother. To counter claims that they were "unwomanly," these women developed the concept of "maternalist politics," arguing that they were simply fulfilling their womanly duties in the larger arena of the community. But if maternalism allowed them to lobby for legislation, head up agencies, and expand women's higher education, it also diminished their use of a claim to equality as an individual right for all. As Cohen notes, today's American women would reject Lathrop's reliance on traditional gender roles to justify voting rights for women.

One of the many strengths of Cohen's book is that she resists any temptation to idealize Lathrop or the progressive women who were her allies. Although she clearly admires Julia Lathrop, she acknowledges that women reformers of the era shared with other privileged white women an often unthinking but damaging racism and social elitism. This can be seen, Cohen points out, in the suffragist argument that giving the vote to educated, native-born women would counterbalance the right to vote given to immigrant men.

In this carefully researched and gracefully written book Cohen has drawn a rich and complex portrait of a remarkable American woman. In the process she has provided a fresh look at the critical role that women like Julia Lathrop played in an era of progressive reform.

— Carol Berkin

ACKNOWLEDGMENTS

In 2001 the Vassar (Alumnae/i) Club of Chicago invited me to speak on some aspect of social reform in the Windy City. I talked about Julia Lathrop, Vassar Class of 1880, who was so important to the history of Chicago's Hull House. Already doing scholarship on the history of the welfare state, I was familiar with many of Lathrop's accomplishments on behalf of children. Preparing for the talk piqued my interest in this woman who contributed to so many social causes of her day. When Carol Berkin suggested I contribute to her Lives of American Women Series by writing about a woman of the Progressive Era, I eagerly proposed Lathrop. The first woman to head a federal agency, Lathrop appears in numerous scholarly works on women and social reform in the Progressive Era. Yet, except for Jane Addams's memoir about her Hull House friend, she has never been the subject of a book-long study. Carol agreed with my choice and has supported the project ever since. A fine historian and a wonderful writer, Carol's advice for improving the manuscript has been invaluable.

Many people have helped me during the time I have been working on Lathrop. Mary Pryor, the Rockford University archivist emeritus, acquainted me with the various aspects of the Julia Lathrop Papers. My wonderful colleagues in the Vassar College Department of History encouraged me along the way; the department's incomparable administrative assistant, Michelle Whalen, provided crucial help. Vassar College Dean of the Faculty office facilitated my work through research funds; I especially thank Dean of the Faculty Jonathan Chenette for his ongoing support. Recognizing Lathrop as a distinguished Vassar alumna, the college library, at the suggestion of former president Catherine Bond Hill, purchased a microfilm copy of the Julia Lathrop Papers to be housed in our own Special Collections. Thank you to Ronald Patkus, associate director of the libraries for Vassar's Special Collections; Laura Streett, archivist; and Dean Rogers, library specialist, who assisted me and my students as we mined the Lathrop papers and Vassar's own holdings on Lathrop. Thanks to Colton Johnson, Vassar College Historian, for his insights and suggestions.

The staffs of the Special Collections Research Center at the University of Chicago Library and the National Archives in Maryland made my work in both collections productive and pleasant. My trip to the archives in Chicago, my hometown, was special because my Aunt Daila Shefner provided me with food, shelter, and love. My dear friend Meryl Silver and her husband, Steven Korn, offered hospitality and so much more while I worked in Maryland.

My Vassar students are thoughtful and engaging; their discussions about women, the Progressive Era, and Julia Lathrop contributed to my own thinking. I was especially blessed to have outstanding student assistants. Adrienne Phelps first collected materials for me from the Vassar Collections. My Ford Fellow, Thomas Renjilian, located materials on Lathrop as I began the book project; our discussions about Lathrop helped me formulate my approach to this study. Rita Carr, Megan Feldmeier, Jessica Roden, and Michael Zajakowski Uhll have provided invaluable help locating materials, discussing the findings, and doing editorial work.

I have lectured on Lathrop over the years and benefited from the responses of Elisabeth Israels Perry and Robyn Muncy. Robyn Muncy generously shared Lathrop documents she had in her possession. Chad Fust taught me the whys and wherefores of the digital camera and how to organize digital documents. My Vassar colleagues Rebecca Edwards, James Merrell, and Quincy Mills offered critical advice on aspects of Lathrop's career. I thank Carol Berkin, Rebecca Edwards, Nora Hanagan, Laura Streett, James Merrell, Kathryn Kish Sklar, and anonymous readers for their comments on draft chapters that made this a better book. My friends Anne Constantinople, Eileen Leonard, Molly Shanley, Adelaide Villmoare, and Patricia Wallace have listened to me talk about Julia Lathrop a lot. I thank them for their support on this project and their help to me in so many other ways. It is a pleasure to work with Nikki Ioakimedes of Westview Press; enthusiastic about the book, responsive to my various questions along the way, and full of excellent ideas about how to improve the work, she has been a wonderful editor. I am also very grateful for the excellent work of Cisca Schreefel and her production staff at Westview.

My parents, Rebecca Slutsky Cohen and Martin A. Cohen, made their own contributions to bettering the lives of Chicagoans. My mother, a social worker trained at the University of Chicago, was inspired by Jane Addams, Julia Lathrop, and the Abbott sisters. My father, a labor economist and arbitrator, worked in a variety of organizations in the Hyde Park–Kenwood community where my brother, Dan, and I grew up. They are no longer with us, and, sadly, my brother did not live to see this project completed, but I believe they would be pleased about this book.

My husband, Michael Hanagan's, help, as always, has been critical. Despite the challenges he faces coping with Parkinson's disease, he supported this project through his enthusiasm, his many readings of draft chapters, and his unflagging confidence in the project. My daughters, Nora and Julia Hanagan, and their spouses, Melanie Priestman and Nate Verbiscar-Brown, are blessings in my life. They are generous, bright, and fun-loving adults. My fabulous granddaughter, Leah Dawson Hanagan, arrived while I was writing the book. My family reminds me of what Julia Lathrop knew—that all people want access to good health care and decent resources so that their loved ones can thrive, and all people should have it.

Introduction

When Julia Lathrop died in 1932 at the age of seventy-four, newspapers around the country carried the news, many with banner headlines. That the press would pay attention to her death was not surprising. In 1912, when President William Howard Taft appointed her as the first chief of the US Children's Bureau created to promote child welfare, Lathrop became the first woman to head a federal agency. Under her leadership the Bureau investigated infant mortality and child labor, provided advice on infant and childcare to women across the country, and successfully lobbied for federal legislation providing prenatal and early infant care.

A leading advocate for children and for women's rights, Lathrop began her career as a social reformer in the poor neighborhoods of Chicago but soon became active throughout Illinois. In 1893 Governor Peter Altgeld appointed her as the first woman on the State Board of Charities. As a member of the board, she conducted statewide investigations of the almshouses for the poor and the "insane" asylums and then pushed vigorously to upgrade the institutions and their staffs. In Chicago she also worked on behalf of immigrant protection and the establishment of America's first juvenile court system. If that were not enough, during her Chicago years she helped found one of America's first schools of social work. In 1922, after her retirement from the Children's Bureau, she became a leader in the Illinois and the National League of Women Voters; she also worked for the League of Nations on behalf of children's welfare around the world. Jane Addams, the most celebrated female reformer of her day, founder and director of Chicago's famous social settlement, Hull House, where Lathrop lived for two decades, hailed her close friend and colleague as "One of the most useful women in the whole country."[1]

In devoting her life to child welfare, women's rights, social research, and building the welfare state, Lathrop was part of a movement of American politicians, journalists, professionals, and volunteers who mobilized at the end of the nineteenth century to deal with a variety of social problems associated with industrialization. Woman activists like Lathrop, mainly from middling and prosperous social backgrounds, emphasized the special contribution that women could make in tackling these problems. With issues of public health and safety, child labor, and women working under dangerous conditions so prominent at the turn of the twentieth century, who better than women to address them?

Focusing on issues that appealed to women as wives and mothers and promoting the notion that women were particularly good at addressing such concerns, many female activists, including Lathrop, practiced what many women's historians call maternalist politics. According to historian Molly Ladd-Taylor, all maternalists believed there was "a uniquely feminine value system based on care and nurturance." They also believed that women across class and race were united "by their common capacity for motherhood and therefore shared a responsibility for all the world's children." By emphasizing that the traditional concerns associated with women as mothers belonged in the civic sphere, the maternalists collapsed the separation between the public world of work and politics and the private world of women and the family. All maternalists, however, did not embrace the same political perspective. Ladd-Taylor terms those maternalists active in the National Congress of Mothers (NCM) as "sentimental maternalists." These women believed that marriage and childrearing were the "highest calling" for every woman; the organization never supported suffrage.

Lathrop and her colleagues at Hull House and in the Children's Bureau also believed that women shared special characteristics as mothers or potential mothers. When Addams referred to Lathrop as one of America's "most useful" women rather than one of America's greatest women or most accomplished women, she reflected traditional notions about women as servants to others. Just as women had traditionally served their families, women had a special affinity for social service to the broader community as well. Not surprisingly, in praising Lathrop in life as well as at her death, people referred to her as a "great public servant."[2] Although famous men could also be termed great public servants, they enjoyed such acclamations as "great leaders" or "accomplished persons" much more often than women.

Historian Sonya Michel tells us that "the relationship between maternalism and feminism has . . . vexed feminist scholars from the outset." Even as Lathrop and her closest colleagues, first at Hull House and then at the Children's Bureau, made use of traditional notions of gender, they, unlike the sentimental maternalists, also pushed at its boundaries. These "progressive maternalists," to use Ladd-Taylor's term, were active suffragists and believed that women could legitimately choose between career and marriage. Female social reformers between 1890 and World War I created new spaces for themselves in local and then national government even before they had the right to vote. They carved out new opportunities for paid labor in professions like social work and public health. Moreover, the progressive maternalists believed "that while women had a natural affinity for issues that involved women and families, they insisted that their 'claim to authority' was based on 'professional expertise.'"

The progressive maternalists also stressed the special needs of poor women and children to build support for America's early social welfare state. In a country with a deep suspicion of strong government, these women appealed to society's sympathy for children in arguing on behalf of new social programs. As pragmatic activists, they adopted more than one strategy to achieve reforms. Like men, their politics were multifaceted and shaped by a variety of concerns. To achieve their ends, they worked with various reform coalitions and tailored their rhetoric to strengthen those coalitions. In promoting suffrage they often emphasized that the vote was necessary to address the problems of industrialization more generally as well as the special needs of women and children, but they also argued that women, as citizens, had the right to vote.

Other historians have termed these reformers "social justice feminists" because they prioritized the problems of poverty, sweated labor, and the growing inequality between the rich and poor while promoting an "expanded view of women's citizenship." Linda Gordon terms the women "social feminists" because of their belief in women's rights, including suffrage, and their commitment to social welfare. "Some of the social feminists called themselves feminist and some did not but all believed that women's [political] power was vital to improve the world."[3]

Lathrop's career, which involved leadership in so many facets of public life, illustrates how women worked both within the bounds of traditional norms about gender as well as pushed against them. A social reformer and a social scientist, she pushed for women's political rights and promoted women's education. Most especially she took on a new role in the federal government and used her power to provide professional jobs for other women as well. Throughout the book Lathrop and her close associates will be referred to as progressive maternalists or social feminists.

Lathrop's personal style also combined traditional traits of woman-hood with a style that was anything but traditionally feminine. Those who knew and worked with her often commented on her brilliance, her quick wit, the way in which she balanced her "ladylike Victorian persona," her poise, her tact—indeed her pragmatism—with a dogged determination.[4] When she retired from the Bureau in 1921 noted progressive journalist William Chenery wrote about Lathrop's "remarkable personality, her flash-ing irony and her human understanding. Few residents of Washington," he concluded, "are better liked. Even reactionary senators who did not under-stand what she was driving at and who had no taste for what they under-stood, count Miss Lathrop among their honored friends."[5]

Dr. Alice Hamilton, America's founder of industrial medicine, noted that her close friend from their Hull House days did not shrink from a fight, whereas "I have always hated conflict of any kind, . . . and would shirk unpleasantness." For Lathrop "harmony and peaceful relations with one's adversary were not in and of themselves of value, only if they went with a steady pushing of what one was trying to achieve." At times, Ham-ilton wrote, she "remembered Julia Lathrop and forced myself to say un-pleasant things which had to be said."

Lathrop's modesty also stood out for Hamilton, as it did for so many others. "When I try to describe Julia Lathrop the word that comes first to my mind is 'disinterested.' This is a rare quality . . . even in people who are devoting theirs lives to others. Julia Lathrop did not see herself as the cen-ter of what she was doing."[6]

Throughout her adult life Lathrop displayed what we might view as undue humility, even for that era, when much modesty was expected of women. But she also took well-deserved pride in her accomplishments. When, in 1944, Lathrop's brother William donated her personal papers to Rockford College, he included at least three honorary diplomas, four cita-tions from American colleges and the governments of Poland and Czecho-slovakia, one medal, and the scroll from President Taft appointing Julia Lathrop as chief of the Children's Bureau. Here we see Lathrop preserving important, material evidence of the public recognition bestowed upon her. Yet Lathrop hated to talk about herself and very much underestimated her achievements. In 1929, three years before her death, Lathrop, a graduate of Vassar College in 1880, filled out an alumnae questionnaire that was circulated to class members in preparation for her class's fiftieth reunion in 1930. Under "Occupational Record" she wrote, "For many years, at intervals a resident at Hull House." Under "Public Record," despite her role in leading so many organizations, she listed only that she was a "member of the Illinois State Board of Charities for about 13 years" and then "For nine years, Chief US Children's Bureau in the Dept. of Labor, a presidential appointment." Under "Literary Record," which asked her to list articles; papers, written or edited; and contributions to the press or to periodicals, this author of hundreds of Bureau publications, many social investigations, and popular and professional magazine articles wrote, "No literary record. I have of course in connection with work . . . written many brief articles. Few are preserved"—which, thankfully, is not true—"and few deserved to be preserved." Under "Other Creative or Productive Work" she answered only, "I have spoken much on the subjects in the social [work] with which I have been concerned."[7]

Lathrop's approach to her own accomplishments reflected her individual personality and the society's contradictory impulses about what constituted proper womanhood. Lathrop also held contradictory attitudes about class and race. Whether she was working in poor Chicago neighborhoods or as head of the Children's Bureau as she worked to improve the conditions for poor mothers across the country, Lathrop, like many of her friends and colleagues, sometimes showed elitism about what constitutes proper family life. These activists could be patronizing when it came to immigrants; their attitude toward African Americans and American Indians could be even more troubling, often steeped in assumptions about the superiority of all European cultures. But more so than most reformers of the day, Lathrop had an appreciation for the real problems faced by the poor, especially poor mothers. Convinced that poverty and inadequate services, not character defects, were responsible for disease, malnutrition, delinquency, and premature death among poor families, Lathrop worked throughout her life to prove it to others. Although her views about race were problematic, she was one of the few white reformers who spoke out throughout her career against racial discrimination, working with such civil rights leaders as W. E. B. Dubois and the National Association of Colored Women; in her later years she championed efforts to improve the lives of Native Americans.

The story of Julia Lathrop is the story of someone who, like all of us, is shaped by the historical context of her times but who also pushed successfully against some of its limitations.

Childhood and Education at Vassar: Old Traditions and New Paths

Born in 1858, the eldest of six children (one of whom died as a baby), Julia Clifford Lathrop grew up in Rockford, Illinois, a small town eighty miles northwest of Chicago. Lathrop came from well-established ancestors on both sides. In 1620 the Reverend John Lathrop, one of the founders of the "Independent" Church of England, known in the United States as the Congregationalists, was arrested and jailed. In the 1920s, when the nationally and internationally renowned Julia Lathrop was fighting against the growing intolerance of political dissent and immigration restriction, she used to joke that "her ancestors did not come in on the Mayflower because they were in jail at the time." Perhaps less often did she add that when the reverend objected to being placed in the common "clink" because it "was not suitable for a person of high degree, the justice of his plea was recognized" and he was moved to a gentlemen's prison.[1]

Lathrop's father, William, was born in Genesee County, New York, where his father had prospered as a farmer but then lost everything on a speculation that failed. In 1851 William settled in Rockford, where he established a lucrative and prominent law practice. As a trial lawyer, he practiced all over the state of Illinois. Lathrop would later recall that as a child she used to hear her father speak of suits in one town or another and wondered why he did not bring them home. William Lathrop was known as a hard worker with a great sense of humor. Lathrop's close friends believed she inherited her "quick and spontaneous" wit from him. She probably also took after her father in her ability to do public speaking almost extemporaneously, with few written notes.

In 1857 William Lathrop married Sarah Adeline Potter, known as Adeline, a member of a prominent and prosperous Rockford family. Born one year later, Julia was named for one of her father's sisters who died in childhood. Anna and then her three brothers, Edward, William, and Robert, known as "the little boys," followed Julia. While Julia was growing up the family employed one servant, and all the children were expected to do some chores. Nonetheless, once grown, Lathrop never showed any interest in housework; she could do plain sewing and crocheting, which also bored her. As for cooking, she was known only for her browned oysters and also made excellent omelets. Lathrop did have an interest in and a special eye for interior decoration that she carried to her residences in Chicago, to Washington, and, later, back to her own home in Rockford. As an adult she also cared a great deal about her dress; she enjoyed purchasing nice clothes, and her friends often remarked about her terrific attire. While living at Hull House, to protect herself on chilly afternoons, she would throw over her skirt and thin shirtwaist blouse a "mandarin coat of blue, embroidered inch-deep in vivid colorings and outlined in golden threads."[2]

Julia attended public school in Rockford; school reports noted that she was a good child and very bright. She was also "timid and shy" in those days, and her concern in adulthood that children be treated with respect and sympathetic understanding may have stemmed from her early school days. Once, when her teacher selected her because of good behavior for an errand that would require her to cross through the school, with its long corridors and stairs, she found herself too afraid to carry out the task, so she declined with a shake of her head. When, despite the teacher's urging, she would not change her mind, the instructor humiliated her by declaring aloud, "Julia Lathrop, you are as stubborn as a mule."

The shyness, however, did not seem to apply at home. The Lathrop family was very close-knit, spending a great deal of time together. Julia took on special responsibility to look out for her brothers, once interceding on behalf of one brother who was expelled from school for breaking a rule against snowball fighting. With a flair for drama, she often made up and then directed plays for the younger children; sometimes she could be a very stern. Apparently one brother once blurted out in frustration to his older sister, "You are not a mother to us as an older sister ought to be; you are a perfect stepmother to us." Years later Lathrop looked back on those experiences with her usual sense of humor. In the 1890s, when testifying at an Illinois hearing against child labor while she was living at Hull House, a hostile legislator challenged her expertise on the issue by asking this single woman, now in her thirties, how many children she had actually raised. "Without a moment of hesitation," Jane Addams, also present at the event, recalled, "with no suggestion of a retort but as if she were answering a commonplace question [Lathrop] replied, 'with a little help from my mother and father I have raised four.'"[3]

Lathrop remained close to her parents until their deaths and close to her siblings throughout her life. She visited her parents' home frequently during her years in Chicago; although her parents were no longer alive by the time she moved to Washington, Lathrop returned to the Rockford home to stay with her sister, Anna. The letters exchanged between Lathrop and her family throughout her adult life reveal their continual connections. During her many travels abroad—sometimes to study welfare services in other countries, sometimes for holiday, and often for both—she wrote numerous letters to her family and sent home various gifts. She received many letters from them as well, catching her up on news from home and expressing concern when she was ill. Family letters often discussed finances—including money that Lathrop had invested and controlled independently—reflecting their importance to her throughout her adult life, as Lathrop relied on these resources for her living or as a supplement to the money she earned.

Julia's relationship to Anna was especially important and remained so throughout her life. Anna, unlike her older sister, married and moved to Charles City, Iowa, but her husband died eight years later; in 1897 Anna Lathrop Case returned to Rockford and lived in the family home until after Julia's retirement from the Children's Bureau in 1921. The sisters then built a home for themselves in Rockford, living together until Julia's death in 1932. But long before that, Lathrop's "angel Ann" was her most significant companion. Anna joined Lathrop during her senior year at Vassar, and they often traveled together in the United States and abroad; Anna nursed Julia when she was sick, and during Julia's final decade, with the former Children's Bureau chief still traveling throughout the United States and the world, Anna tended their home. Lathrop doted on all of her sibling's children, saving numerous letters from her nephews and nieces who corresponded with their Aunt Julia as soon as they learned to write, but she was particularly close to Anna's daughter Bobbie.

The Lathrop family provided more than just good times and support for Julia; in her childhood home Lathrop first learned political and social attitudes that were ahead of their times for most white Americans. Julia's father once turned down the offer of a judgeship because he thought being a trial lawyer was more fun, but he did seek political office, serving one term in the Illinois legislature. An ardent Republican, he was one of forty-six who called for a meeting to organize the Party in northern Illinois in 1854.

Lathrop shared the experience of growing up in an abolitionist household with her close friends and famous reformers at Hull House, Jane Addams and Florence Kelley, who went on to become the head of the National Consumers League. In the nineteenth century, antislavery activists acted on their conviction that the "peculiar institution" was not compatible with republican democracy. The next generation of social reformers like Lathrop acted on their convictions that unbridled and unregulated industrial capitalism, which had taken hold by the end of the nineteenth century, was the greatest threat to democracy.

Although Julia was only seven years old when the Civil War ended, her father's activism exposed her to adults who were deeply engaged in pursuing social justice. The Lathrops and their political allies stood against the criticisms of those who vilified antislavery Republicans as radicals who threatened the social order. Illinois was deeply divided on the question of support for the antislavery cause. Although there were many supporters of antislavery in northern Illinois, in the days leading up to the Civil War many southern Illinois residents were fully prepared to secede from the union. Throughout her adult life Lathrop also fought for causes that were denounced as dangerously revolutionary. Even as she was pragmatic in picking some issues to push over others, she did not shrink from fighting for those aspects of the social welfare agenda she deemed most important.

If William Lathrop's radical Republicanism was unconventional, so too were his views on established religion. Julia's mother was quite religious; she came from an observant Congregationalist family and was herself active in the Second Congregationalist Church, but her husband was not a church member. While every other Potter household in Rockford engaged in family prayers, William Lathrop would have none of it, to his wife's regret. However, he did not always act on his personal views in public, a trait Julia would imitate later in her life. On the issue of religion, for the sake of his wife, William played the more traditional role as head of the family who sets an example; he attended church regularly, and the children were sent to Sunday school. Absorbing their father's attitude rather than their mother's when they became adults, none of the children became church members, at which point, according to Addams, "he whimsically declared that he would attend church no more for his painfully achieved example had been a failure."[4]

When it came to views on women's roles, Julia's parents were in accord. One of the first graduates of Rockford Seminary, Adeline combined a life devoted to domestic duties with an ongoing interest in literature and politics; she formed the Monday Club, a discussion group that focused on the important books of the day. She and William fervently believed in women's suffrage, a cause that Julia pursued as an adult; Adeline was an active member of the Universal Suffrage Association. Both parents encouraged all their children to express political opinions. William Lathrop employed Alta Hulett, Illinois's first woman lawyer, in his Rockford law office, and he helped draft the 1872 bill permitting women to be admitted to the Illinois Bar.

The Lathrops' belief in women's rights included education. After graduating Rockford High School, Lathrop first attended her mother's alma mater, Rockford Seminary, but then decided she would like to attend Vassar College. Since its founding after the Civil War Vassar had sought students from beyond the eastern seaboard. By the mid-1870s it had already established a national reputation as a pioneer institution, offering women the most advanced opportunities for education. In the middle of the nineteenth century teacher's seminaries like Rockford, which provided the chance for women to receive education beyond high school, already dotted the educational landscape on the East Coast and the Midwest. The expansion of teacher training since the 1820s took place in the context of the growing demand for mass education of white Americans in a land where the population was exploding and pushing west. With such a need for teachers, who better than women, the traditional nurturers in the family, to fulfill this new public role? This was a particularly attractive solution to the problem of staffing schools because women could be paid less than men. By midcentury a few of America's public universities in the Midwest admitted women, along with a small handful of private colleges, but the majority of women who gained an education beyond high school did so in the teachers' seminaries.

In time some of the teachers' seminaries, such as Mount Holyoke and Rockford, became full-fledged comprehensive colleges. In 1865 Vassar Female College (the name changed to Vassar College in 1867), located in the mid-Hudson Valley, New York, opened its doors to students, promising something new. Its founder, Matthew Vassar, was a prosperous Poughkeepsie brewer. Never married and with no children, by the time he was sixty his thoughts turned to what kind of monument he could establish to preserve his memory. With $400,000 and a group of twenty-eight trustees he had selected and despite the advice of his own nephews in business with him in Poughkeepsie, Vassar opened the first college to offer a liberal arts education for women that matched the most elite male schools. Admiring her ambition and her sense of independence, William was pleased and willing to let his "shy" daughter Julia travel almost one thousand miles to further her education.

When Lathrop arrived on the Vassar campus in the fall of 1877 she joined classmates who, like herself, came from prosperous families of businessmen or lawyers. Not only had she finished a year at Rockford Seminary to aid in her preparation for Vassar, but her family had also hired tutors in German and mathematics. Yet she entered Vassar as a sophomore feeling very unprepared. A look at her courses during her first year at Vassar might reveal why: they consisted of botany, composition (for both semesters), German (both semesters), ancient history, Latin, zoology, math, literary criticism, physical geography, and drawing. Her last two years, when students were provided with some freedom to choose a few of their courses, featured a similar set of classes, although Julia had dropped drawing and added philosophy. Such coursework was typical for this early generation of students. The curriculum's rigor reflected Matthew Vassar's desire to "accomplish for young women what our colleges are accomplishing for young men."[5]

Lathrop studied hard at her courses and graduated on time with her class. Hard work may have been one reason she often felt lonely, but it was probably not the most significant. By the 1870s forming friendships was an important aspect of college life for what was a growing number of college women, who now had the opportunity to pursue education away from home. Women often entered into very intense relationships with one another that they understood as crushes, or "smashes," referring to the fact that the pair seemed inseparable. Students exchanged flowers, special gifts, even locks of hair. College students, both male and female, took note of smashing but did not seem at all concerned that there was anything im-moral about it, perhaps because at the time proper young women were not viewed as sexual beings capable of passionate emotions. Nonetheless, some faculty members fretted that these liaisons were a distraction from the se-rious business of education, and administrators and others worried that such relationships, possibly involving physical intimacy, were unhealthy. Although we do not know whether Lathrop had such intense relationships with her Vassar classmates, it seems doubtful because she had difficulty making friends at Vassar. Many of her classmates in those days had en-tered Vassar through the college's own preparatory school. The prep school, housed on the campus, opened soon after the college's founding, when the faculty discovered that so many of the young women were ill-prepared to do the work expected of them. By the time Lathrop joined her class as a sophomore, friendships were already well formed. One of the older students, who was a close friend of Lathrop's in the years after Vassar, re-called that she was a "shy, retired young woman" at Vassar "who had no confidence in herself. . . . Julia Lathrop made no impression on her fellow students in college. The eastern girls were not particularly interested in a quiet girl from a middle-western town. . . . When she came back in 1905 for her twenty-fifth reunion of her class few remembered her."[6]

College life picked up for Lathrop during her senior year when her sis-ter, Anna, Vassar class of 1882, arrived on campus. Seniors usually roomed together in one section of the student living quarters and enjoyed certain privileges, but Julia was happy to live in the garret of the living quarters, where she and her sister could reside side by side. The college, sensitive to the charges that higher education was too taxing for women's delicate nature, mandated physical exercise for all students, reflecting the convic-tion that such activities would help maintain women's health. All Vassar students had to spend one hour a day doing some physical activity; unless the weather was truly terrible, they had to do it outside. Some students complained in letters home about their compulsory one-hour walks, but Lathrop embraced the task. As a senior she usually did them with her sister, arranging in advance so they could do this activity together, but she also walked with two students from Japan whom she befriended. Lathrop re-mained a walker throughout her adult life, going well beyond the one-hour requirement of her Vassar years. On Thanksgiving Day, 1919, Lathrop, then sixty-one, and chief of the Children's Bureau and living in Wash-ington, DC, walked three miles with her close friend and protégé Grace

Abbott to the new Army and Navy building to check on an International Labor Conference; they then dined on Chinese food with another friend before returning home to do some laundry and mending—"altogether a good six miles," she proudly reported to her sister—before attending a 5:30 Thanksgiving dinner at the home of another friend, followed by the theater![7]

If her physical stamina was honed at Vassar, Lathrop also learned something about strong and well-accomplished women from her teachers. She developed close relationships with several faculty members, in particular Vassar's beloved astronomer Maria Mitchell. In later life Lathrop was outspoken about what she and others saw as the shortcomings of the dry, classical curriculum that was the hallmark of college education for women of her generation. "Dry as dust," she once recalled about her ancient history course, "and without purpose. Nevertheless," she went on, "one got a splendid educational impulse from the stimulating personalities in Vassar then. . . . Maria Mitchell, Dr. Webster [the school doctor who taught physiology] and the other great teachers of the school knew thoroughly what they sought to impart was an inspiration, if the curriculum itself was not."[8]

The first professor hired to teach at the college when it opened, Mitchell was already internationally famous when she arrived with her father to take up residence in the Observatory, having discovered a comet in 1847 that was later named for her. Mitchell was devoted to her students, encouraging their pursuit of science. Mitchell shared with her students her many interests beyond her subject matter, influencing many more Vassar students beyond her own classes. More than one alumna recalled the guests Mitchell brought to campus, especially activists promoting women's rights, such as Elizabeth Cady Stanton, Lucy Stone, and Julia Ward Howe. Mitchell encouraged her guests not only to lecture on issues of the day but to mingle with students as well.

Although Lathrop might not have made much of an impression on her classmates while she was a Vassar student, clearly attendance at Vassar made an impression on her. She remained interested and involved in the college throughout her adult life. In the 1890s, in the midst of an economic collapse that placed extra responsibilities on all of the residents of Chicago's Hull House, Lathrop made time to lead a subcommittee on scholarships for the Chicago chapter of the Alumnae Association. While head of the Children's Bureau in Washington, she served for six years as the alumna representative on the Vassar Board of Trustees, where she worked on such issues as faculty empowerment and reform of the curriculum. Later, when the college erected a building to house some of the new educational programs Lathrop helped to implement, her alma mater honored her with an engraved stone tablet at the entrance of Blodgett Hall, saluting her accomplishments; it remains today. Julia and Anna both visited the campus many times for various events. In 1930 Lathrop was a featured speaker in Poughkeepsie at the fiftieth anniversary reunion of her own class of 1880.

Lathrop's attendance at Vassar during her formative years was an important prelude to a lifetime of navigating between traditional gender roles and pushing against them. By the late 1870s Vassar was no longer the only women's college offering a comprehensive liberal arts education—Wellesley and Smith opened their doors in 1875. At all of the women's colleges contradictory attitudes about gender were plentiful. On the one hand, Vassar boasted that its curricular offerings reflected the college's belief in women's unlimited intellectual capacities. On the other hand, early on, President Raymond, at the helm of the college when it opened until 1878, made it clear that if Vassar was to offer an education as excellent as that at Harvard and Yale, it was not necessarily to be the same. The curriculum he wrote was one "specifically appropriate to women," and the amount of work expected of the women would not be comparable to the expectations for men. With careful attention to the required courses in mathematics, science, and modern languages, Vassar also offered courses in flower gardening, and special care was taken outside the classroom to make sure students learned how to sew and take care of their homes.[9]

The rules and regulations dictating so much of college life in Lathrop's time reflected traditional assumptions about the proper environment for women students. In order to assure families that their daughters would be properly supervised, almost all college activities took place in one building. Students lived, took classes, ate, and even exercised during bad weather in the building; moreover, all faculty (an exception was made for the esteemed Miss Mitchell) and administrators originally lived in the building as well. Meal times, class times, and, during the earliest days, all recreational time, study time, and even silent time were scheduled and tightly enforced. Attendance at daily chapel was compulsory, and the students had relatively little free time until the weekends; yet even during the weekends students were required to attend chapel and to exercise. While Lathrop was at Vassar all students except seniors lived in residential halls supervised by corridor teachers who, in addition to assisting the professors in teaching, enforced rules but also comforted the women when they became homesick and tended to them a bit when they became ill.

The corridor teachers reported to the lady principal, the chief assistant to the president and, according to President John Raymond, the "immediate head of the Vassar family" who "takes charge of deportment, health, social connections, personal habits, and wants of the students."[10] A ten o'clock curfew was strictly enforced in the very earliest years, especially because of the very aggressive approach the then lady principal, Hannah Lyman, took when it came to all manner of rules. Each evening included a lecture from Miss Lyman about the misbehavior she had observed during the day.

The fact that the lady principal had to continually admonish students about breaking rules suggests that from the beginning the Vassar students, like their peers at other schools, found ways to enjoy some of the freedom that came with living among their peers and away from home. Rule breaking tightened friendships. Students wrote letters, usually to friends or siblings rather than parents, about sneaking into one another's rooms during study break or after curfew.

By the time Lathrop arrived at Vassar, Lyman was no longer the lady principal and most women were ignoring the ten o'clock curfew. And from the beginning students used what free time they had to form extracurricular organizations. They organized the Philaletheis (seeker of truth) Society in 1865, at first as a literary society that, in the 1870s, turned to drama. In the early days faculty members led the organization, but just three years into its history it was under student control. In 1868 the students who founded the first student government association informed President Raymond that they would elect a chair only after he left the room. Until the late 1880s the association could not act to affect college policies, but this was also true of male colleges that instituted student government at the same time. Some of the early student organizations, such as the Floral Society and the Society of Religious Inquiry, which encouraged Christian missionary work, were in keeping with traditional gender norms. But students defied President Raymond's intention that Vassar students not learn debating, which he saw as unsuitable for women, by organizing two debating societies. By Lathrop's time students were also putting out a yearbook and a literary magazine; they were holding celebrations on holidays such as Valentine's Day but also had developed celebrations for annual Vassar events, such as Founder's Day and commencement. In Lathrop's day riding had been discontinued as being too expensive. Bowing in this case to public opinion that it was too rough for women, baseball was also discontinued just before Lathrop arrived, but students participated in skating, toboganing, and lawn tennis, which were just gaining popularity. Students also could take off-campus trips into the town of Poughkeepsie or to visit family friends who lived in the region or professors who by then lived off campus. By contemporary standards such traveling privileges do not seem like much, but in the late 1870s "respectable women" rarely traveled unchaperoned; these activities stretched traditional views.

Vassar College was not only a place where women could test their intellectual and physical capabilities as never before; students also grappled with political issues. After the mid-1880s and until 1914, while President James Monroe Taylor was at the helm, students and faculty found it more difficult to bring controversial speakers to campus, but in the early days women's rights activists, including but not limited to Maria Mitchell's guest list, came to campus. Most Vassar students did not endorse women's suffrage until the early twentieth century, but the issue was openly debated on campus. Although they could not vote, Vassar students participated in mock elections during presidential election years.

Many Vassar graduates predicted that they would pursue a range of careers, including academia, medicine, archeology and astronomy, and social reform. But they also expressed concern that their high hopes for postgraduate careers might be dashed, given traditional expectations that women would marry and then retire from the public sphere. Certainly many Vassar graduates did not have plans for postcollege careers and were happy to use their education to enrich their lives as married women, but some who were planning to marry resented the notion that they had to choose between marriage and career. Moreover, in the late nineteenth century a high percentage of college-educated women never married; between 1865 and 1890 40 to 47 percent of the Vassar graduates remained single. The high rate of single women among the elite native-born population was a subject of much discussion at the turn of the twentieth century, with such luminaries as Theodore Roosevelt weighing in with concerns that not enough women of the old stock were having children while their inferiors among the foreign born were having many.

Beyond the lack of opportunities for postcollege careers, educated women of the day faced other problems. We can see this expressed in Lathrop's senior prophecy. In Lathrop's time fellow seniors delivered little prophecies, often witty, for each senior at the annual Class Day Exercise that took place the day before graduation. The prophecy for Julia was based on a scandal much in the news in the late 1870s concerning the criminal conviction of a Reverend Edward Cowley, superintendent of a New York City children's orphanage, the Shepherd's Fold, on charges of cruelty to the children. Here's an excerpt from the prophecy:

> Upon the conviction of the Rev. Mr. Cowley, the field lay open for Julia Lathrop. In the Shepherd's Fold she at last found children who were actually . . . destitute enough for her longing. She did not send them to [public] school as her illustrious predecessor had done, but she educated them herself, teaching first in the realm of Moral Philosophy and afterward in the more advanced branches. From their little Primers, she regaled them with theories on freedom of the will.[11]

The elitist tone aside, the prophecy is useful because, first, it indicates that already Lathrop's classmates knew about her deep commitment to poor children. But the prophecy addressed, in fun, another issue: the irrelevance of her Vassar education for the kind of social service work Lathrop wanted to do. It was that problem—how to make advanced education for women relevant, especially for those women interested in social reform— that was to motivate Lathrop's later suggestions for changing women's education, including the curriculum at Vassar.

Lathrop returned to Rockford after graduation to face the problem of so many of her generation—what to do now if one did not wish to pursue that most obvious of careers: marriage and motherhood. It would be another decade before she would find an answer, one that would take her to Chicago and Jane Addams's Hull House.

2

"J. Lathrop's Here!" Single Womanhood and a New Life at Hull House

Julia Lathrop returned to the family home after graduation without a clear idea of what she wanted to do with her life. Her choices for the next ten years reflected the limited options available to women, but she stretched the boundaries of what was considered acceptable work for women. For a while Lathrop did administrative work at Rockford College; she never pursued the most common occupation for educated women of her day—teaching; instead, she found work in another job available to women: she became a secretary in her father's law office. In the second half of the nineteenth century office work expanded as new forms of management emerged along with the expansion of American industries. Business expansion generated more jobs for men in law and insurance as well as sales. As office work expanded, so too did the need for office assistants; by the end of the nineteenth century the vast majority of office assistant jobs was women's work.

Office employment required literacy and some mathematics; by the early decades of the twentieth century women were preparing for the jobs by attending commercial schools or high schools. Lathrop was far more educated than most office assistants. She first took on writing tasks for her father, as he disliked the work. Soon thereafter stenography—the process of taking notes in shorthand—and the typewriter became fixtures in American offices, including William Lathrop's. With these advances Lathrop could now use her newly found free time to "read" law, as it was known in those days. Before the 1890s, when the American Bar Association began limiting entrance to the profession, it was possible—in fact, most common—to practice law without attending law school; instead, one learned the law through an apprenticeship with an experienced attorney, such as Mr. Lathrop. She worked at the Lathrop firm intermittently in the 1880s and made some money working two other jobs. She was a secretary for two companies founded by inventors in Rockford—one manufactured the lemon juice extractor, and the other produced the first air brush. Julia Lathrop invested in both companies, and her work made money for the stockholders and for herself. "Shrewd and careful in business," Jane Addams notes, Lathrop "enjoyed the sense of independence that her own income gave her."[1]

Lathrop probably spent little of her income for recreation in those days. Jane Addams tells us Lathrop's father "did not understand the need for a definitely arranged playtime." The family spent summers in Rockford; besides taking part in the family hobby of reading, Lathrop took drives and, in the winter, skated.[2]

During the winter of 1888–1889, in a life-changing moment, Lathrop attended a speech in Rockford given by Jane Addams, who along with her friend Ellen Gates Starr, was traveling to publicize their new initiative just underway—the founding of Chicago's Hull House. Starr and Addams were no strangers to the town; they had become friends attending Rockford College together. Lathrop had known Addams a bit already; some years earlier, while Addams was in school, she and her classmates implored Lathrop, a recent Vassar graduate with somewhat of a reputation for drama, to help them with a scene from *Macbeth*. Addams later recalled that she and her classmates "greatly admired this brilliant young woman [two years older than Addams], from a real women's college, carrying her honors with such a quick wit and disarming charm."[3]

This time, after hearing Addams speak on the subject of social settlements, Lathrop came away with admiration for Addams. The settlement movement was part of a larger mobilization of activists at the end of the nineteenth century, both women and men, who were concerned about a variety of social problems associated with the spread of industrial capitalism. Advocates of change, progressives did not always value the same reforms nor did they always agree on the nature of the problems, but as part of the progressive movement, their concerns shared some basic characteristics. Historian Daniel Rodgers argues that progressives drew on three "distinct clusters of ideas." One was the deep distrust of growing corporate monopoly; the second involved the increasing conviction that in order to progress as a society, the commitment to individualism had to be tempered with an appreciation of our social bonds. Progressives also believed that modern techniques of social planning and efficiency would offer solutions to the social problems at hand. Their ideas did not add up to a coherent ideology, but as Rodgers notes, "They tended to focus discontent on unregulated individual power."[4] As the nineteenth century closed, periodic economic downturns served as wake-up calls to the dangers of relying solely on the workings of the free market to ensure the general prosperity.

Women were especially prominent in a number of progressive efforts. At a time when the social problems of working-class families were so high on the national agenda, women activists emphasized the special contribution they could make in tackling these problems. Many historians refer to the women who focused on social problems of special interest to women as wives and mothers as maternalists. Lathrop, Addams, and their closest allies are examples of what Ladd-Taylor has termed "progressive maternalists." In emphasizing women's special ability to address some of the critical problems of the day, they stretched the boundaries of acceptable behavior for women. The progressive maternalists carved out new professional opportunities and created new spaces for women in government, and they pushed for women's suffrage. Like most political activists, these women adopted more than one strategy to achieve reforms; they did not always emphasize women's special role as mothers. Emphasizing maternalist concerns was one strategy they used to help build public support for important social welfare initiatives.

The women of the Progressive Era were not the first generation to engage in the social problems of their day. Since the antebellum era middle-class white and black women engaged in various forms of civic activity related to the social and moral welfare of those less fortunate. Temperance, abolition, and moral reform activities dominated women's politics before the Civil War. By the 1870s women were broadening their influence, working in national organizations such as the Woman's Christian Temperance Union (WCTU) and the Young Women's Christian Association (YWCA), which helped single women in America's cities. During the Progressive Era a moral-reform agenda motivated many women, who intensified their activities on behalf of a national ban on alcohol and against prostitution.

After 1890 the issues surrounding social welfare took on greater urgency. The depression of 1893 along with the increasing concerns about industrialization—the growing slums across American cities, the influx of new immigrants from southern and eastern Europe, the increase in labor strife—contributed to that sense of urgency. Within a decade vast networks of middle-class and wealthy women were energetically addressing how these social problems affected women and children. Responding to the problems associated with urban industrial life, American reformers looked to their counterparts in Europe who were struggling with similar issues.

One such initiative was Toynbee Hall, an institution named to honor the recently deceased social reformer Arnold Toynbee. Established in London's poverty-stricken East End in 1885, Toynbee Hall was the first settlement, in this case, of university men who lived among the poor in order to learn about and promote remedies for the social conditions facing the community. Although Addams had already contemplated establishing a settlement house by the time she and Starr visited Toynbee Hall in 1888, they were inspired by the efforts of its residents to reach across the class divide. In 1889, using Addams's considerable inheritance from her father— about $1.3 million in today's buying power—the two women cofounded what was to become America's most famous social settlement, Hull House on Halsted Street in Chicago's Nineteenth Ward.

The settlement house movement soon took hold throughout the United States. Many were affiliated with Protestant churches; some relied on the support of colleges. Others, including Hull House, depended on private donations. Located in urban, poor, often immigrant communities, the houses were residences for young middle-class and prosperous women and some men who wished not merely to minister to the poor and then go home but to live among them, to learn about social problems directly from those who were experiencing them, and to participate with their neighbors in bettering their communities. Addams and Starr had acquired the Hull mansion (named for Charles Hull, who built the home in 1856) in 1888, and after refurbishing it and hiring a housekeeper, they were now looking for other residents; in particular, they were looking for college-educated women. In the early years Addams used her speaking engagements to recruit people to Hull House.

Although we have no record of the Rockford presentation, Addams preserved other versions of her early recruitment speech. The struggle for democracy that had begun in the eighteenth century in Europe (and in the United States) had focused on the ballot, on the assumption that "the franchise would secure to all men dignity and a share in the results of civilization." Addams told her audiences that now we all must make democracy social—that is, we must ensure that social conditions allow for all to share in the fruits of modern society. Those of us, she continued, who are able to participate in civic affairs, who have the chance for leisure and are educated, are "unmindful of the commonweal" because the rich and the poor live far apart in every large town and city. Staying away from the poor and then, in ignorance of the true conditions, blaming the poor for their own misfortune, as wealthier Americans tended to do, is the great paradox. The answer is to end the separation between the rich and the poor. Those who are more prosperous "need the thrust in the side, the lateral pressure, which [like settlement house residents] comes from living next door to poverty."

Addams also argued that settlement house work offered privileged, educated, young people an important outlet for their pent-up desires to do good. Young girls, she pointed out, feel cut off from a meaningful life most in the early years after school; although she has freedom from care, she, for the most part, feels miserably useless. "The desire for action, the wish to right wrong, and alleviate suffering haunt young women daily. We smile at it instead of making it of use to society." Addams was offering new recruits such as Lathrop a chance to be of use and a new idea of what she might do with her life. Addams established Hull House to remedy this sense of uselessness so "young women who had been given over too exclusively to study might restore a balance of activity" and "learn of life from life itself: where they might try out some of the things they had been taught and put truth to the ultimate test of the conduct it inspires."[5]

Addams wrote about her personal "maladjustment" during her post-college years and her feelings of uselessness; it was this sense of despair that led her to her larger critique of higher education. As a prominent activist first in Chicago and then on the national stage, Lathrop also critiqued traditional education, particularly for women. But unlike Addams, she never spoke—at least to her close friends, let alone to a wider audience—about any personal despair she might have felt during those first ten years after college. Her quick response to Addams's invitation to visit her at Hull House suggests that Lathrop had high hopes that settlement house work would be a positive alternative to her current life in Rockford. Although her father expressed reservations about the settlement house idea (we have no record of her mother's wishes), he did not object when Lathrop joined Addams and Starr at Hull House. However, in keeping with her somewhat cautious approach to new endeavors and possibly in accordance with

Addams's expectation that potential residents undergo a probationary period, Lathrop decided to try out the possibility of settlement house work through a number of long-term visits to Hull House. Beginning in 1890 Lathrop commuted between Hull House and her family home in Rockford before taking up permanent residence approximately two years later.

If Lathrop was looking for destitute children to help, as her Vassar class prophecy suggested, she found them in her new Chicago neighborhood. Chicago's Nineteenth Ward, located on the near West side, housed approximately fifty thousand people representing eighteen nationalities. Dominated by Bohemians (today, we would refer to them as Czechs), Italians, and Russian and Polish Jews, this back-of-the-stockyards neighborhood—indeed, the stockyards employed many of the residents—contained dirty streets and overcrowded wooden houses with inadequate and unsanitary water supplies. Instead of school, many children spent their days in sweated factory labor, hawking goods, or roaming the streets.

Within the first few years of its establishment Hull House residents were hard at work getting to know their neighbors, providing kindergarten classes for neighborhood children, extending relief to destitute families, and working with labor organizations to improve the conditions of labor in the factory and sweatshops of the neighborhood.

Living alongside their poor neighbors did not mean the educated, upper-middle-class women of Hull House or the residents of the other American settlements actually lived with them under the same roof. Although the residents disdained a life of materialism associated with many elite American women, they nonetheless embraced a version of gracious living that echoed their own upbringing. "Life was simple," Dr. Alice Hamilton, a resident and close friend of Lathrop, recalled in her autobiography, "as far as luxuries went, but it was full of beauty."[6] The home featured marble fireplaces, French windows, and a long, paneled dining room. Addams used some of the Victorian furnishings from her family home but, in keeping with progressive impulses of the time, also embraced the designs of John Ruskin and William Morris, which emphasized a new simplicity, functionality, and an appreciation of the artisanal craft. The dining room featured a sixteen-foot table, chandeliers of Spanish wrought iron, and an attractive rug. Lathrop's room, like that of the other residents, contained only a few furnishings—a bed, bureau, bookcase, two chairs, and a desk. With her good eye for home decoration, she likely adorned the room with pictures and small items from the family home. During the early years residents had rotating responsibilities for some household chores and for serving communal meals, though the settlement always employed a full-time cook. Eventually a paid staff took on most of the household work. Like other prosperous Americans, the settlement house residents escaped the heat of the big city in the summer months, vacationing in such places as Bar Harbor Maine or by the shores of Lake Michigan.

But if it seemed an upper-middle-class home, the lifestyle the settlement house women carved out for themselves challenged middle-class notions of gender. Traditionally women who remained unmarried were expected to live with relatives, but Hull House provided the women an opportunity to live among close friends. In the words of historian Kathryn Kish Sklar, the residents "joined a small cohort who were reconstructing their gender identity by refusing to replicate their class identity through marriage."[7]

By the early twentieth century American settlements were, "in contrast to England, conspicuously feminine organizations." Men comprised only about one-fourth of the residents, with many coming from the ranks of the clergy. Hull House provides an example of this female-dominated space. In Britain, according to Sklar, with its longer history of government programs on behalf of social welfare, settlement houses were "training grounds for reform-minded" young men who would later join government as civil servants. In the United States at the time men gained access to government jobs largely through party patronage rather than training in social service. Lathrop would attack the patronage system throughout her career. In the meantime, with settlement houses not operating as entrees to government jobs in the United States, women could dominate the space.[8]

In the early years, along with Addams, Starr, and Lathrop, the core of the Hull House community included Florence Kelley, who arrived at the settlement house soon after Lathrop. By that time Kelley was already known for her involvement in social reform and her translation of the renowned German socialist Frederic Engle's writings. At Hull House she soon became an agent for the Illinois Bureau of Labor Statistics and then Illinois's first state factory investigator. In 1899 she moved to New York to become head of the National Consumers League, an organization devoted to eradicating sweated labor conditions through consumer boycotts and state and federal law. Lathrop, Addams, and Kelley were approximately the same age—about thirty—when they joined Hull House. They had come from families who had been involved in the antislavery cause; they were all well educated and single. When Kelley divorced her husband she was the mother of three children; she raised them with the help of her Hull House companions as well as her friends Henry Demarest Lloyd and Jesse Lloyd. As Sklar writes, the three women, having spent nearly a decade trying to find satisfying work, now found that "what others could not provide for them, they could supply to one another . . . a livelihood, contact with the real world, and a chance to change it." In 1897 Dr. Alice Hamilton, later the great expert on occupational diseases, joined the core group of women who were not only colleagues but also close friends.

Like colleges, settlement houses provided the space and opportunity for close and sometimes intimate partnerships among educated women. At the turn of the century, before the popularization of Freudian psychology, educated Westerners did not believe sexual desire was a meaningful part of women's lives—at least not proper women. Many women entered into life-long partnerships, known as "Boston marriages." Jane Addams, for example, had an intense personal relationship with Ellen Gates Starr since their college days. That relationship cooled in the last decade of the nineteenth century as Addams entered a lifelong partnership with Chicago widow and Hull House benefactor Mary Rozet Smith. By the end of the decade they had purchased a summer home together in Bar Harbor, Maine. In the twenty-first century we might well term the relationship between Addams and Smith as lesbian, but as Sklar argues, the term seems anachronistic for the era; because we do not have direct evidence of a sexual relationship, she uses the term "homoerotic" to describe the partnership.[9]

Members of their social and political circles, both female and male, did not condemn Boston marriages; it was not until the 1920s that psychologists and others openly characterized women in such relationships as deviant. It is quite possible, as the historian Estelle Freedman has written, that throughout the early decades of the twentieth century middle-class and prosperous women distinguished between their own woman-centered relationships and those considered to be "homosexual perversions"—that is, relationships based on women pursuing other women for sex, which many people associated with the working class.[10]

Lathrop, Addams, Kelley, and Hamilton were peers and colleagues as they did battle for social justice as well as dear friends, often providing the love and support of close sisters. In Lathrop's case, her widowed sister, Anna, was her closest companion. All during the years when she resided at Hull House and in Washington Lathrop frequently spent time with her sister in Rockford, and they often traveled together. After she retired from the Children's Bureau, Lathrop lived with Anna in a house they built together in Rockford.

Hull House friends addressed one another with terms that reflected closeness and a respect for women who had broken out of Victorian conventions. At Vassar Lathrop was called "Miss Lathrop." All the women used this proper form of address, even close friends, an approach that struck her as rather formal compared to the conventions of Rockford where she was known as Julia. At Hull House Addams conferred upon her the name "J. Lathrop," which the others took up as well. In turn Addams was J.A. to her closest friends and sometimes was referred to as "Lady Jane." Kelley became Sister Kelley; sometimes Lathrop addressed her as F. Kelley. In some of their quick letters to each other about one or another political development that needed to be communicated or about advice sought, they might refer to someone only by their last name: "Kelley and I had a friendly talk with Richmond."[11]

With Addams setting the tone, the atmosphere among these close friends shed the sentimentality associated with women; indeed, as Sklar notes, "The emotional landscape at Hull House was more reserved than intimate."[12] Their letters, however, like the correspondence of many women at the time, often revealed the strong affection they had for one another; Kelley's letters to Lathrop many times began with "Dearest J. Lathrop" and ended with such salutations as "Your devoted FK."

The friendships, though not sentimental, were warm and filled with good humor and good times. Kelley and Lathrop became good friends soon after Kelley's arrival in 1891. Kelley's personality was nothing like her friend's from Rockford. If Lathrop was patient and deliberate, considered the diplomat, Kelley was much more the zealous fighter with a fiery tongue. The two women were known for their many riveting conversations, often debates, about one or another issue of the day. Often their disagreements reflected their very different temperaments and divergent approaches to social reform. Thus, for example, at the turn of the twentieth century they disagreed about the unwillingness of the US Supreme Court to sustain the constitutionality of legislation regulating working hours and wages, with Kelley dismissing all concerns that the Court expressed about following precedents and Lathrop contending that the courts could only go slowly in changing their approach, gradually broadening the power of government to regulate the workplace.

But if Lathrop was a diplomat, she was also determined and, like Kelley, pursued her side of any issue with logic. One reason they were such good friends was because both appreciated good humor, though each practiced it differently. Addams's nephew, James Weber Linn, who spent some of his youth at Hull House, wrote that "one flashed, the other scorched. When both were at Hull House together, arguing some problem or correcting a social injustice, . . . it is doubtful if any better talk was to be heard anywhere." High-ranking politicians, philosophers, labor leaders, or neighbors of the Nineteenth Ward eagerly listened at dinner to the "odd half-reluctant meandering sentences of Miss Lathrop, with their often marvelous Mark Twain–like twists into high philosophy or sudden nonsense at the close, and to the interrupting thrusts or quick, close and yet sweeping logic of Mrs. Kelley and were glad to be there."[13]

Lathrop's sense of humor was an endless source of entertainment for her Hull House friends. "Her brown eyes so sincere, but with a sparkle lurking in them [and] her slow redolent voice with a flavor of Illinois, gave her a richness which was valued by colleagues who had less vitality." She often amused her friends with stories gathered during her many trips throughout the state of Illinois as a member of the State Board of Charities. Lathrop saw the humor in so many aspects of her work as a social reformer because, according to one Hull House resident, "she had a roguish sense of the tragic comedy of American politics. You felt she enjoyed the game . . . without losing sight of the big end she had in view."[14]

Sometimes Lathrop used her humor to poke fun at Victorian conventions. Addams recalled "an early incident at Hull House when an old friend [of Lathrop's] brought a parrot as a present to our then new day nursery." The friend detailed his many virtues and ended with a boast that he knew not one single swear word. To Addams' astonishment, Lathrop said, "That lack of education was soon to be rectified in our nursery." Later, Lathrop noted, "[I]t was stupid to impute virtue to a heathen bird whose ugly beak was obviously fashioned for the most outrageous oaths." At other times Lathrop's humor served to strip away pretensions of the well educated. On the eve of her appointment to the Children's Bureau she was interviewed for a special profile in a Chicago newspaper. Not surprisingly she was asked what her favorite reading was. "Trash—late at night!" was the reply. "I wish there was more of it . . . and that it all turned out well—that all books had large print and a good ending."[15] It is not hard to imagine that when Lathrop returned to Hull House from her many trips either to Rockford or to

Illinois charitable institutions downstate, "one of the clearest and fondest recollections of [Hull House residents] . . . is of coming in at the end of some day's work and being met in the hallway with the cry, 'J. Lathrop's here!' It was as if their weariness fell from them at the news."[16]

If the Hull House women fashioned a lifestyle that combined traditions with innovations, so too did they embark on work that combined elements of older approaches to aiding the poor with new endeavors. Early on the residents instituted a variety of adult enrichment programs, including lectures, concerts, and education clubs. Lathrop started the Plato Club, a weekly gathering of neighbors, residents, and distinguished local professors such as University of Chicago philosopher John Dewey for discussions of the *Dialogues*. Thinking about Lathrop teaching Plato to the poor residents of the Nineteenth Ward, one might be reminded of the tongue-in-cheek Vassar prophecy that Lathrop would someday teach the classics to poverty-stricken orphans. Was the Plato Club an elitist project in which Hull House residents tried to bring "high culture," traditionally defined as European high culture, to the masses? If so, how was this in any way a departure from rather traditional approaches of wealthier women trying to "uplift" the poor? Certainly there are echoes of long-established methods. But to dismiss this as continuation of something old is to miss the political and social ferment of the times that motivated the activists. "Access to high culture was enthusiastically sought by the workers themselves, who occasionally extended the two-hour Sunday sessions, which were to end at six o'clock, to ten o'clock."[17] Inspired by Toynbee Hall's commitment to working-class education, Hull House residents instituted discussion groups on subjects such as Greek philosophy, painting, literature, French, and even Latin and Greek because they believed that making democracy social meant providing opportunities for all adults, not just the privileged and the professional, to participate in the life of the mind. Reflecting innovative ideas about education that Dewey pioneered, Hull House courses did not replicate traditional classes, with students sitting passively, expected to absorb the information imparted to them by the "expert"; rather, Lathrop and the other teachers encouraged the students to participate in a joint enterprise where all discussed, analyzed, and argued about the texts they were studying.

Moreover, Hull House did not confine its studies to traditional subjects. Early on Hull House instituted the Working People's Social Science Club, scheduled on Wednesday evenings at eight so that workers on the day shift could come. Workers, labor activists, socialists, anarchists, young professionals, and women interested in social reform attended lectures on such subjects as trade unionism, socialism, unemployment, and "the Negro problem," often with Florence Kelley presiding. Addams believed that the club was the source of Hull House's reputation for radicalism. For Lathrop the discussions at the club were the inevitable result of the residents' desire to understand the root causes of poverty. "Welcoming every point of view," Lathrop told the audience of the National Conference of Charities and Corrections in 1896 in her speech on "What the Settlement Work Stands For," "the settlement stands for a free platform. It offers its best hospitality to every man's honest thought."[18]

At Hull House the progressive maternalists were literally working to break down the barriers between the so-called private world of the family home and the outside society. To examine the internals of Hull House, Shannon Jackson writes, "is to see the spaces of public and private redefined in several directions and on different scales." This was a "space of everyday life that was intriguingly unsettled, with doors opening, bells ringing and chairs moving as the push and pull of settlement practice dictated." Early activities at Hull House reflected the residents' special concerns about the circumstances of poor immigrant women and their children. Working mothers dropped their children off at the nursery and kindergarten before heading off to factories. The Hull House Women's Club provided information on health, including contraception, for neighborhood women.[19]

Lathrop was particularly interested in the new field of domestic science. At Vassar she had heard of the pioneering work of Ellen Swallow Richards, also a Vassar alumna, who, after graduating in 1870, went on to earn degrees in science from MIT, where she was the first woman to be admitted, although as a special student. Richards later directed a laboratory at MIT where she, along with other women scientists, used the innovations in modern chemistry to promote safer American homes, including work on steam heating and cooking. Richards's work went well beyond traditional housekeeping improvement; she and her Boston colleagues were practicing early ecology, producing pioneering studies of water pollution and water purification, and studying the effects of air quality and poor nutrition. Along with Mary Hinman Abel, Richards opened the New England Kitchen in 1890 to serve take-out meals for the urban wage earners and to provide hot lunches to Boston schoolchildren. Lathrop spent a few months training with Richards and Abel in Boston in the early 1890s and returned home to open in 1893 a public kitchen at Hull House with a take-out section for workers to pick up food and a restaurant section designed to attract residents of the Nineteenth Ward.

Efforts to "improve" the eating habits of the neighborhood were problematic from the beginning. Immigrant Americans who sampled the fare were less than enamored with recipes that were variations on standard Anglo-American food such as codfish balls and mutton stew. Lathrop and the others who ran the restaurant soon renamed it "The Coffeehouse." They wanted to offer an alternative to the saloon for working-class men. But the potential male customers were reluctant to patronize an establishment that—unlike the saloon, which provided space for men to congregate—now served men, women, and children. Most problematic for the neighbors was the fact that no liquor was served. Many reformers, including Lathrop, thought drinking was a problem for the working class, draining away family funds and contributing to domestic violence; for the residents of the Nineteenth Ward, eliminating alcohol in a public place for eating made the Hull House enterprise a decidedly unattractive place to dine. The Coffeehouse decor, which had been designed to evoke the rustic images the residents associated with the lives of immigrants in their native countries, actually appeared as a rather somber space. Lathrop herself told the Hull House architects that in seeking to provide a wholesome alternative to the "base saloon" they had produced "a crypt . . . inducing reflections so somber as to inhibit indulgence in our proffered ginger-ale and grape juice."[20]

The public kitchen movement never caught on at Hull House—or elsewhere. The Coffeehouse soon became not a space for industrial workers and their families but rather a a gathering place for schoolteachers at the local schools and businessmen connected with local factories. As Addams herself noted, "The experience of the coffee house taught us not to hold to preconceived ideas of what the neighborhood ought to have, but to keep ourselves in readiness to modify and adopt our undertaking as we discovered those things which the neighborhood was ready to accept." Addams spoke many times and published widely on her philosophy of the settlement house as an experimental enterprise. One of the most important statements came at a conference of applied ethics in Plymouth, Massachusetts, that took place in the summer of 1892, which Addams attended along with Lathrop. "The only thing to be dreaded in the Settlement is that it lose its flexibility, its power of quick adaptation, its readiness to change its methods as its environment may demand. . . . Its residents must be emptied of all conceit of opinion and all self-assertion, and ready to arouse and interpret the public opinion of their neighborhood." Like her friend and Hull House teacher John Dewey, who was just beginning to articulate his views associated with the philosophy of pragmatism, Addams was setting forth a philosophy rooted in engagement and adaption to one's environment. One's ideals and values must be understood not as timeless but in light of the particular social historical context.

As she felt her way toward suitable activities as a resident of Hull House, Lathrop embraced a similar guiding principle. She told an audience in 1896, "As an acquaintance between the residents and the settlement and the neighborhood grows, and the character of its need becomes more evident, the sort of work undertaken depends upon the ability of the settlement to furnish from its residents or its friends people to undertake the work."[21]

Once she saw "the needs" of the neighborhood, Lathrop was fearless in responding, especially if she believed an emergency was at hand and no one else was providing aid. In fact, it was Lathrop who encouraged Addams to adapt a pragmatic approach to their work. In the beginning Addams often insisted that settlement house workers tread carefully before acting, lest they proceed without adequate training. But sometimes the situation at hand required action. On one occasion during Lathrop's early days she and Addams assisted a young unmarried woman in labor who was giving birth in a neighborhood tenement; at the moment no family, neighbors, midwife, or doctor could or would come to her aid. Afterward, when Addams forcefully told Lathrop they really had gone too far in doing things "we don't know how to do," Lathrop replied, "If we have to begin to hew the line of our ignorance, don't let us begin at the humanitarian end. To refuse to respond to a poor girl in the throes of childbirth would be a disgrace to us for evermore."

At the Plymouth conference Lathrop saw that Addams had now worked out cogent and articulate views about the experimental nature of the settlement house. Lathrop argued to her friend that now was the time, just as the settlement house movement was taking off, to get across the notion that despite the inevitable failures or half-successes, reformers ought not let the perfect be the enemy of the good. Already on the East Coast the two traveled to New York City to ask Walter Hines Page, editor of the acclaimed monthly periodical *The Forum*, to publish the Addams talks. Recalling this visit, Addams wrote that it was Lathrop, ever valiant, who was pushing her friend forward when Addams, "embarrassed and weak-kneed," said aloud to herself as they entered the building housing the journal that she felt like a "callow writer, peddling her wares." As they waited in Page's office for "the great man to appear," Lathrop "adjured me once more 'Don't cave in, J.A., this is our chance to give the public the pure milk of the word.'" During the interview with Page, Lathrop argued for immediate publication. "Much to our astonishment," Addams recalled, Page took both speeches and soon "sent us a generous check in payment which astonished us even more."[22]

The discomfort Addams felt in seeking recognition for her work and the surprised reaction of the two women to the compensation suggests just how unusual it was for women in the late nineteenth century to achieve recognition as serious writers and as participants in a discourse about politics and political philosophy.

Women's reluctance to promote accomplishments was certainly a factor in understanding Lathrop's approach to her own achievements. She was always more forceful and fearless when it came to promoting something or someone other than herself. Responding to an epidemic of smallpox that swept through Chicago in 1893, Lathrop and Kelley fearlessly marched into the tenement apartments in the sweatshop district of the West Side when garment manufacturers, fearing both lawsuits and the disease itself, refused to destroy infected garments. The two women burned the infected clothes in the streets and eventually succeeded in getting manufactures to destroy thousands of garments so that their circulation would not spread the disease. In entering these sweatshops both Lathrop and Kelley were risking their own lives, and the incident was often told as an example of their courage, yet Lathrop characteristically downplayed the episode. Asked in 1930 to look over a draft of the entry for her in the National Cyclopedia of American Biography, she told the editor that the entire reference to the epidemic "should be omitted because while we were in the midst of an epidemic none of us suffered from it nor did I."[23]

Lathrop, like so many women in the early settlement house movement, accepted—indeed, embraced—the traditional image of woman as servant when it came to describing her work rather than the persona of a distinguished achiever. In turn-of-the-twentieth-century America, however, something new was at work. Lathrop and the other women associated with America's settlement houses were creating professions for themselves in a world quite inhospitable to the idea that upper-middle-class women would play a prominent role in the world of paid labor. Addams expected all Hull House residents to be self-supporting; the women of Hull House were part of a national movement of women developing new opportunities for themselves as they launched new helping professions. But whether it was preschool education, art, music, physical education, directing a lodging house, or work in public health, the women, unlike most male professionals, served clientele who did not pay them. Thus, they were dependent on philanthropists, most often wealthy women, to sponsor their work. Throughout her career Lathrop spent much time and energy soliciting private sponsors for a number of initiatives, which included professional opportunities for women. As Robyn Muncy has noted, women's need to solicit philanthropists meant that the workers had to emphasize their work on behalf of others. "After all, the true object of patronage of elite women was to aid the downtrodden—not to subsidize the careers" of these middle-class women.[24]

If the women were carving out their own niche in the professional world by inventing new professions that emphasized traditional female traits, they were also pushing at its boundaries. For Lathrop and her colleagues the progressive maternalist approach meant something much more than a reliance on women's natural sympathies for children; they believed that the problems of the poor in general and children in particular must be approached with hardheaded research. Soon after her arrival Lathrop began putting most of her energies into improving private and public charities. In doing so, she stressed that women must become trained experts and not succumb to sentimentality. As she said in 1894 when discussing the participation of women on state boards of public charity that supervise state institutions, "I do not believe that solely because we are women we shall necessarily have more light of inspiration on the Board than men have. I have a suspicion that the common dust of which men and women were made enjoyed no spiritual transmutation when it passed through Adam's rib. . . . I am sure we do not monopolize any of the finer qualities of human nature . . . the powers of tenderness and sympathy and adaptation are those that belong to choice individuals and not to man and woman as such."[25]

Investigate, study the facts, and then publicize them to bring about social change. For Lathrop and her colleagues at Hull House the purpose of research was action. It was not enough to learn about horrible conditions; you had to do something about it. What Lathrop did as a social investigator and a social activist at Hull House is the subject of our next chapter.

3

Social Research and Progressive Government

"The era of rule by thumb and a kind heart must give way to trained individuals, whose kindness is rendered more effective because governed by intelligence."

—Julia Lathrop, 1912

Describing Hull House activities at the National Conference of Charities in 1894, Julia Lathrop told her audience that while the settlement house initiated educational programs and became involved in social issues affecting its neighborhood, it did not "dispense charity. There are hospitals and relief societies and asylums enough; and the best service we can perform is to co-operate with them, and, if possible, increase their usefulness."[1] By the time she addressed the conference, Lathrop, more so than any other resident of Hull House, was spending her time providing that service. Learning about the various relief agencies in Illinois and working to improve them occupied much of her time for the next decade. Lathrop took seriously the responsibility of learning about these institutions. A hallmark of progressive activities was the conviction that attacking social problems required systematic social investigation, which meant gathering as much empirical data as possible. But like other progressives, Lathrop saw the social investigation as a necessary prelude to social change.

During the depression of 1893 Lathrop began her efforts to improve relief services for poor Chicagoans, whether it be what we call outdoor relief—that is, aid in the form of money, food, or clothing to people living in their own dwellings—or indoor relief, which is institutionalized care provided by the poorhouse, the orphanage, or the public hospital. The worst economic downturn the United States had experienced to date, the Panic, affected the entire country, but in Chicago the winter of 1893–1894 was particularly harsh. During the previous summer Chicago was host to the spectacular Columbian Exposition, a World's Fair to celebrate the four hundredth anniversary of Columbus landing on the shores of the so-called New World. The fair garnered praise for its beautiful neoclassical buildings, the latest in modern technology, and commercial amusements for the masses as well as the elite. But all was not rosy; the fair brought with it the terrible smallpox epidemic that swept through the Hull House neighborhood among others. When the extravaganza ended in the fall of 1893, five months after the Panic set in, thousands of men who had been hired for the event were now stranded in the city, joining the many already unemployed.

The following winter Cook County, which included Chicago, appointed Lathrop to be a volunteer visitor, investigating within a ten-block radius of Hull House cases of needy families as possible candidates for public charities. She also reported on the relief institutions as well. This meant thoroughly studying the operations of the Cook County outdoor relief agency, where poor Chicagoans went to pick up aid, as well as the indoor relief agencies. The indoor institutions included the county poorhouse, known as the infirmary and located in Dunning, Illinois, just north of Chicago, for men, women, and children who could not care for themselves. The other indoor relief institutions, the public hospital and the public detention center for the mentally ill, were both located in the city.

Lathrop's description of the crowds at the County relief agency on Clinton Street is a poignant description of the impact of economic downturns on those already struggling to make ends meet: "It was a solid, pressing crowd of hundreds of shabby men and shawled or hooded women, coming from all parts of a great city . . . standing hour after hour with market baskets high above their heads, held in check by policeman, polyglot, but having the common language of their persistency, their weariness, their chill and hunger. The crowd stood unsheltered from the weather . . . Now and again a woman was crushed—in one instance it is reported was killed, and the ambulance was called to take her away."

Lathrop assessed the quality of the services provided by the relief agencies by focusing on the clients' point of view, paying special attention to the indoor relief institutions. "Ward B [of the infirmary] with beds crowded together, others made on the floor, and filled with a melancholy company of feeble and bedridden men and idiot children, must haunt the memory of whoever has seen it." For Lathrop the standard should be not what these very deprived Americans had been used to but rather what "experience and modern science show to be essential to the proper care of such a mass. The absolute lack of privacy, the monotony and dullness, the discipline, the enforced cleanliness—these are the inevitable and, in the opinion of some, wholesome disadvantages of the infirmary from the standpoint of the inmate."[2]

In 1893, at the behest of Governor Peter Altgeld, a leading progressive of the day, Lathrop became the first women to join the State Board of Charities, which oversaw the operations of relief agencies throughout Illinois. In this capacity she now widened her investigations of relief institutions. Serving on the board from 1893 until 1909, with an interruption of four years, Lathrop managed to visit every one of the 102 poorhouses in the state.

In her "dark blue tailored suit and shirtwaist blouse," almost a uniform for her investigating trips, Lathrop conducted herself in her trademark manner, combining tact, charm, and fierce determination. Attending to traditional assumptions about proper female behavior allowed her to disarm those whom she meant to confront. One day, while on an inspection tour of a mental health asylum, the manager proudly showed Lathrop a circular chute, a fire escape that had been installed a few years earlier. Lathrop voiced her approval but then asked, "Does it work?" The manager replied that of course, it would empty the building instantly in case of fire. "But we haven't had any fires so it hasn't been tried." So Lathrop gathered up her skirts and spiraled to the ground, four stories below.

Lathrop's friend Alice Hamilton, who accompanied her visit to one of the large mental hospitals in the state, described another encounter with asylum authorities:

> The superintendent was at first distinctly hostile, but Julia's tact gradually softened him until at last he was pouring out all of his many grievances and difficulties. She listened with sympathy and I thought that would be the end, that we should depart feeling we had conquered his hostility and left him friendly and well-disposed. But to Julia that was only the preparatory spade-work.

She then proceeded to tell him gently, but with devastating clarity, what was wrong with his administration of the asylum, for which he, after all, was the only one responsible. He took it, with startled meekness and I learned a lesson I never forgot.[3]

Lathrop was quite conscious of her approach. By 1905 other volunteer visitors, mostly women, were fanning out across Illinois, investigating state charitable institutions. Lathrop published a set of guidelines for approaching the work, and she began by emphasizing the need to approach institution officials with friendliness and openness. "Try to understand, then, first of all, the official point of view," she advised the visitors, "and the official difficulties. A critical, suspicious bearing will defeat your purpose to learn the facts."[4]

Lathrop and her Hull House colleagues, like other progressive reformers, combined their determination to learn the facts with an optimism that once conditions were known, the American public would support their reform agenda. Modern historians have hailed one of the earliest projects at the settlement house, *Hull House Maps and Papers*, produced in 1895, as both a classic in the field of early social science and the "most important work by American women social scientists before 1900."[5] The maps of the Nineteenth Ward, created under the direction of Florence Kelley, at the time an Illinois factory inspector, detailed the ethnic composition of the residents and their wages earned. The maps anchored the book; they appeared along with a series of essays on the various social problems associated with the conditions of the neighborhood, all written by Hull House residents, including Lathrop.

The book was published by Richard Ely, economist at the University of Wisconsin, for his series the Library of Economics and Politics, which reflected Ely's belief that social science ought to reflect moral convictions. The women pioneers in this early social science fit into this approach quite well. Theirs was a social science that combined investigation and advocacy. Whereas male social scientists, often affiliated with research universities, were sometimes subject to institutional pressures to tone down their activism, women, shut out of these positions, were freer to express criticisms of the status quo. Moreover, the women conducting the early social investigations, like the Hull House residents, did so as part of their work within the communities; unlike most of the male social scientists, they were not cloistered members of the academy. The women, including Lathrop, in the tradition of such philosophers as John Dewey, embraced a social science rooted in experience.

Lathrop's article in *Hull House Maps and Papers* was a systematic look at the indoor and outdoor charities of Cook County and was based on her work as a volunteer visitor in 1893. For Lathrop, interested in learning about the realities of poverty, nothing surpassed a trip to the public charity institutions. "There is, doubtless, a certain satisfaction to the philanthropist and the sociologist alike, in having touched bottom, reached ultimate facts; and this in a sense we have done when we visit the county institutions."

In keeping with the determination to render "the facts," Lathrop provided her readers with lots of statistics, including the number of inmates at the poorhouse (about fifteen hundred people), the large number of foreign born, and the gender distribution, which showed that women constituted about a third of the clients. In addition to the statistics, Lathrop thoroughly described the buildings, the wards, the food, and clothing provided to the residents, how the inmates spent their time, and their moods. The descriptions include both facts and judgments, and they are intermingled throughout. For example, she reported that "few persons could see the food [at the County insane asylum] as prepared and served . . . without a sense of physical revolt."

Lathrop often illustrated her policy prescriptions with examples based on her personal interactions with individuals. Thus, in discussing what she thought was the heartless policy of separating husbands and wives in the poorhouse within sex-segregated wards, she wrote, "How painful this separation may be indicated by the attitude of an old Irish couple of my acquaintance. . . . When Dunning was suggested to them they were panic stricken, and the old woman, who is ninety odd said, 'Oh, he'll have to go in with the men; I'll have to go in with the women, and all our own clothes will be taken away from us. . . . I'll feel sorrier for him than for me. I am older than he is, but I can get along better'n he. Let us stay here.'"

In her conclusion Lathrop turned to policy prescriptions. "We need a children's home," she argued, "or some provision so that no child shall be in a poorhouse. We need a home for convalescents" so that patients discharged from hospitals who are still not well enough to work will not end up in the poorhouse. Like other progressives, she ended with the optimistic conviction that educating the public will create change: "There is no mal-administration so strong that it can persist in the face of public knowledge and attention."

Lathrop's tremendous compassion for the wards of the state motivated her work on the charity institutions; she believed that all were entitled to better care. However, along with what we might see as her more advanced ideas, her views in 1895 reflected an acceptance of traditional notions about the culpability of many poor people for their circumstances. Lathrop shared with her close friends at Hull House a particular suspicion of what she called "the intermittent husband" as an important culprit and ongoing problem in understanding the plight of poor women and children. As she noted in 1895, "By some curious law of pauperism and male irresponsibility, whose careful study offers an *interminable* task to any loving collector of data, men are in a great majority in poorhouses."[6]

In the early years Lathrop and sometimes Jane Addams embraced the traditional idea that some of the poor seeking aid, particularly outdoor relief, should be denied help lest they be encouraged in their dependency. Such a view was characteristic of nineteenth-century approaches to charity. The private Charity Organization Society (COS), active first in England and then in the United States, pioneered what it saw as a scientific approach to philanthropy. Systematic investigation of each case under consideration could be done by charity workers who would make hard-headed, not sentimental, evaluations of whether aid was justified.

Lathrop found the COS approach of systematically investigating relief cases appealing, along with its efforts to coordinate the relief provided by various charity organizations. Lathrop's views on the responsibilities of the poor for their circumstances, however, were contradictory. She never abandoned completely the notion that for "tens of thousands" poverty could be understood as a result of "drunkenness, idleness, ignorance, desertion, all the personal, mental, or moral defects which would drag a family below the self-sustaining average."

By 1908, however, Lathrop was articulating clearly her belief that the modern approach to philanthropy must focus on the larger social conditions, not on individual blame. In the predemocratic age, she argued, the rich gave to the poor out of a sense of duty and a belief that the various stations in society, ordained by God, would always be with us. Next, she argued, in the early democratic era a new approach to philanthropy, which lasted even into her own era, put the responsibility on the individual. The purpose of charity was to make the poor as uncomfortable as possible in accepting aid so they would cease their dependency. Such an approach, she declared, has been "a cruel failure in abolishing poverty and a truer failure in relieving distress." Now, she said, we must embrace a "third stage" in our effort to help the poor. "This time the load is laid upon the shoulders of society and it is held that the problems of philanthropy are social problems and can only be solved as such." To illustrate her argument, Lathrop detailed the story of one young widow who comes to the philanthropist seeking aid because her husband has just died of tuberculosis. The husband had worked for fifteen years in the same factory in which his father had also worked. The man was prone to tuberculosis and knew his work was hazardous to his health; so too did neighbors who entreated the employer that he be assigned an outside job, but to no avail. Hence, the hardworking employee risked his own life in providing for his family and now left his survivors dependent on the state. The modern philanthropist, according to Lathrop, recognizes that this tragedy is not an individual problem but a societal one; the family ended in dependency because of a preventable and curable disease. An improved understanding of occupational hazards, industrial insurance, health insurance for ordinary Americans, and wages that would have allowed "healthful living" for the family could have saved the breadwinner.[7]

Like so many progressives, Lathrop's vision of the interdependent society where government took on more responsibility for social welfare was reinforced as a result of social investigation abroad. Reformers on both sides of the Atlantic met frequently to share ideas about efforts to deal with the social consequences of industrial capitalism. Lathrop and her friends had the resources to frequently tour abroad, and Lathrop often took trips with friends, professional colleagues, and her siblings. The trips combined recreation and the serious business of learning about what she and other American reformers viewed as the more advanced European approach to social welfare. As a commissioner on the Illinois Board of Charities, Lathrop visited Scotland and Belgium in 1898 to study new forms of care for the insane. She was especially interested in the growing trend of allowing mentally ill patients to be boarded out to families inhabiting small villages. The families lived in close proximity to asylums and to doctors and nurses who could supervise the patients. Two years later she added to her knowledge about such practices by visiting a similar effort in a small village in France.

Lathrop's report on these investigations, published in 1902, combined detailed descriptions of what she found with her strong argumentation. If at all possible, she argued, poor adults should be spared the poorhouse, children should be spared the orphanage and the poorhouse, and the mentally ill could be better cared for outside the asylum. Boarding out was less costly than institutional care, and both family members and the patients benefited from these new arrangements.

Lathrop was particularly interested in the European approach to occupational therapy. In Ainay, France, some of the boarders worked on the farm, but if they didn't want to do such work, patients could assist other villagers in such activities as furniture refinishing, shoemaking, tutoring children, or giving music lessons. Women patients boarding in Dun, France, worked in sewing rooms. Lathrop became a strong advocate of occupational therapy for the mentally ill, a cause she was to champion for the rest of her life. To emphasize the positive aspects of occupational therapy, she recounts the story of one Scot, John, who helped a relative of his host family by tending to a fretful baby. "The young mother said . . . she did not know how ever she could get through her work without John to 'mind' him. That baby was John's supreme interest and patient care." By contrast, according to Lathrop, on a visit to an insane asylum in downstate Illinois she found an elderly woman, a skilled knitter, in a locked ward, surrounded by violent patients. "I asked her where she learned to knit," Lathrop recalled, "and she said with a jerk of her thumb, 'About forty mile [sic] over there.' When I confessed that I could not knit, she said 'Well, where was you raised?' and when I answered 'At the northern end of the state,' she retorted with a jovial smile to take out the sting, 'Well, do they work or do they steal for a living up there?' The attendants said she could live perfectly well outside 'if only had some one to look after her a bit.'"[8]

With the publication in 1905 of *Suggestions for Visitors to County Poor Houses and to Other Charitable Institutions*, Lathrop established her reputation as an expert on not only how to conduct investigations of public charities but also the best practices for institutional care of the poor. But for Lathrop writing and speaking about conditions were not ends in and of themselves. The purpose of spreading knowledge was to generate action; improving the situation, not merely writing about it, was her highest priority.

Lathrop struggled to improve the quality of Illinois's charity institutions against mighty odds; only meager public resources were available for services to the poor. Illinois was no different from the rest of the country at that time. The United States was born out of conflict with a tyrannical government, and suspicion of powerful government remained. Although in the nineteenth century state, local, and even the federal governments assisted entrepreneurs as they expanded businesses, when it came to aiding the poor, America, more so than other developed countries, relied on voluntary associations, including religious organizations and private philanthropies. To deal with the social crisis of the 1890s, Cook County was providing $100,000 dollars of outdoor relief yearly (worth close to $3 million today) and about $700,000 (worth $18 million today) to pay for the salaries of about five hundred attendants *and* the services at all of the institutions providing indoor relief.

To help during the 1893 Panic, Chicago, as in the past, turned to private organizations, including Hull House, which provided small funds for desperate neighbors. Most especially, under Lathrop's leadership Hull House residents decided to set up a temporary relief bureau to screen applicants for private charity. When it became clear that the Hull House efforts were not enough, Lathrop, with the help of Addams and another important activist in Chicago, Lucy Flowers, set up a relief organization under the supervision of the newly formed Central Relief Association (CRA) to coordinate the efforts of the charities throughout the city.

Lathrop, Addams, and Flowers were all prominent members of the Chicago Women's Club, an organization that not only raised money for Hull House and other settlement house initiatives but also pushed for social welfare programs. Founded in 1876, the Chicago Club, like so many women's clubs across the country, originally had focused on edification in the arts and literature; by the 1890s it turned its attention to learning about and then addressing the crises of the urbanizing society.

Women's clubs, along with settlement houses, were critically important resources for promoting social welfare partly because, as Kathryn Kish Sklar has noted, they were filling "in gaps in the political culture." With few men in the civil service bureaucracy and with most male-dominated organizations, such as labor unions, and male politicians uninterested in expanding a social welfare state, Lathrop and her allies stepped in to promote a reform agenda for Cook County charities.[9]

Lathrop's agenda centered on proper staffing for the charities providing indoor relief. She concluded in her piece for *Hull House Maps and Papers*, "The comfort, the recovery, the lives, of all these thousands of dependent people, hang upon the knowledge, the kindliness, the honesty, and the good faith of those hired to care for them." Most of those both supervising and staffing the charity institutions were recipients of political patronage;

this was true throughout the United States and was very much the case in Cook County and throughout Illinois. County boards, whose composition could change from election to election, appointed the staffs of the charity institutions. Nothing seemed more obvious to machine politicians than that loyal supporters should have access to public jobs, including those available in the public charitable institutions. Such jobs not only provided lucrative rewards to those in supervisory positions; politicians also provided stable working-class jobs for many ordinary citizens.

For Lathrop and her allies care for the poor and the mentally and physically ill should be in the hands of trained professionals placed in jobs because of their qualifications, which could be measured by civil service examinations and reinforced by the recommendations of those considered knowledgeable in their respective fields. Is a "man or a woman overcome with an infirmity. . . . placed in the constant care night and day of nurses trained in such care?" Lathrop asked. "Not at all." They were cared for by "some one who has a 'pull.' . . . The remarkable thing with our present system of appointments is, not that abuses occur, but that more do not occur."[10]

Throughout her tenure on the State Charities Board, Lathrop and her allies worked to break the lock hold of patronage when it came to staffing the public institutions for dependent care. To replace men who were not qualified, Lathrop often championed male professionals; this was particularly true in the case of institution directors because men overwhelmingly dominated the upper ranks. But the entire thrust of her approach involved pushing new job opportunities for women. She consistently argued that skilled women, such as nurses and physicians, should care for women and children. She also argued on behalf of what was then considered a new trend—the use of female nurses for male patients.

Under Governor Altgeld, Lathrop could point to some achievements in reforming dependent care in Illinois. A separate school for delinquent girls was established in Geneva, Illinois, in 1896, and rather than continuing the usual practice of increasing the size of existing hospitals for the mentally ill, the state built two new ones. Lathrop also had some success in putting medical staff into the state hospitals based on competitive examination. Altgeld's most important effort on behalf of civil service reform involved his backing of the state's first Civil Service Law in 1895. The law was not very strong, however, merely calling on cities to adopt the reforms voluntarily; it would be ten more years before Illinois legislation compelled the state institutions to appoint staff without regard to political considerations.

During her work under the administrations of Democrat Altgeld and his successor, Republican John Tanner, Lathrop obtained cooperation from some of the charity superintendents and much resistance. She herself admitted that during those eight years under both administrations, the care institutions continued to be used for political goals. However, when political considerations became even more blatant under the new administration of Richard Yates Jr., governor from 1901 to 1905, Lathrop resigned along with Rabbi Emil Hirsch, of Chicago's Sinai Temple, one of the pioneers in the founding of Reform Judaism and another activist in reform politics. In resigning she made public her reasons. At the time Lathrop's Hull House friends were startled she would take such an action, given her years of investment in the work of improving state care for the poor. "J. Lathrop I didn't think you could do it," Addams told her. To which Lathrop replied with a suspicious terseness, "I am not sure that I can."

But Lathrop did. She was deeply disappointed that despite his public statement during his campaign supporting civil service reform, once in office Governor Yates made no effort to promote changes; on the contrary, he scuttled a 1901 measure in the Illinois legislature designed to take the state institutions out of politics. Moreover, his own appointments to the Charities Board showed his determination to reward political friends. For the all-important job of board secretary, a paid position for someone who communicated to the board all the information about the use of funds for and the conduct of the various institutions, the governor saw to it that the board elected the former governor Tanner's son by the slimmest majority. Such an appointment for Lathrop represented a commitment to all the "standards and traditions" that constituted the problem of the state institutions. "My continued presence on this Board," she concluded, "will appear at least to indicate a complacency towards methods whose evils I have seen too long, and which I have tried earnestly, but of course vainly, to overcome."[11]

Lathrop spent the next four years campaigning against the patronage system, particularly as it applied to the charity institutions. To assist in her efforts to publicize the poor conditions at these establishments and to help her campaign on behalf of civil service reform, she turned to her allies in the women's club movement. Lathrop, like other women social reformers, was extremely effective in mobilizing volunteer organizations such as women's clubs to help her fulfill her goals as a public official. In 1902 Lathrop chaired the Illinois Federation of Women's Clubs Committee on Civil Service Reform. The committee exhorted the individual-affiliated local clubs to promote the committee's statewide essay contest for high schoolers on the subject "The Civil Service and Why It Should Not Be Political," to hold public meetings on the subject, and to contribute to a traveling speakers fund.[12] In Illinois and later, as a federal official in Washington, DC, Lathrop would turn to women's organizations whenever she was interested in pushing reforms.

Lathrop's campaign paid off. In 1905 Illinois elected a new governor, Charles Deneen, who reappointed Lathrop and Hirsh along with Addams and two physicians to make up a newly reorganized board. The Chicago reform community hailed the appointments as a new signal that professional standards, not political needs, were to be the guiding principles for supervising the charity institutions.

Lathrop's efforts to reform the public charities exemplify some of the contradictions that surrounded ideas about women as public activists. All along, Lathrop pushed for professional standards and expanding opportunities for women's work. Yet in relying on club women and other female volunteers, Lathrop tapped into the notion that precisely because they operated outside the arena of paid labor and, unlike men, were not motivated by monetary concerns, women volunteers could be more objective about the needs of caregiving institutions. Thus, although Lathrop had been mentioned widely as the possible new secretary to the board appointed by Governor Deneen, she didn't want such a position because it was paid for by the state; indeed, Lathrop's friend and ally in social reform, the Reverend Graham Taylor, director of the Chicago Commons settlement house, specifically praised her service to the board because it was "without compensation, other than the heart's own reward for duty well done and opportunity well met."[13] That prominent citizens, whether female or male, because they serve without pay, somehow are disinterested representatives of the larger good is an idea needing critical scrutiny. Certainly civic leaders from the corporate sector represent the views of their community, labor leaders the same, just as women social reformers like Lathrop represent viewpoints and assumptions rooted in the world they inhabit.

In addition to professionalism, the rhetoric surrounding civil service reform emphasized the importance of taking politics out of social welfare services. In pursuing the nonpolitical agenda, however, Lathrop was extremely political. In an era when women were not even permitted to vote in state elections, Lathrop not only lobbied politicians on behalf of her agenda, she was intimately involved in—indeed, in charge of—fashioning legislation to advance her objectives. Before her resignation from the State Board, Lathrop took the lead in drafting the 1901 proposed law that would have taken politics out of the appointments for the various public charities.

From 1904 through 1908, while again serving on the board, Lathrop continued to push legislation. She worked on countless drafts of the law that ultimately passed in 1908, which put the charities under a new Board of Control. To supervise the work of the salaried experts, a new Charities Commission of distinguished citizens, including a prominent and experienced physician, replaced the old Board of Charities. Most important to Lathrop, the new commission supervised small boards of three volunteer visitors, including one woman, for each state charitable institution. The commission also took control over the county visitors required to inspect county jails and poorhouses.

Once the salaried board was instituted in 1909, Lathrop ended her official charity work for the state of Illinois. She left with some disappointments but could nonetheless take pride that during her second stint on the board the medical administration of the hospitals for the insane had been standardized. In 1907 the state established a Psychopathic Institute to train doctors who tended to the insane.

In 1908 Lathrop devoted a considerable amount of time to a subcommittee appointed by the old board that worked, successfully, to increase training for nurses and attendants at mental hospitals. Since her earliest days at Hull House, Lathrop viewed her work on behalf of training social welfare workers as inseparable from her efforts to improve social welfare services. Like most of the women she worked with, Lathrop believed that generous experts would provide the answers to many of the problems her neighbors confronted. Such an attitude reflected both older assumptions about the superiority of middle-class values and a new belief that training would enhance the efforts of the middle class to truly understand the problems of the poor. In lauding Chicago's Visiting Nurses, who worked in poor communities, Lathrop told an audience in 1894, "One is not surprised by the grateful affections of patients nor by the deference to their gentle authority. . . . It is a revelation to see the ease and delicacy with which [the visiting nurse] performs tasks impossibly repulsive to the untrained person and the skill with which she evolves approximate order out of tenement house chaos."[14]

Because gentleness was traditionally associated with women, Lathrop used that idea to carve out an important place for women in the public sphere. She consistently argued that women were critical additions to any efforts to improve social services. She pushed for women to be appointed to state boards of charity throughout the country because there were so many women who were under state care, and there were so many available women who contribute important service. But as a progressive maternalist, Lathrop resisted the notion that women's special sentimental natures necessarily made them good servants of the state. In fact, in 1894 she argued that women, precisely because they are susceptible to sentimentality, must guard against acting out of such emotions alone. "Tenderness, sympathy, and adaption," powers that belong to both men and women as individuals, combined with proper training, was the indispensable combination.[15]

In promoting the formal training of social welfare workers, Lathrop was part of a larger professionalization of social work taking place in Chicago and elsewhere. Training charity workers in the Windy City, in any formal sense, began in 1903 when Graham Taylor of the Chicago Commons settlement house offered one extension course (for students not regularly enrolled in school) for twelve students already doing social welfare work. One year later Lathrop joined Taylor's Social Science Center for Practical Training to teach a class on the public charities she knew so well from her own work. By 1905 the school, with private funds provided by the president of the University of Chicago, was able to pay Taylor a stipend as director as well as for his various guest lecturers.

The purpose of the school was not only to educate its students on the social conditions of the larger society but also to train both professional and volunteer social service workers catering to families. During the early years of social work, education disagreements erupted among faculty throughout the country about whether the emphasis should be on the study of social conditions, the training of caseworkers, or both. Taylor's school in Chicago was one arena where that debate took place. In the wake of the economic crisis of the 1890s many charity workers had moved away from the notion that poverty was a result of individual failings. Larger economic and social forces needed to be changed, and those who wished to improve the lives of the poor needed to be educated about these forces and how to change the conditions. Yet, as Robyn Muncy has pointed out, many charity reformers still believed that welfare workers needed to be trained practitioners, help-ing the "suffering, who, after all, could not wait for massive economic restructuring."[16] In 1908 Lathrop herself, in accordance with the new pol-icies of the State Charities Board she helped to create, offered a summer school course for attendants at mental hospitals.

Lathrop was also critical in developing a social science research agenda for the Chicago school. By 1906 the school, hard-pressed for money, had to rely on the trustees of Taylor's own settlement house for funding to keep it afloat. At the time Lathrop proposed that the institution commit to social research; by obtaining a grant of $100,000 for five years from the Russell Sage Foundation to develop such a program, she was able to solve, at least for a while, the school's financial problem. In 1907 Lathrop became the first director of the newly created Department of Research at the school, which was soon renamed the Chicago School for Civics and Philanthropy. To assist her in the Research Department she turned to So-phinisba Breckinridge, a coresident at Hull House. With a PhD in political science from the University of Chicago as well as a law degree, she was at the time an assistant professor in the Department of Household Economy at the University of Chicago. In 1908, when Lathrop took on the position as vice president of the school, Breckinridge took over as the director of the Research Department. Almost immediately Lathrop and Breckinridge recruited Edith Abbott, also a product of the University of Chicago with a PhD in economics, to share in their new enterprise.

The newly reorganized school in Chicago now emphasized both the practical training of social service workers and research into the conditions that created the larger societal problems. Courses involved sending stu-dents out to apprenticeships in various relief agencies, mental hospitals, settlement houses, and the juvenile courts. Students also took practical courses, such as the one Lathrop taught for attendants at mental hospitals. But Lathrop remained active in the Department of Social Investigation, the new name of the research program, even after she relinquished her post as director, supervising student projects. Breckinridge and Abbott them-selves conducted studies of the housing conditions in Chicago, the prob-lems of juvenile delinquency, and truancy in Chicago's public schools.

Although not all faculty members or all students were women, the de-velopment of social work schools could be viewed partly as an effort to in-vent a new profession for women. Traditionally distinguishing themselves as volunteers in service to their community, women could now approach the work as trained experts. Like the one in Chicago, research departments were instituted at the New York School for Philanthropy, founded in 1903 as America's first full-time school for training social workers, as well as at the Boston School for Social Workers. Together these programs not only represented a commitment to student training but also provided critical opportunities for women scholars who wanted to pursue social science research projects. Until then such work was pretty much a male enterprise, available to men as professors in universities. When Edith Abbott gave up her teaching position at Wellesley College to take a job at some unknown new Chicago school, her older colleagues at the prestigious women's college thought she was a bit crazy, but Abbott welcomed the opportunity. Neither Breckinridge nor Abbott until that point had jobs that allowed them the chance to pursue advanced-level research. Lathrop assured Abbott that at the Chicago School "we can promise you full opportunities for your ability and full recognition for your work."[17]

Lathrop's enthusiasm for graduate education in social work, which offered opportunities for faculty to pursue sophisticated research and students the chance to train for social service professions, motivated her to push for a new program at her alma mater in Poughkeepsie. In 1912 Lathrop, who was at the height of her fame and about to become chief of the US Children's Bureau, joined the Vassar Board of Trustees as an alumna member. The second decade of the twentieth century was the high point for progressive reform, and so it was on the Vassar campus. By then most students considered themselves suffragists; social reform organizations such as the College Settlement Association and the National Consumers League claimed active Vassar chapters. The students, stimulated by professors such as historian Lucy Maynard Salmon, who began outreach programs for college employees, and Herbert Mills, who taught courses on social problems, embraced the new enthusiasm for social work.

It was in this atmosphere in 1915 that the college celebrated its fiftieth anniversary. One of the most important themes for the celebration was the significance of higher education for women; the celebration included an address by Lathrop, widely covered in the press, where she outlined her views on the subject. She believed that rather than modeling higher education for women after the traditional male approach, which she termed either "unspecialized training along cultural lines, or preliminary to specialized training," she hoped to see women in higher education "apply their training in original research to a study of the life and the interests of the family, to the end that the family may be developed to its greatest strength through the fullest individual development" of the student.

The idea of elevating household tasks to the status of a profession was not new. In her speech Lathrop acknowledged that the public universities of the Midwest, some other women's colleges, and technical institutions all had courses in applied household economics. But her vision was something different. She wanted a graduate school, a research center, where "choice minds are devoting their powers" in various fields connected to the study of the family. Doing work out in the field and working with actual mothers, students, and teachers at the new school could "correlate and inspire the many scattered educational activities that now existed." The new research center would not control the practical instruction (at other schools) already under way but instead be an institution where people could "turn for . . . help." She proposed that Vassar consider "instituting a graduate school for such a study of the family," something akin to the Chicago School of Civics and Philanthropy, where she had played such a leadership role.

Although a graduate school was never instituted, Lathrop did see a partial fulfillment of her dream with the institution of the Vassar Euthenics Program in 1924. The term "euthenics" was invented by Ellen Swallow Richards, Class of 1870, the pioneer in America's public health and home economics movements who had inspired Lathrop in her early days at Hull House. Euthenics referred to the science of improving the human species through the control of environmental factors. The short-lived Euthenics Program—it ended in the mid-1940s—allowed students to major in the social and scientific study of family life as preparation for their own careers as mothers or to concentrate on courses that would be pretraining to graduate work either as teachers or in social welfare.

Euthenics was controversial from the beginning. Lathrop and her allies at Vassar, which included the college president Henry Noble McCracken, saw it as an extension of the ideas behind progressive education, which sought to make education relevant to the lives of its students. Was euthenics an important vehicle for providing women with an education more relevant to their lives and a way of promoting professional opportunities, or was it a retreat for women?

Similar debates about the direction of women's education took place at women's colleges across the country and among women alumnae. The women graduates of such schools as Vassar, Wellesley, and Mount Holyoke were marrying at a higher rate than the women of Lathrop's generation. Increasingly the women of the Progressive Era expected to work before marriage and children and planned to return to work later in their adult lives. Teaching and social work careers allowed women to leave their work and return later in life. Although Bryn Mawr, as early as the 1890s, took the position that any courses related to home economics were sex-stereotyped efforts to move away from the commitment to education equal to male schools, Wellesley and Smith incorporated a few courses on domestic science. The elite women's schools were, however, wary of any courses linked to the profession of home economics, which they associated with the inferior land grant universities of the Midwest. However, by embracing graduate schools of social work during the Progressive Era, Bryn Mawr and Smith addressed career opportunities for women and the desire to contribute solutions to the social problems of the day.

From the time when Lathrop first proposed the idea, national press coverage reinforced the concerns of those who worried that this sort of education reinforced women's traditional roles. Laura Hillyer's article in the *Boston Herald* of March 1915 about Lathrop's plan carried the banner headline, "'Babyology' College Uncle Sam's Latest; Pet Idea of His $5000 a Year Woman 'Chief,'" with an accompanying cartoon. Underneath the cartoon the caption read, "Not Yet Reality, but 'Twill Be Soon if Julia C. Lathrop Has Her Way."[18] But one cannot fully understand the Vassar program without appreciating the original vision of its founders, including Lathrop, who thought education ought to be a training ground that would encourage young people to make a contribution to the larger society. As the Vassar Board of Trustees noted at Lathrop's death in 1932, "Her dreams of Vassar were that it should become not merely a great college but a great social institution."

In the age of industrialism, the progressives believed, in which the growing economic and political power of some were threatening important democratic rights of all, individual freedom had to be balanced by a notion of social responsibility. Education should foster an understanding that social cooperation was critical to the successful modern society. Progressives like Lathrop believed that the best education was one in which students could see the connection between their studies and the concerns of the larger society, one that could link theory and practice. Lathrop's vision for the new study of the family was meant to do just that. It would provide women with an education that would be relevant to their personal lives.

But the best education about family life would be one in which all students could see the connection between their individual lives and society as a whole. Or, as Lathrop put it in her anniversary speech, "The mother would come to look upon her own door and find that the doors of all homes open on the highway, and that no home prospers or perishes unto itself."[19]

Many faculty objected to euthenics because they were—rightly— concerned the program might represent a retreat from the commitment that women were capable of pursuing any profession they might want, not just those traditionally associated with their sex. Then too, by the 1920s, the overall curriculum at Vassar had already been influenced by the progressive thrust—the college boasted many more courses that addressed the problems of the real world than there had been in 1880 when Lathrop graduated, so euthenics was addressing a problem—reforming a stale curriculum—that no longer existed. Perhaps most important euthenics was not instituted in an era characterized by progressive reform but rather in the 1920s, and times had indeed changed. Reform impulses emphasizing social responsibility were in decline, and the embrace of individual fulfillment was paramount. Most euthenics majors studied the "science of family life" in preparation for raising their own families, not for a career in social reform.

In the 1920s some of the established social work schools, including the Chicago School of Civics and Philanthropy, were also addressing the role of social reform in the graduate school curriculum. Lathrop's protégées Breckinridge and Abbott embraced the idea that research and scholarship ought to contribute directly to new policies that addressed current problems. Lathrop's whole career reflected the conviction that social research ought to be connected to social policy, and she promoted the research agenda of the Chicago School, even after she left the city to become chief of the US Children's Bureau. Lathrop wrote the introduction to Abbott and Breckinridge's famous treatise, *The Delinquent Child and the Home*, an investigation of the juvenile justice system in Chicago. As head of the Children's Bureau, Lathrop provided federal funds for the school so faculty and students could do research on child welfare issues that interested her agency.

By contrast, Graham Taylor continued to believe that training caseworkers for practical service to individuals and families was critical. He feared that the abstract approach of problem solving minimized the importance of personal relationships that developed between caseworkers or settlement house workers and the poor they were meant to serve. Breckinridge and Abbott, for their part, were "skeptical about the ability of personal relationships between social workers and the poor to be anything but meddling middle class intrusions."

Regardless of their commitment to social reform, Breckinridge and Abbott felt that practical training courses under Taylor's direction were too informal and not systematic, an inferior education that did not enjoy "the academic prestige or social value" of the research department. Their conflict came to a head in 1920. Finding it hard to raise funds for its operation through private donors or research foundations, one answer for the school was to pursue an affiliation with a university. With Taylor on a leave of absence in 1920, the two women, with the approval of the Chicago School's Board of Trustees, entered into negotiations with the University of Chicago. Over Taylor's objection, the university took over the school, making it a graduate school for professional training. Both Abbott and Breckinridge became professors and leaders in the new University of Chicago School of Social Service Administration (SSA), while Taylor received no position.

As ever, Lathrop's views on the conflict between Taylor and the two women over the future of social work education reflected both an older approach as well as the embrace of the new. At the time of the showdown in 1920 Lathrop had already been in Washington for eight years, but she had remained active at the school as a member of the Board of Trustees. She was close to Taylor and, like Addams, also on the board, so she was reluctant to have the school lose its independence. Influenced by John Dewey, she was committed to the notion that education be rooted in practical experience. She believed in the casework model of serving poor families and had also promoted the training of the volunteer investigator. Moreover, she believed that personal relationships and sympathy for individuals remained critical components of social service. Yet Lathrop was a transitional figure who pioneered in embracing the social investigation for the field of social work and the increasing professionalization of social service. In the end she endorsed her mentees, Abbott and Breckinridge, telling Abbott that "your judgment as to the best practicable turn is backed by such generous devotion that I accept it and feel grateful for what you have done and will do to uphold the standards of applied social science."

Ultimately Lathrop had to embrace the Abbott/Breckinridge approach; she fervently believed that elevating the training for women in the helping professions was connected to elevating the status of the work and improving working conditions. Instructing Dr. V. H. Podesta of the Elgin State Hospital for the Insane on what would be appropriate for his lecture on the occupational therapy at her 1908 summer school course, Lathrop told him that "what we want is to make the girls feel that they are doing an important and dignified thing, and although the present hours and pay are not inviting, in the very fact of their doing extra time and study in such a way as this will tend to improve their standing and remuneration."

When she was once challenged that all this training and standardization could breed bureaucracy, Lathrop answered, "Let us deal with bureaucracy when we get it. We can afford to run the risk of that danger for a time. We need orderly teaching for those going into public work."[20] Yet she never lost the conviction that personal feelings and individual relationships were critical to social welfare work.

Lathrop herself tried to provide that individual attention in helping Illinois families dependent in one way or another on the charity institutions. She responded to constant personal requests that she find out about this or that relative being cared for in the poorhouse or at a mental hospital. "Dear friend to the unfortunate," began one such letter addressed to her from an eighty-one-year-old Chicago woman writing in 1908 to inquire about the condition of her forty-five-year-old son. The son had been in one of the Illinois institutions for the "feebleminded" for fifteen years. Mrs. DeSisla had heard that he had been working on the institution farm, which would be something he would "find congenial." Neither she nor her daughter had the means to visit him in all these years, and she was hoping Lathrop could inquire as to how he was doing. Aware of Lathrop's battles with local politicians about staffing at the asylums, the mother told her that "I need hardly say that I know of you and your Christ like work, and I recognize how much we parents of the helpless are indebted to you." In response Lathrop had a staff member at the institution write to the mother to tell her that her son was getting along well; the staff member sent along a photograph. Lathrop herself assured the mother that he was being attended to by kindly people, not those who, as the mother wrote, "fail to realize the mental condition of their charges and [who have] tempers impatient of control." "I now call you [and the staff member who also wrote to her] friends," Mrs. DeSisla told Lathrop in her letter of profuse thanks, for "Service makes friendships. . . . Please to accept my sincere sorrow for your mother's condition," she concluded in her thank-you response, "and to assure you of my hope that she will speedily recover. . . . had I known of your cause for anxiety . . . I would have spared you the additional task."[21]

Lathrop and Mrs. DeSisla were not friends, of course. The mother was one of the "helpless parents" who felt indebted to Lathrop as someone more powerful who could gain information that she, an ordinary parent, could not. The obsequious tone of her letters to Lathrop helps us understand Abbott and Breckinridge's skepticism about the possibility for true friendships between welfare workers and those who needed aid. Molly Ladd-Taylor's assessment that "despite her genuine respect and sympathy for the poor, Lathrop's interest in reform was motivated more by her belief in the responsibility of privilege than by any personal identification with their troubles" is fair. But for Lathrop, an intense sympathy for the poor was critical to the growing movement for social change. "The justice of today," she once remarked, "was born of yesterday's pity."[22]

Nothing aroused Lathrop's sympathy more than the plight of children. The miserable conditions of children in Illinois poorhouses and orphanages shocked her, as did the deplorable conditions of the detention schools for "wayward" boys and girls. A look at Lathrop's work on behalf of poor children and immigrant families completes our story of her contributions to social reform in turn-of-the-twentieth-century Chicago.

4

Juvenile Justice, Immigrant Aid

"The great primary service of the [juvenile] court is that
it lifts up the truth and compels us to see that wastage of
human life whose sign is the child in court."

—Julia Lathrop, 1912[1]

Arriving at the poorhouse in Dunning, Illinois, in 1893, Julia Lathrop was
shocked by much of what she saw, but she was especially distressed about
the children. There were young children with their mothers, but there were
also some "whom no one cares to adopt because they are unattractive or
scarred or sickly."[2] In addition to the young ones in the poorhouse, Julia
discovered poor children arrested for delinquency who ended up in jails
with incarcerated adults because their parents could not afford to furnish bail. Almost as bad, many judges, reluctant to sentence youth to the
dreaded city jail for adults, often sent juveniles to industrial schools meant
only for poor and neglected children. So-called troubled youth would now
be mixing with and influencing the innocent. Lathrop's concern about
poor children in general and the treatment of youth who ran afoul of the
law would put her at the forefront of developing new laws and social services for America's young people.

Lathrop's work reflected new ideas about child development and the
role that government ought to play in providing for the general welfare.
Nonetheless, her approach to children also reflected some traditional notions about the superiority of elite and middle-class ideals. When Lathrop
and her allies acted on their ideals, they did not always respect the rights

of poor parents, nor did they adequately appreciate the resources that poor parents could bring to bear in rearing their children.

Who were the troubled children who landed in the Cook County courts? They were mostly young men between the ages of twelve and fifteen, arrested for stealing and such things as "incorrigibility" or "disorderly conduct." Girls made up about 20 percent of the total; most were sixteen or seventeen years old and were arrested for "immorality," which usually meant prostitution. Like other interested citizens, Lathrop viewed the growing numbers of poor troubled children as part of the so-called immigration problem that dominated so many aspects of American urban life. True, delinquent children were disproportionately from families with foreign-born parents. However, the Hull House reformers understood that immigrant children were not necessarily more criminal. They knew that white middle-class Americans tolerated the indiscretions of native-born American children more than those of the foreign born or the children of the foreign born. Children in immigrant families tended to live in crowded neighborhoods that were under police surveillance. This meant that youngsters involved in rather minor offenses were more likely to come to the attention of the authorities. Native-born American parents could protect their children from run-ins with the law.

Many Americans believed that the problem of juvenile delinquency among immigrants could be addressed by stopping the influx of foreigners. To bolster their cause, they often called on the new "science" of eugenics, which held that immigrants' negative traits like criminality were associated with inferior genes. Lathrop and her allies believed that immigrants bore certain racial characteristics, but they did not embrace eugenics as it was promoted in the early twentieth century. Lathrop once noted that it was impossible to know what sort of combination of biology and environment shaped behavior. Most important Lathrop and her Hull House sisters believed that immigrant behavior and immigrant culture could change. They rejected the exclusionary approach in favor of efforts to help immigrants adapt to American urban life.

Lathrop and her closest associates also believed that the troubles of African American youth were largely a product of the discrimination they faced in so many aspects of their lives. The women worked with civil rights leaders, including activists in black women's clubs, to combat racism. Nonetheless, they spent far less time and energy on helping poor blacks in comparison to immigrants. This was partly because poor immigrants commanded more attention as so many foreigners arrived in northern cities at the turn of the twentieth century, whereas the influx of poor blacks from the American south, although steady and growing, did not explode until World War I. But numbers are not the whole story. Most white reformers, including those promoting juvenile justice, did not concentrate on poor African Americans because they believed blacks could not adjust as easily to modern American life.

Lathrop was part of a larger movement redefining the meaning of childhood. By 1900 enlightened Americans, along with their European counterparts, had embraced the notion that children and young teenagers were not little adults. Children and teenagers were born innocent and, with the proper upbringing at home and education at school, could become happy and constructive members of society.

In the Progressive Era both men and women focused on children, but women were at the center of the "child saving" movement. With her usual modesty Lathrop refused to take the credit that she and Lucy Flowers deserved for bringing about America's first juvenile court; instead, she attributed its success to the wide mobilization of Chicago women. In 1924 Jane Addams was serving as the chair of the committee organizing the silver anniversary celebration of the Cook County Juvenile Court. One evening she reported with sarcasm to her friend Lathrop, that she, Addams, "had the honor officially to inform her that every woman in Cook County except Mrs. Flowers . . . [and Julia] had been personally responsible for the existence of the court." Lathrop responded that in a sense "it was true, that the court could not have been secured without the backing of thousands of women."[3]

The historian Linda Gordon has written that the "alliance between professionals and volunteers was a defining practice of . . . early twentieth-century women's political culture."[4] Nothing illustrates this better than the story of Lathrop's role in developing Chicago's juvenile justice system. As a member of the Chicago Women's Club (CWC), the Hull House settlement, the state Board of Charities, and the Chicago School of Civics and Philanthropy, she embodied the intertwined alliance; Lathrop leveraged her position in all of these organizations to help create the nation's first juvenile justice system in Cook County, Illinois, that became a model for the country.

In the 1890s, spurred on by Lathrop and Flowers, the CWC began a sustained effort to reform Chicago's treatment of both delinquent and neglected children. The club helped to fund and manage a school for boys who were either serving sentences or waiting at the jail pending trial. In 1892, at one club meeting, the teacher at the jail school riveted her audience with her disturbing report that her pupils had been in an "excitable condition . . . owing to an execution held in the jail." Soon after, the club began pushing for a separate justice system for juveniles; it also worked for stronger compulsory school laws and for a reconsideration of the state and county's treatment of all dependent children.

By agitating in public and privately pressuring lawyers and judges, the CWC won speedier hearings for juveniles so they would not have to languish in jails alongside adults. Judge Richard Tuthill, an important ally in the fight for the juvenile court, agreed to hold special court sessions for boys in order to speed up the process. Lathrop and sister Club members Flowers and Mary Ellen Martin knew that the informal approach to dealing with juveniles was not enough. They drafted a state law in 1895 that would institute a separate judicial system so that the larger history of the child, including his particular family circumstances, could now be considered.

Borrowing from a system put into place in Boston, the bill called for a staff to work with children who would be put on probation rather than sent to jail. On the advice of lawyers who were pessimistic about the bill's success, the CWC abandoned this first effort to implement a new law, but not the cause. As before, whenever she faced opposition, Lathrop swung into action; in this case she worked with reform organizations and prominent Chicagoans to publicize the plight of delinquent and neglected children. As a member of the State Charities Board, she obtained a great deal of "first-hand information" as she put it, "on the conditions of children throughout the state who were in poorhouses or otherwise neglected." The CWC held their own monthly meetings in 1896 to study current Illinois law regarding women and children and also convened a congress of women's clubs in the city to focus on the plight of Illinois children.

In 1898 Lathrop, as head of a CWC committee on probation work, put forth a plan to keep as many children out of the city jail as possible. She recommended that judges dealing with a child offender appoint one of the club members as his or her guardian, keeping the child in his parental home if he lived up to the agreement reached in court. At year's end Lathrop's committee, in cooperation with the Children's Aid Society, had secured the services of two probation officers. Paid by the volunteer organizations and working under the auspices of Hull House, Carl Kelsey and Hull House resident Alzina Parsons Stevens investigated cases and, if they thought appropriate, secured suspended sentences.

All the while Lathrop had not given up on legislation. In 1898 she persuaded Jenkins Lloyd Jones, her colleague on the Illinois State Board of Charities, then serving as the president of the Illinois State Conference of Charities and Corrections (ISCC), to organize its yearly meeting around the topic of neglected, dependent, and delinquent children. Years later Lathrop recalled that at the conference "papers were given by authorities of national standing."[5] In fact, many of those authorities were part of her particular network. Members of Lathrop's Board of Charities, along with the superintendents of the various charities overseen by the board as well as CWC members Lucy Flowers and Mary T. Bartelme delivered papers that addressed the theme "Who are the Children of the State?" A representative of Illinois governor John Tanner, the current secretary of the State Board of Charities Frederick Wines, assured the participants that the governor would respond to the public as "soon as the public knows what it wants." He noted out loud what Lathrop and the other reformers knew: "It is in meetings like this, that public opinion is formed and public sentiment is developed." Lathrop then zeroed in on what she and her allies wanted; she put forth a resolution calling for a new committee to work with other organizations in the state to bring about suitable legislation on juvenile delinquency and dependency.

In fact, even before the conference Lathrop, always the politician, understood that the ISCC committee and the CWC needed other organizations with greater power. She asked lawyer and fellow member of the State Board of Charities, Ephraim Banning, whether he would enlist the aid of Chicago's powerful and politically influential Bar Association. In the fall of 1898, at the annual Bar meeting, Banning put forth exactly the views held by Lathrop and the CWC regarding the problems of delinquent children. The Bar in turn set up its own committee of five to draft the bill for consideration.

Lathrop was, as ever, the pragmatic fighter. She deliberately enlisted the help of prominent men because, as she told Flowers, the bill would have a better chance in the legislature if it wasn't labeled "a woman's measure."[6] Yet in classic Lathrop fashion she worked behind the scenes to ensure that she maintained control of the bill. In deciding which men to appoint to the Bar Committee, Banning and Judge Harvey Hurd, who headed the committee, discussed each possible choice with Lathrop, and she herself met with each prospective member to solicit their participation. All were reformers who had been active in such issues as civil service reform or anti–child labor campaigns. As soon as the committee was formed, Hurd invited Lathrop and Flowers, as representatives of the CWC, back into a newly enlarged group. Lathrop once stated that two leaders on the committee, "Mrs. Lucy Flowers and Judge Harvey B. Hurd worked together with perfect accord, yet in their respective fields. Mrs. Flowers was a leader in the Chicago Women's Club . . . and in many other civic, philanthropic and educational activities. Judge Hurd was a jurist of distinction."[7] Here we see Lathrop bowing to traditional norms, emphasizing the distinctly gendered contributions the two reformers brought as members of different sexes. But in fact Lathrop had worked hard to make sure that this was a committee of very like-minded people, regardless of gender.

The Juvenile Court Bill was introduced in the Illinois House and Senate in February 1899 with the strong backing of progressive politicians, most of them Republicans, the Chicago Bar Association, women reformers, and the powerful *Chicago Tribune*, which provided many articles favorable to the bill. As originally drafted by Lathrop, Flowers, and the other committee members, the "Act to regulate the treatment and control of dependent, neglected, and delinquent children" was much broader in scope than what emerged for signing by Governor Tanner the following April. Nevertheless, throughout the process Lathrop forged ahead with determination to see that a bill to establish a separate juvenile court system, however imperfect, took hold.

Indeed, although the bill was known as the Chicago Bar Association Bill, Lathrop and the women directed much of the lobbying. Using her position as a member of the State Board of Charities, Lathrop wrote to and visited county officials, urging them to press their legislators. Lathrop and Ellen Henrotin, another delegate from the CWC, met with the legislative committees responsible for the bill, and when passage of the bill seemed lost, Lathrop and Flowers, along with others from Hull House and the CWC, put extra pressure on the House speaker and Governor Tanner.

The Illinois Juvenile Court Bill of 1899 defined a new and wide role for county courts throughout the state. They were given jurisdiction not only for delinquents in trouble with the law but also for dependent and neglected children, including all youth under sixteen who were homeless or "without proper parental care" or children under eight deemed to be living with unfit parents. Anyone could petition the court about a child whom they deemed a candidate for possible investigation. Parents would then have to appear in court, and a probation officer would be appointed to investigate the case so that she could supply the judge with information to make a decision. The percentage of boys and girls brought before the court for investigation as dependent or neglected, as opposed to delinquent, was extremely low; for the first ten years of the court's existence it ranged from between 1 and 3 percent. However, if the court judged a child as neglected, he or she could be committed to a state institution, an industrial school, or one of the agencies that could "care for or obtain homes for children" or to some reputable person.[8] For those children arrested as violators of state or local laws, the court often committed them to stay at home while under the supervision of a probation officer. Those children found guilty of serious criminal offenses might be sent to a reform school until they came of age.

Much to Lathrop's disappointment, the bill did not provide for the public payment of probation officers, so the CWC continued to pay the salaries of those in Cook County already at work as well as the added staff. The "work," insisted Lathrop, must depend on "paid volunteers," a statement that nicely embodied her willingness to both embrace an older vision of women as volunteers with a new insistence that they be paid.[9] To raise funds for paying the court officers, Flowers organized the Juvenile Court Committee (JCC), a group of Chicago citizens, with Lathrop as its first president, who quickly turned over the reins to Louise deKoven Bowen, another activist in the CWC and a wealthy benefactor of Hull House. The court relied on the JCC's philanthropy until 1908, when Cook County finally took over the funding of the probation officers.

During the earliest years of the juvenile court, Hull House work, CWC and JCC activism, and the responsibilities of Cook County government were inseparable. The JCC was headquartered at Hull House, which was also the site for its meetings. Within a few years of its establishment the court was placed in a building on city land, which included not only the court but also the probation department, a detention home for boys and girls awaiting adjudication. Naturally enough, the building was diagonally across from Hull House. At the Hull House coffee shop Lathrop lunched with judges and other officials of the court as well as the volunteers, discussing all aspects of the enterprise. The women of the CWC and the JCC not only raised money to pay for probation officers, with so little money allocated by the state and county officials in the early years, they pretty much paid for the detention home and took responsibility for administrating it as well.

The women also had a hand in running the court. First, they ensured that Judge Tuthill would be appointed to head the first official court. The CWC, along with Judge Tuthill and other judges, met together to draw up the plans for court procedures. In the first years Lathrop and other CWC women literally sat with Judge Tuthill to help him decide sentences. The JCC selected the probation officers and met the officers at Hull House to discuss their duties. "We really knew absolutely nothing about such duties," Bowen once admitted, because "there was really no literature on juvenile courts at the time, nor on probation officers and those of us who had the training of these officers had to fall back on our own knowledge of human nature and on our best thought as to their duties."[10]

The JCC didn't question its right to train the probation officers because the state of Illinois Board of Charities in 1904 certified it as a duly incorporated charity organization. In issuing its approval the board noted that JCC members "are reputable and responsible persons, [and] . . . the proposed work is needed and that the incorporation of such association is desirable and for the public good."[11] In the twenty-first century we would be troubled that Lathrop was a member of the State Board of Charities that approved the organization *and* a member of the JCC Board of Directors that managed the organization itself. Lathrop herself was very disturbed by the conflicts of interest that arose when political officials gave jobs at the public charities to their patrons, who in turn were subject only to supervision by those same officials. Yet in the case of the juvenile court Lathrop, like other elite activists, reflected a confidence that their interests and goals put them above the need for truly independent supervision.

Writing later about the early juvenile court, Addams once noted that "never was a social experiment watched with more anxious care than that which Julia Lathrop followed its growth year by year." Lathrop had much to be concerned about; the program was woefully underfunded at the beginning, the industrial (also called reform) schools were crowded, and often the children were placed in situations that were inappropriate to their needs. Moreover, with a new law that now defined the terms "dependent" and "neglected" quite vaguely, Lathrop relied on a juvenile court that was given wide latitude to intervene in the private lives of families.

Lathrop believed that if parents could not raise thriving children, the state ought to assert the principle of *parens patrie*, which gave the government the power to act as guardians for those who could not care for themselves. If possible, they would be placed in other homes, but sometimes in institutional settings. One day in Chicago Lathrop sat in on a juvenile court case regarding the disposition of a twelve-year-old girl. The youngster had lived for five years as a foster child of a woman who ran a hotel, and she had put the girl to work from dawn to dusk, doing arduous work as if she were an indentured servant. A prostitute living at the hotel tried to rescue the child by running away with the girl to another county. Because the court deemed that neither of these circumstances was suitable, Lathrop agreed to become the child's legal custodian, assuming the responsibility for finding a suitable placement. As they were leaving the courthouse together the child asked Lathrop, "Are you going to be my mother now?" Lathrop replied, "No. You have had enough mothers. The judge said, didn't he, that the State of Illinois was going to take care of you now. The Governor has asked me to do such things for the state." In truth Lathrop agreed with her close associate, Judge Julian Mack, that the juvenile court was now doing "the work of the wise and loving parent."[12]

Lathrop believed that most children in trouble with the law, regardless of their social background, could be redeemed. Probation officers, teachers, and others working with children and their parents could turn youth away from a lifetime of crime and help neglected children succeed in living happy and productive lives. Her optimism was born of a conviction that juvenile delinquency was more a product of the social problems confronting Chicago's poor than individual character flaws. In 1912 Lathrop's appointees to the Chicago School of Civics and Philanthropy, Abbott and Breckinridge, published their study of the delinquent children of Cook County, emphasizing the social factors that explained troubled youth. Writing the introduction to the study, Lathrop conceded that the efforts of the court to combat the social problems "wholly restore some children, partly restore others, and sometimes fail." Nonetheless, regardless of the complexities of the problem, "the great and memorable fact must remain that all children need for successful rearing the same conditions: homes of physical and moral decency, fresh air, education, recreation, the fond care of wise mothers and fathers."[13]

Ten years after the founding of the court Lathrop was pleased that probation officers were now civil servants, paid for out of public funds and subject to civil service examinations. The citizens of the JCC, however, still exercised an important role because they were appointed to direct the exam. After the county took over the funding of the court officers, the JCC reconstituted itself as the Juvenile Protective Association (JPA), continuing to provide volunteer probation officers to assist the paid staff. In an effort to prevent delinquency in the first place, the JPA turned to "elevating" the wider neighborhood as well as individual families. As Ethel Sturges Drummer, one of the leaders of the JPA, noted, "The children were not to blame . . . we adults, having leisure, should see to it that the environment was improved. Prevention is better than cure."[14]

Drummer and Lathrop wanted to understand why some children continued to appear in juvenile court with repeat offenses. They were convinced that a number of the children were "psychopathic" cases. As an advocate for the mentally ill in Illinois institutions, Lathrop was already involved in the fledging national movement to promote modern treatment of psychiatric disorders. Such an approach focused on both environmental and biological factors as components of mental illness. Lathrop was one of the founding members of the National Committee on Mental Hygiene in 1909 and the Chicago Committee for Mental Hygiene. Lathrop and Abbott arranged to have psychologist Dr. William Healy give a course at the Chicago School of Civics and Philanthropy on "The Mental and Physical Factors in Delinquency and Dependency," which, according to Abbott, was the first course in social psychology ever given at a school of social work. In 1909 Lathrop, under the auspices of the JPA, hired Dr. Healy to head the newly organized Junior Psychopathic Institute, financed by Drummer, to study the causes of delinquency.

Once the juvenile court took hold in Chicago, Lathrop and other founders crisscrossed the country urging other cities to follow suit. By 1902 four more cities, New York, Cleveland, Milwaukee, and Buffalo, instituted similar courts, with nineteen other cities, including Denver, following the next year. Nine years later twenty-two states had passed juvenile court laws, and some fifteen years later every state but two had some sort of juvenile court, although in many states separate juvenile courts were only available in the larger cities.

In 1925, when Lathrop, Healy, Bowen, Drummer, Addams, and Judge Mack and others gathered to celebrate the twenty-fifth anniversary of the Cook County Court and the fifteenth anniversary of the Psychopathic Institute, they could look back with pride at their accomplishment. They had established that the state had an obligation to care for abandoned and neglected children. In our times the juvenile justice system itself is under threat, and children are increasingly being tried as adults, even as biologists and psychologists are showing that children and adolescents do not have the same brains as adults and cannot make the kinds of judgments expected of adults. Many people today can appreciate the humane impulses motivating the pioneers of the juvenile justice system.

Nonetheless, with the power of the state behind them, Lathrop and her allies sometimes acted without taking into account the rights of parents and without appreciating the important ties between children and parents even in troubled families. The definition of a neglected child, subject to court supervision or, in some cases, removal from the home ranged from such offenses as the drunkenness of parents or the very vague term "lack of care."[15] Lack of care might mean that the child literally had no home, but it also could mean that probation officers and social workers deemed the care not suitable. As the JPA confidently stated in 1909, "If delinquency on the part of the parents in the home reigns supreme, and the children are left to go where they will, do what they will, and grow up as they will, then it is that some organization sincerely interested in the welfare of the children must act as a civic and social conscience, and if necessary stand in *loco parentis*."

The JCC instructions to probation officers show how middle-class expectations about family life and gender roles influenced the reformers' attitudes: "Find out the kind of work the breadwinner is doing; if he is earning as much as he is fit to earn. Teach him how a man ought to carry his responsibility. Advise the mother as to how the home may be made more attractive, cleaner, and better ventilated."[16]

Lathrop believed that poor mothers working outside the home was the single-most important explanation for delinquency. "There can be no question, that a mother cannot be expected to succeed in the duty of keeping her house and children while she uses up in earning money time and strength all of which are needed to discharge the more fundamental duty." All maternalists, according to Ladd-Taylor, believed that "ideally men should earn a family wage to support their 'dependent' wives and children at home." Lathrop sympathized with mothers who sought employment outside the home; they worked because husbands were either dead or had deserted or perhaps the father had been injured on the job, had suffered illness, or did not make a livable wage. She admired the working women but, reflecting both her understanding of the realities for poor working mothers and her own gender ideals, believed that few women could succeed in

combining mother work and wage work. Lathrop and most of the reformers in her circle did not fully appreciate the fact that many immigrants
came from communities in Europe where all members of the family, including mothers, often contributed earnings to help sustain the family.
Moreover, by concentrating on the elimination of wage work for married
women, Lathrop and her close colleagues failed to appreciate its importance to mothers in the African American community. In comparison to
whites, African American mothers, out of necessity, were employed outside the home to a much greater extent than white mothers. Black activist
women at the turn of the twentieth century understood this. While, like
the white reformers, they also "held up the breadwinner husbands and unemployed mothers as ideals . . . black acceptance of married women's employment as a longterm and widespread necessity was much greater than
among whites so much so that it requires a redefinition of 'maternalism.'"
The black maternalists prioritized day nurseries and kindergartens to meet
the needs of working women in their community.[17]

The women reformers preferred that children brought before the juvenile court remain with their families whenever possible. Nevertheless, they
believed that officers of the court had to consider what was the best interest
of the child regardless of the desires of parents or relatives. It was not until
the 1960s that the US Supreme Court stepped in to guarantee that parental rights were respected when mothers and fathers faced the prospect that
they might lose their children. Today many Americans still have concerns
about whether parental rights are respected. And many people have less
faith than Lathrop showed when she told her young charge that "the state
of Illinois" would take care of her. Historians have shown that the powers
given to new government institutions like the juvenile court did not always
translate into better lives for working-class people. Nevertheless, juvenile
courts were not only employed by elites to impose their values on the poor;
poor Americans also made use of the courts for their own needs. Working-
class parents often turned to the juvenile courts to discipline their children.
Parents brought sons to court for failing to turn over needed earnings to
the family or daughters to court when they could not control how and
with whom they socialized and because the girls were not helping mothers
in domestic tasks. In the case of girls, according to historian Mary Odem,
the court system in the Progressive Era was "a complex network of struggles and negotiations among working-class parents, teenager daughters,
and court officials."[18]

As the court developed in the early decades the emphasis on the environmental causes for juvenile delinquency lost ground. While the faculty at the Chicago School of Civics and Philanthropy focused on poverty and the home conditions of the child, the court-appointed probation officers tended to focus on what they viewed as psychiatric problems of the individual delinquent. Lathrop's own approach to the problem put her somewhere in the middle. Although deeply interested in the psychiatric problems of the individual, Lathrop never lost her commitment to the idea that social research ought to lead to social reform.

The JPA shared Lathrop's commitment to social reform, concentrating its efforts on poor neighborhoods to keep children out of trouble. "Police duty in the interest of children" is what Grace Abbott, Edith Abbott's younger sister, also a resident of Hull House, termed the work of the JPA, where she was temporarily employed in 1908. Paid staff and volunteers for the JPA worked in neighborhoods to help factory inspectors root out illegal child labor or to remove children from the Dunning poorhouse. Many JPA efforts to tackle what they saw as the "demoralizing conditions" of a neighborhood might strike us today as prudish, elitist, and censorious. In addition to the presence of saloons, the JPA worried about the immoral influences of the 5-cent movie theaters (nickelodeons), where children could be found crowding outside to look at suggestive posters, or amusement parks with their "suggestive and immoral shows." The JPA staff was happy to report that in 1908 they succeeded in banning penny slot machines and limiting the sales of "obscene post cards." Throughout her life Lathrop worried about the immoral influences of some of the more risqué films of the 1920s and early 1930s; she and Jane Addams endorsed efforts to regulate the content of movies in order to spare children from their negative effects.[19]

The JPA paid so much attention to immigrant neighborhoods because the women firmly believed that immigrants could, with help from interested citizens, adapt to and succeed in the modern industrial city. Providing badly needed social services to newly arrived immigrants could address problems of criminality and help immigrants find adequate housing and employment.

Juvenile justice reformers especially worried about the numbers of young immigrant women brought to court on charges of prostitution. Here again traditional norms about natural characteristics of boys and girls influenced their understanding of the problem. The women believed that boys, naturally rambunctious and mischievous, could be saved from a life of crime with relative ease. Boys were arrested for such offenses as stealing coal from railway yards, setting bonfires or junk heaps, perhaps illegally jumping trains, or gambling. Girls more likely found themselves in court on charges of immorality. Once girls entered into prostitution, most people, including family members, regarded them as deviant and disgraced girls, less likely to be "rehabilitated" and more likely to enter into an "unseemly" life. By contrast, Lathrop wrote in 1912, "If a boy's will is the wind's will, and the period of willful adventure must have its gusty way, it is quite as true that the wind often quiets."

Lathrop herself was ahead of many reformers; she did not necessarily believe that girls arrested on charges of immorality were deviant, but she acknowledged the opinion of the larger society at the time. Comparing the girls to the boys, she noted, "It is not so easy to speak of his elder sister's return, and we are still too unused to regarding her waywardness as of like quality with his, however different its manifestation—a difference, which increases so inexpressibly the difficulty of her return to orderly living." This assumption about the depravity of delinquent girls meant that once brought before the court, girls were much less likely than boys to be put on probation and more likely to be placed in reform institutions. Studying the first ten years of the Chicago court, Abbott and Breckinridge reported that close to 60 percent of the boys who appeared before the court "were returned to their homes and only 21 percent were sent to institutions. With girls the proportions were reversed. More than half (51 percent) were committed to institutions, while only 37 percent were placed on probation."[20]

Lathrop and her sisters in the Chicago reform movement wanted to prevent immigrant young women from falling into prostitution in the first place. A group of women active in building the Chicago labor movement first focused on unaccompanied immigrant girls who arrived at Ellis Island in New York, bound for Chicago. The activists feared that the girls would be picked up by male traffickers in the sex trade posing as helpers to the women looking for friends and relatives. To combat the problem, the reformers began a program of assistance to help the new arrivals unite with their kin. In 1907 Lathrop, along with Hull House residents Breckinridge, Addams, and Judge Mack, founded the Immigrants' Protective League (IPL) to assist both immigrant men and women with a variety of problems that they faced as newcomers to the United States.

Grace Abbott, one of the younger Hull House residents, was especially close to Lathrop, eventually following her to Washington to work at the Children's Bureau. Happy to leave the work of the JPA, Grace became the first director of the League. A fierce advocate for immigrants, she expanded the League's work in countless ways, from reuniting single women with families to providing housing for stranded arrivals, to helping immigrants send money to relatives abroad, safe from embezzlers.

The history of the IPL illustrates the permeable boundaries of public and private work that was a hallmark of the era. It began as a volunteer organization, but thanks to the work of Lathrop and the other board members, in 1919 the state of Illinois established a commission with state responsibility to help immigrants. The IPL then merged with the commission, under the leadership of Grace Abbott. In 1921, when the new governor abolished the commission, the IPL returned to its work as a volunteer organization. Before she went to Washington and after she retired from the Children's Bureau, Lathrop served as a very active member of the League Board.

Lathrop's attitudes toward immigrants show once again a reformer who embraced innovative ideas even as she clung to the more narrow-minded views of her social class. During the bleakest months of the 1893 depression Lathrop worked hard with the National Council of Jewish Women in Chicago, a group of prosperous women of German Jewish background from families that had emigrated in the mid-nineteenth century. The council established an office at Hull House to provide food to poor and newly arrived Russian Jewish immigrants. Lathrop voiced enormous sympathy for the plight of the immigrants. On one occasion, however, a group of the immigrants, through an interpreter, arrived at Hull House to complain that the food provided for them by the Canal Street soup kitchen was made with lard, which was forbidden in the kosher Jewish diet. Lathrop became indignant, exclaiming, "Of course, you would rather starve!" Addams, more appreciative of immigrant values than her friend, attributes Lathrop's reactions to her lifelong impatience with religious ritual, but it also reflects a lack of appreciation of other cultures and different norms.

In her early writings about poor Chicagoans, Lathrop emphasized that certain ethnic traits, whether cultural or racial, contributed to the difficulties they might be having. In 1894 she noted that "here is a foreign population living in every sort of maladjustment—Russian Jews, whose two main resources are tailoring and peddling, quite incapable in general of applying themselves to manual labor . . . here are Germans and Irish, largely of that type which is reduced by drink to a squalor it is otherwise far above."[21]

Lathrop and her closest companions included men and women from immigrant backgrounds among their wider circle of friends. Yet their own words revealed their preferences for ethnic minorities who looked and acted in ways that conformed to the reformers' own sense of hierarchy. In 1921 Lathrop wrote to Grace Abbott for suggestions as to candidates for a position as coordinator of a newly formed Committee on the Welfare of Immigrants. Her younger friend did have a candidate, recommending appointing a John Valentine of Chicago. "While of Southern Italian origin," she wrote Lathrop, "he is American in looks (not dark) and in manners (excellent) and one of the ablest young persons I have met in a long time" who can get along with wealthy citizens and with immigrants. Lathrop replied to her friend, "I take great note of what you say about John Valentine." Lathrop socialized with the leading settlement house activist in New York, Lillian Wald, as well as Josephine Goldmark, who, like Wald, was of German Jewish background, an activist on behalf of protective labor legislator, and the sister of the famed attorney, Louis Brandeis, appointed to the US Supreme Court in 1916. During the 1920s, with antiforeign sentiments sweeping the country, she and her close allies fought against anti-Semitism. Yet among themselves the women could engage in anti-Semitic stereotyping. Once, in the 1920s, when Lathrop asked her friends about the advisability of appointing Sophie Loeb to the League of Nations Committee on Child Welfare, she received a number of negative responses. Some may well have been right on the mark in terms of Loeb's unsuitability for the job, but they included such statements like the following from the always blunt Florence Kelley: "Miss Loeb is a typical New York Jewess of the most 'pushful kind.'"[22]

Whatever her negative views about ethnic culture, Lathrop believed immigrants were adaptable and that she and other motivated reformers could help the newcomers adjust to American life. At Hull House Lathrop gave talks to the older native-born Americans living in the neighborhood about their pioneer past; she made a special point of linking the histories of her audience to the experience of the new immigrants. She and Addams talked together about their own families who built the towns of Illinois. They believed that like their immigrant neighbors in Chicago, their ancestors arrived in their new homes with little understanding of the circumstances that might await them. Eastern Europeans faced adjustments when they moved from rural work in Europe to factory work in Chicago. So too farm youths around Rockford faced challenges when they had to give up a life of self-directed work on the farm for summer work in the local watch factories. Speaking to her audience of older Chicagoans, Lathrop, according to her friend Addams, made "human and understandable not only the pioneers but their successors as well."[23]

If Lathrop and Addams could identify with European immigrants, they had a harder time identifying common human experiences across the color line. As racial liberals, more so than most white progressive reformers of their day, the women of Hull House actively worked on behalf of civil and political rights for African Americans and condemned the lack of economic opportunities available to black Chicagoans. But as historian Khalil Gibran Muhammad points out, for white liberals, African Americans' "ancestral victimization as the children and grandchildren of ex-slaves tied them both to an exceptional past and a peculiar present."[24] Lathrop and her peers believed that the so-called problems of black culture, rooted in the experience of slavery, were especially intractable, making it harder for blacks, in comparison to European immigrants, to adapt to modern American life.

From its earliest days Hull House welcomed individual African Americans through its doors. At a time when most whites refused to socialize with blacks, Florence Kelley roomed for a while with an African American doctor, Harriet Rice, and in 1899 Jane Addams invited delegates to the National Association of Colored Women convention meeting in Chicago to lunch at Hull House. Hull House frequently hosted prominent African Americans for dinner and invited speakers such as W. E. B. Dubois to give major addresses at the settlement. Addams joined with the great black freedom fighter and Chicago resident Ida B. Wells to protest the possibility that the Chicago public schools would embrace segregation. After the founding of the National Association for the Advancement of Colored People (NAACP) in 1909, Addams spoke publicly to her neighbors as well as nationwide audiences of her work as a leader of the new organization.

Black clubwomen, along with their white allies, pushed the juvenile court in Chicago to improve services to black children, including providing reform schools for black children that were a far better alternative to jails and necessary because so few black children were admitted to white reformatories. Marcia Chatelain points out that "with few institutional options specifically for orphaned or abandoned black girls, city authorities sometimes sent them to juvenile detention facilities, essentially criminalizing them for being black."[25] Black women fought to become probation officers so they could protect black children not only from crime but also from discrimination by the court system.

Lathrop herself intervened on behalf of African American social workers in Chicago. In 1911 the court and its founders faced sustained attacks by the president of the Cook County Board of Commissioners, Peter Bartzen, and others who wished to wipe out the entire system. One target of attack was the fact that the JPA appointed the probation officers, rather than political officials who, Barzten asserted, better understood the needs of immigrant communities. Thus the fight about the juvenile court was embroiled in the ongoing battle between Lathrop and politicians over political appointees. In campaigning against the juvenile court system Bartzen enlisted an ally, Winifred Black, who wrote a series of columns in the *Chicago Examiner* exploiting racial fears to generate opposition to the court. The articles, as historian Joanne Goodwin has written, "captured two points about which Americans shared great anxiety—the social relations of sex and race—and wove them into a public criticism of the activist state." One "outrage" was the fact that an African American probation officer took charge of Irish families. "Whose brilliant idea," asked Ms. Black in one article, "was it to put a colored woman into a district of Irish people as its probation officer. A good woman, a highly intelligent woman . . . but who can have the entire confidence in the common sense of the people who send that woman out to look after the destiny and welfare of an Irish widow who would rather die than to admit that any one not of her own particular race can possibly give her any kind of advice that would be beneficial?"

Apparently Lathrop thought it was a good idea. When the story broke, Joanna Snowden, an African American probation officer who had been working out of Hull House, wrote to Lathrop, asking for her help in countering the attack by speaking with the county officials who had criticized the arrangement. "You have no doubt observed it at Hull House and may have noted with what freedom of friendship and good will have gone on between myself and the parents and children as well as older boys and girls of the other race who visited me. . . . I love my work and have only been aware that those I was given charge of needed my help and lost sight of color and class." We do not know whether Ms. Snowden was able to keep her job, but Lathrop and her allies successfully fought off the efforts to put the appointment of probation officers in the hands of Cook County politicians. Lathrop did intervene with County officials to provide personal testimony of Snowden's excellent work. "My heart is full of thanks," Snowden wrote again to Lathrop, "for your bravery and friendship and I close with deepest and continued gratitude."[26] Snowden would go on to become a leader in the African American women's club movement. Lathrop intervened with public agencies on behalf of black individuals throughout her life, both in Illinois and in Washington. She also broadened her work against racism through her lifelong, active membership in the NAACP.

Whereas many Americans, including leading progressive reformers, believed inferior genes explained the problems of African Americans, the pioneers of the juvenile court emphasized environmental explanations. For example, because of their efforts to rescue girls from prostitution, the JPA learned that most of the maids working in houses of prostitution were black. Employment agencies refused to place white maids in these establishments because if the white women became prostitutes, the agency might be held responsible for pandering. "In an attempt to ascertain the causes which would account for a great amount of delinquency among the colored boys and the public opinion which would so carelessly place the virtue of the colored girl in jeopardy," the JPA, under the auspices of Bowen, launched an investigation into the industrial and social status of blacks in Chicago. Their publication, "The Colored People of Chicago," concluded that African American children were disproportionately arrested because segregation confined them to neighborhoods where vice flourished. Black children were barred from participating in "wholesome" leisure activities. Moreover, black fathers had little access to adequately paying jobs, and black mothers, even more so than their immigrant counterparts, were away at work. Finally, the investigators pointed out one hundred years ago something that resonates in the twenty-first century: African American children are more often arrested and convicted for crimes, both serious and petty, on extremely flimsy evidence: "that any negro who happens to be near the scene of a crime of disorder is promptly arrested and often on evidence upon which a white man would be discharged."[27]

Nevertheless, despite their sensitivity to racial discrimination, Lathrop and her sister reformers of Hull House viewed African Americans as vastly different from white Americans, immigrant or native born. They believed that slavery had left African Americans with an inferior cultural inheritance in comparison to Americans of European descent, which contributed to greater delinquency. They also thought that blacks were more likely to steal, and because of sexual exploitation in slavery, black women were more inclined to engage in illicit sex. It is not surprising, therefore, that despite the commitment to integrated schools, even liberal settlement house workers did not embrace social integration. They did not challenge segregation in housing and, during its first four decades, neither the Hull House boarding house for girls or its summer camp included African Americans. In their private writings the Hull House women engaged in racist stereotyping. Thus, in the early 1920s Lathrop, now retired from the Children's Bureau, wrote to Grace Abbott that she accepted a last-minute request to fill in for Addams at a dinner because the Hull House leader was ill. "I had fondly intended to 'nig' and spend Sunday at home," she confided to her friend. In this context we can conclude that the shortened version of the 'n-word' is being used as a synonym for being lazy, a troubling example of how racial liberals such as Lathrop could so casually make use of the worst racial slurs. Lathrop's good friend, Florence Kelley, was perhaps the most outspoken champion of African American rights among the original Hull House circle, yet even she, writing to Lathrop in 1914 about her concerns regarding Congress's appropriation of funds for the Children's Bureau, asked, "'Is there a 'nigger in the wood pile' in the restricting of the House appropriation to infant mortality and dangerous occupations?"[28] This common racist phrase, heard in song, seen in theater, and found in fiction, was meant to connote something hidden and unpleasant that might surprise someone. The ease with which the reform women made use of such racist language in their private writings may be clues as to why they did not prioritize social welfare for the black community. As Chatelain has shown, many white reformers involved in Chicago's juvenile court system "doubted the ability of African Americans to lead their own institutions."[29] Nor did white liberals have the same faith that they could help the black community in comparison to recent immigrants.

One might conclude that given her many commitments, Lathrop could hardly take on more issues. However, because she took a holistic approach to the problems of troubled and neglected youth, Lathrop worked on many other campaigns to improve children's lives. She fought for state aid to widowed mothers, often called "mothers' pensions," so that women in fatherless families would not be forced to work for wages and thereby neglect their children or have to surrender children to public institutions. In 1911 Lathrop, Addams, Abbott, and Breckinridge, along with the juvenile court justices, worked with mothers' pensions leagues, mounting a successful push in Illinois to enact one of the first such laws in the country. By 1920 most states had enacted some form of mothers' pensions. The Illinois State law, known as the Funds to Parents Law, authorized the juvenile court to provide public funds for children who were then placed on probation in their homes. To administer the program, juvenile court Judge Merritt Pinckney appointed a committee on mothers' pensions, consisting of representatives of the local private agencies and volunteer organizations. Lathrop, representing the Federation of Settlements, was one of six members of the executive committee. She also promoted stronger laws to prohibit truancy and child labor because she believed that both contributed to juvenile delinquency.

Lathrop lauded the Cook County juvenile court because it tackled so many aspects of child welfare. "For the first time in history," she wrote in 1912, "the so-called juvenile court reveals a great social situation and thereby bestows the greatest aid toward social justice which this generation comprehends—*the truth made public*."[30] She was convinced that once the truth was made public, the country would act to improve the lives of its children. That same year, at the height of progressive reform, the US Congress created the first federal agency to "investigate and report on all matters pertaining to the welfare of children and child life." The president of the United States, William Howard Taft, consulted with the two most famous settlement house leaders, Jane Addams of Chicago and Lillian Wald of New York, about who he should appoint as the first head of the US Children's Bureau. Although some child welfare activists put forth male candidates, Addams and Wald wanted a woman for this important job. They told the president that Julia Lathrop would be the perfect choice, and he agreed.

5

"Chief"

> "Miss Lathrop . . . was the first woman to be made head of a Federal Commission in this county and she will be paid the highest salary of any woman in the Government employ. Hers will be unquestionably the most important position held by any woman in this country."
>
> —*New York Times*, September 29, 1912

"America's First Official Mother"—that's how the *Chicago Daily American* referred to her in the banner headline that introduced its profile of Julia Lathrop. The article appeared in May 1912, three weeks after the Senate confirmed her as the chief of the Children's Bureau, the first woman ever to go through the confirmation process reserved for high-level government appointments.

Like the *New York Times* article published in September, the *Daily American*'s profile of Lathrop lauded her appointment as an important milestone in the history of women. Directing a federal agency meant a national platform to publicize the social conditions of millions of American families. Lathrop used her position to promote and to lobby on behalf of innovative laws at the state, local, and national level. She could offer hundreds of paid jobs to women, a long-held goal of hers, and she moved quickly to do so. She also used her national celebrity to promote such issues as woman's suffrage. An administrator and political player on the national scene, she was an important model for other women, especially young women who could now imagine themselves doing political work on a national scale and paid labor that was widely recognized.

Yet the Chicago headline reminds us of the contradictions that surrounded women in the political arena. Lathrop's new job carried with it the comforting notion that even as officials, women in government would confine themselves to affairs traditionally associated with motherhood. Just as she had done in Chicago, Lathrop accepted the idea that women had a special interest in and affinity for issues involving family and children. Sometimes she embraced this assumption because she believed it. But Lathrop also wrapped her work around women's traditional roles for pragmatic reasons. She understood that many Americans, including many Washington politicians, disliked the idea of women working as paid professionals and participating as government workers, not to mention as voters. After twenty years of experience in Chicago she knew that many people opposed her entire agenda. They would resist all efforts of the Children's Bureau to expand government responsibility for the health and welfare of American citizens. In responding, Lathrop, true to form, was both bold and cautious.

Lathrop's appointment as chief came rather suddenly, but the creation of the Children's Bureau did not. Lillian Wald and Lathrop's old friend Florence Kelley began the effort in 1903. Wald, a nurse, was head of Henry Street Settlement House in New York; Florence Kelley, by then the head of the National Consumers League (NCL), now lived in New York at Wald's settlement. Wald often told a story that one morning at breakfast the two women were discussing a letter they had just received about the high rate of infant mortality during the summer. Wald told her friend that she really did not know of any source of information on the problem. By contrast, she saw in the morning newspaper that the government was financing an investigation into the reasons why the cotton crop was vulnerable to damage from the boll weevil. Wald asked, "If the Government can have a department take such an interest in what is happening to the cotton crop, why can't it have a bureau to look after the nation's child crop?"[1]

Of course, Wald, Kelley, and the entire social settlement community understood that in comparison to agriculture, it would be far harder to develop a federal government interest in children. Many Americans still believed that child welfare should be the responsibility of parents, not government entities. By 1903 states and localities had expanded government services. The idea that federal government might have a role in social welfare was even more controversial and seemed a great departure from the American tradition of deferring to the states.

Kelley and Wald believed the time was ripe to push officials in Washington, especially with a new president, Theodore Roosevelt, at the helm. Roosevelt was openly committed to an activist federal government. Sometimes this meant federal investigations to shed light on problems; at other times investigations could lead to passing new laws. In 1906 Kelley, Wald, and sociologist Edward Divine of Columbia University, Roosevelt's close friend, pressed the president to back a children's bureau. Although Roosevelt endorsed the proposal privately, he waited until early 1909, one month before he was to leave office, to publicly back the legislation.

Undaunted, Wald and Kelley turned to the organized reform community to help publicize and promote their idea. They mobilized Kelley's own organization, the NCL; the Chicago JPA, so important to Lathrop; and many other women's organizations. Like Lathrop, who relied on important men when she wanted the juvenile court bill passed in Illinois, Wald and Kelley knew that for this campaign, which involved passing a bill in an all-male US Congress, they needed men at the forefront. They turned to the National Child Labor Committee (NCLC) to broadcast the need for a bureau. Although Kelley and Wald were both active in the organization, the NCLC was overwhelmingly a male association. The NCLC also drafted the legislation that went to Congress in 1906 and steered the legislation through its ups and its downs until it was finally passed in 1912.

After years of attending conferences at the local level, state boards of charities and corrections, private and religious agencies, and the settlement movement finally gathered in Washington in 1909 at the invitation of President Roosevelt for the first White House Conference on Dependent Children. Only 30 of the 210 delegates were women; at the time women, so active in the states, were only "inching onto the national platform."[2] The conference centered on the issue that had long preoccupied reformers, including Lathrop: how to keep troubled, orphaned, and neglected children out of institutions. But the president, in order to maintain pressure on a Congress that had repeatedly failed to implement the Children's Bureau, now asked whether the conference could also consider the issue of a federal children's agency.

The conference unanimously endorsed the need for the bureau, but delegates disagreed on exactly what it was meant to do. Most attendees believed that the new agency should investigate the conditions of American children but not promote an agenda; lobbying should be left to voluntary groups. Historian Kriste Lindenmeyer notes that possibly some of the men

who were leaders in "already existing and nationally recognized child welfare agencies did not have the same degree of desire for a federal children's
bureau as Wald, Kelley, and Addams, whose influence came largely from
outside the male-dominated child welfare associations."[3] Wald had no intention of allowing the agency to focus only on data collection. Like the
Hull House women, she disagreed with the emerging trends in academia,
mostly among men, that there should be a dichotomy between social investigation and social advocacy. Wald investigated problems in order to gain
the tools necessary for promoting the proper course of action. Despite their
differences, however, the leading advocates of the legislation closed ranks to
lobby for passage of a bill. With a few fits and starts, Congress authorized
the Children's Bureau in 1912, and President William Taft, recognizing the
surge of progressive idealism, signed the bill. Taft, running for a second term
that year, faced three candidates, Teddy Roosevelt of the newly formed Progressive Party, Woodrow Wilson of the Democrats, and Socialist Party candidate Eugene Debs; they all campaigned for a more activist government.

Once selected by the president, Lathrop had no hesitation about declaring her loyalties to the female reformers. She telegrammed Wald just
after she heard the news: "I am still dazed by appointment. If Senate confirms I fly to consult you. Remember, hence forward I am your chief[.]
Responsibility the people who made the Bureau must now make me[.] I
will try my best to make good." After her Senate confirmation Lathrop
had to wait for the congressional appropriation of funds for the agency.
She used her time well, embarking on her usual exhausting schedule. Over
the spring and summer she met with her own boss, the head of the Department of Commerce and Labor and the chief statistician of the Census
Bureau in Washington. She met with Homer Folks of the NCLC in New
York and, of course, as promised, Lillian Wald. She also attended a Vassar
Board of Trustees meeting in Poughkeepsie, "dashing" back to Washington
to be sworn in. She then went to San Francisco to address the biannual
convention of the General Federation of Women's Clubs (GFWC). A trip
to California in those days was not only time-consuming; Lathrop had to
pay for these travels out of her own pocket. But she knew her success at the
bureau depended on the women's reform community, which could mobi-
lize on behalf of her initiatives.[4]

When Julia took up her post in late August at age fifty-four, she arrived in style, with the well-appointed look that she had cultivated in Chicago. Wald later joked that before moving to Washington Lathrop came to

New York "for two urgent reasons." One was to consult with Wald about her upcoming work; the other was to find a good New York dressmaker so she might "becomingly appear for the Bureau." Julia dressed well because she enjoyed it. Many letters to her sister recount various shopping expeditions in the United States and abroad. Once, after she arrived in New York for a variety of activities, including a speech, Lathrop found that she had left her violet dress for the occasion back in Washington. "Hence a bold gamble," she wrote Anna. "I went to the Flambeau shop and ordered a one piece black satin very simply and soft and not too youthful and going on overhead. . . . Also ordered at Altman's a quite horribly costly jet bead collar to go with it and expect to be inconspicuously decent and to have for comfortable friend for long time. Dress to cost $75.00," which is an amount worth over $900 today. In a follow-up letter that same evening Julia told Anna that a nasty cold forced her to cancel the speech scheduled for later in the week. "This does not make me really regret the new clothing. It rather reconciles me."

Lathrop believed that female reformers "must be careful about their hats and all that goes with them" and that it was an accomplishment to "show that a becoming frock is not inconsistent with a commitment to social justice."[5] Many politicians accompanied their attacks on the social reform agenda with personal comments about Lathrop and her friends. Conservative congressmen called the women unsexed, unhappy individuals who interfered in the lives of American families as a substitute for raising their own children. From Lathrop's point of view dressing well in conformity with traditional norms was partly a defensive strategy.

Lathrop settled in at an apartment hotel in Washington. A beautiful structure—the Ontario, built in 1906 in the Beaux Arts style—had just the kind of living quarters that suited her. Most of the women who came to work in the Children's Bureau or other government agencies found accommodations in boarding houses or apartment hotels that, like the settlement houses, allowed the women to escape cooking chores. Lathrop's apartment contained a kitchen where she ate breakfast in private or sometimes with friends. But she ate dinner in the common dining room, with meals provided. When Lathrop retired from the bureau, bequeathing the job of chief to her friend and protégée Grace Abbott, she also turned over the apartment to her.

Only a few months after taking office Lathrop faced the real possibility that the newly elected president of the United States, Woodrow Wilson, might replace her. Many Democrats thought their work on behalf of Wilson's election in November should now be rewarded by an appointment of one of their own. Even as Lathrop's promoters argued that her appointment was not based on politics, at least one person pointed out that she had publicly identified herself as a supporter of Roosevelt during the 1912 campaign, even marching in a Chicago parade on his behalf. Lathrop took Lillian Wald up on her offer to intercede on her behalf with the president. In her usual way Lathrop wrote to Wald that her concern was not so much what would happen to her; she knew it was the president's right to appoint their own bureau chiefs. Lathrop even added to her typed letter, in her own handwriting, that when speaking with the president, Wald should "Please make clear that I want nothing."[6] But, as she told Wald, she was concerned that all of her newly appointed staff, already embarked on important projects, not be replaced. The diffident words notwithstanding, not only Wald but also Lathrop's entire reform network, including the GFWC, went to work on her behalf, with a massive letter-writing campaign that ultimately convinced the president to renominate her to the post; the Senate quickly confirmed his request.

Lathrop had to cope with more than a change in the political landscape. The Children's Bureau was originally housed in the Department of Commerce and Labor. On the day he left office President Taft signed a bill that elevated the importance of labor in American public policy by establishing a separate Department of Labor; Lathrop's bureau now was transferred to the new agency. Lathrop took the change in stride, telling Wald she did not think it would do either temporary or permanent damage, but it did require a move to new quarters. The move took place during a particularly difficult time for Lathrop, who became ill at the end of her first summer vacation.

Lathrop came down with typhoid in September 1913; in October a very sick chief returned to her sister's home in Rockford so Anna could care for her. Anna became Lathrop's secretary as well, keeping in contact with the bureau staff in Washington, reporting the progress of her illness, and relaying instructions from her sister about bureau affairs. In mid-October bureau staffer Fanny Fiske wrote to Anna, telling her, "We are only saying here at the office that Miss Lathrop was run down from the year's work and is resting at home for a few weeks." Anna wrote right back to Fiske to tell her "Miss Lathrop's illness is a straight case of infection" and that "the Associated Press had now announced it as para-typhoid [similar to regular typhoid without as high a fever]; not exhaustion due to overwork." Anna's quick response might have reflected her sense that in those days exhaustion was a diagnosis all too commonly made about women who exerted themselves beyond their traditional roles as wives and mothers. By the third week in October Lathrop was improving and wanted to let her staff know; true to her professional training, she instructed her sister to send almost-daily charts to Fiske, which tracked Lathrop's temperature throughout the day. [7]

While Lathrop was convalescing in Rockford, Fiske kept her updated on happenings in Washington. She reported that by mid-October the bureau had finally moved to their new offices in the Department of Labor. Although the rooms in the Willard Building "were pretty good . . . ours is rather sad—a front room, but small and the Willard Hotel cuts off any sun or sky. But we have a fine view of ladies and gentlemen dressing at their windows in the hotel."[8]

Lathrop's friends and associates in Chicago often remarked about her comfortable relationships with those she worked with, particularly her younger colleagues. She brought that same sensibility to Washington. Working at the bureau under Lathrop was hard, but it was also fun. She often entertained her staff at her home and at those gatherings, and as one participant recalled, there was no "shop talk." Once, on the occasion of a trip abroad by Lathrop and bureau employee Grace Abbott, the staff sent them off to England with a six-stanza poem, signed by some seventy staffers, entitled, "To J.L. and G.A. on Leaving Home." The last stanza was a humorous nod to their reputation as humorless reformers:

Oh the C.B. may be highbrow and the C.B. may be cold
But the C.B.'s loyal to its own,
And neither time nor distance can break its loving hold
On those it sends to England on a loan![9]

The informality among bureau staffers was not to be confused with the flexible work style at Hull House. While she was recovering in Rockford, Lathrop's assistant chief Lewis Meriam reported to her about the number of staffers taking leaves of absences. Three weeks after he wrote to Lathrop, Meriam issued a memorandum to all bureau employees stating that he feared "we are laying the Bureau open to some very unfavorable criticism because of our lax observance of the usual attendance regulations." Perhaps as a male, Meriam found it easier to issue strict directives about rules and regulations. But Lathrop took on this role when needed. Of a new set of directives issued by the Labor Department in 1914, outlining the detailed procedures for requesting absences in advance, Lathrop told her staff that they "seemed reasonable and implied no lack of confidence." Lathrop was reluctant to become mired in formal rules and regulations, however, so she added to her memo about the new Labor directives that "the Bureau is conducted on the honor system and a general statement [about absences] will be vouched for by me."[10]

Lathrop's appointment of Meriam as assistant chief and Ethelbert Stewart as statistician, both from the Census Bureau, reflected Lathrop's philosophy, already well honed in Chicago, about sentiment and social science. As she told her audience at the GFWC meeting in San Francisco, "the Bureau needs . . . the sternest statistical accuracy because its appeal to the human passion of pity must never be founded on anything but truth . . . and must be able to present all its statements dispassionately with scientific candor and faithfulness."[11]

But Lathrop also knew that every social investigation was intertwined with politics. Although activists against child labor had fought hard to establish the bureau, the agency could not tackle that subject right away; it was simply too controversial. Instead, Lathrop began a campaign to improve birth registrations throughout the country, and she initiated studies of infant mortality.

In early 1913 four bureau investigators embarked on a case study of infant mortality in Johnstown, Pennsylvania, a factory town that was home to many poor immigrants; soon after, the bureau conducted six other studies of factory towns. Using the information from the local government and from church records, the staff interviewed as many mothers as possible who had given birth to babies in 1911, regardless of whether the babies had survived the first two years. With a small staff and meager resources, Lathrop, continuing in the tradition of her investigative work in Chicago, relied on local volunteers, including women's clubs, to assist her staff.

The bureau's approach from the onset emphasized its respect for the mothers in the factory towns. Interviewers were expected to convey that the bureau "recognizes mothers and that it plans to build its future work to a considerable extent on their advice, testimony, and cooperation." To put women at ease about what could seem a very intrusive project, Lathrop hired only women investigators. Lest they seem to mimic the judgmental approach of many workers, they were told not to inquire about whether children were born out of wedlock nor about possible alcoholism or venereal disease in the family; rather, they focused on family income, housing conditions, mother's maternal history, and ethnicity. The mothers, for their part, wanted to know why so many of their children died and how they could prevent future tragedies. In Johnstown the bureau staff sought to interview about fifteen hundred mothers; only two refused an interview. Foreign-language interpreters participated in a number of the interviews so that the voices of immigrant mothers could truly be heard.

The infant mortality studies confirmed for the progressive reformers that poverty, not poor genes and bad mothering, accounted for significant differences in infant mortality among families. Children of fathers making less than $550 annually were twice as likely to die as those in families with the father earning about $1,200. Medical conditions might be the proximate cause for these deaths, but the larger social conditions, which, among other things, often forced mothers to work, were the true culprits. Not satisfied to merely investigate the problem, the Children's Bureau, true to Lillian Wald's vision, used the results to publicize the poor standard of living in many working-class communities. For Lathrop, the Johnstown report showed "the imperative need of ascertaining a standard of life for the American family, a standard which must rest upon such betterment of conditions of work and pay as will permit parents to safeguard infants within the household."[12]

In order to tackle all the issues that concerned Lathrop—infant mortality, poor school attendance, and illegal child labor—the country needed an adequate system of birth registration. The Census Bureau set a mark of a 90 percent registration rate for inclusion in their national birth registration area. At the time only eight states and two cities, New York and Washington, DC, met the criteria. The Children's Bureau launched a national campaign for complete registration.

The campaign, like so many bureau initiatives, involved a two-pronged approach to publicizing a problem. First, it relied on publications—its own and others. In 1913 the bureau published *Birth Registration: An Aid in Protecting the Lives and Rights of Children*. The bureau also used the newspapers to argue the need for birth certificates. "Can You Prove Your Right to Vote?" one press release asked in 1920. "The right to vote is only one of the many important rights which may be difficult to prove without legal evidence."[13]

The second approach came straight out of Lathrop's old toolbox. In the spirit of Hull House and the Chicago School of Civics and Philanthropy, the bureau launched detailed local investigations in the various states to call attention to the problem. Because of her own scarce resources, Lathrop once again turned to the volunteer social reform organizations. Kelley mobilized the NCL and the NCLC, and the GFWC joined the cause, as did the YWCA, among others. By 1915 over three thousand women had participated in the campaign across the country. After canvassing houses throughout cities and states in the country, the bureau and their volunteer helpers compared their findings to the official government statistics of birth to show the vast differences between the number of children actually born and the number officially recorded. Data collection was only part of the initiative; once the discrepancies were revealed, the local organizations lobbied their state officials to improve their registration programs. The intense political pressure produced impressive results; by 1920 fifteen more states had met the Census Bureau's standard of 90 percent registration.

Mobilizing support for improving the social welfare of working-class families meant that the bureau had to maintain close ties with reform organizations. Lathrop very much saw herself as a lobbyist for social reform, and she enjoyed the enterprise. She once told her friend Florence Kelley that "I try to remember that lobbying is an alluring indoor sport if properly played." At the Children's Bureau she proved a master of the game. About a year after she arrived Lathrop requested the appropriation for the fiscal year 1914–1915 be increased to $165,000, which does not seem like much to us today, but the year before it was $25,000. The House Appropriations Committee refused to recommend the increase, so Lathrop sprang into action, mobilizing her "generals," Jane Addams and Mary McDowell in Chicago and Kelley and Wald in New York, to "gain the full support of her troops," according to historian Robyn Muncy.[14] They in turn contacted others—the NCLC, various labor unions, charitable organizations, the YMCA, the Mother's Congress, and juvenile court judges. Soon editorials backing Lathrop appeared in newspapers and magazines throughout the country. The House approved Lathrop's request 276 to 47. Then, in 1916, when appropriations were threatened, Lathrop did the same thing, appealing to the GFWC, the American Association of Collegiate Alumnae, and the Women's Foundation for Health, to name a few, and again she won. The successful lobbying was especially impressive given that women did not even have the vote!

Lathrop earned a salary of $5,000 in 1915, which would be about $115,000 in today's money. She now occupied the highest-paying federal job of any woman, but her ambitions went beyond this singular achievement. With an expanded budget, Lathrop could now provide employment for many more women. Just as she had done in Chicago, Lathrop often framed her efforts to hire women as an extension of traditional values. Women, not men, were the appropriate people to investigate issues regarding childbirth, pregnancy, and childcare—they, not men, could ask questions of mothers about their health and their children. Early on, she obtained permission from the US Civil Service Commission to hire only women for most of the jobs she controlled.

In addition to professional opportunities for women, Lathrop worked on behalf of women's political rights. She was a lifelong supporter of women's suffrage; as Children's Bureau chief, her views on the subject took on greater significance. Only a few months into her tenure, in November 1912, Lathrop addressed the National Convention of the National American Woman Suffrage Association (NAWSA). Like many in the Progressive Era, she thought that giving women voting rights would help the fight for reform. She viewed her outspoken support for suffrage, just like her job as chief of the Children's Bureau, as one more vehicle for achieving social justice.

By the time Lathrop appeared at the NAWSA convention the suffrage movement was in high gear. In 1890 the two major suffrage organizations, the National Woman Suffrage Association and the American Woman Suffrage Association, put aside their differences that had emerged in the post–Civil War era over the issue of black male suffrage. For the next two decades NAWSA met with little success, but the second decade of the twentieth century saw a reversal in fortune partly because progressive reform was at its peak. In the antebellum era the early pioneers on behalf of women's suffrage were also fierce antislavery advocates. At the turn of the twentieth century the mobilization for women's political rights was also tied to the upsurge in social reform. Broad coalitions of women— including settlement house leaders, working-class trade union women, and black and white club women—tied the cause of women's political rights to expanding social justice. Progressive women and their male allies promoted women's suffrage as a way to obtain social welfare legislation, improve working conditions, fight political corruption, and, for some, enact prohibition.

The progressive maternalists often used arguments about women's special needs and attributes to increase women's political rights. Addams's famous piece on women's suffrage, published in the *Ladies Home Journal* in 1910, appealed to her middle-class readers by pointing out that women in modern society no longer produced for their families all the goods they would consume at home; if they cared about the health and safety of their own families—the food they ate, the water they drank, the diseases they might catch—they ought to care about the conditions all around them, and they should want the right to vote on these public concerns.

Lathrop took a similar approach in speaking to the NAWSA convention. "My purpose," she began, "is to show that woman suffrage is a natural and inevitable step in the march of society forward; that, instead of being incompatible with child welfare, it leads toward it and is indeed the next great service to be rendered for the welfare and ennoblement of the home."[15] Today most women would reject Lathrop's reliance on traditional gender roles to justify voting rights for women. One hundred years ago, however, the prosuffragists faced considerable opposition. As historian Victoria Bissell Brown points out, "both sides in the debate were shaped by the other." Antisuffragists argued that allowing women to vote would destroy the family. Advocates like Lathrop turned the argument on its head and argued that, on the contrary, "if we are right in thinking that the emphasis of political thought today tends towards protecting the family and upholding the standards of comfort and decency for the upbringing of the next generation, may we not believe that women, long primarily concerned by habit and experience with the welfare of the household may safely be called upon to vote on questions which . . . affect the welfare of any household?" For years historians recognized as feminist only those arguments that emphasized the rights of all individuals to full political rights. But today many feminist scholars appreciate the arguments of Progressive Era suffragists that focused on "the common good rather than individual autonomy."

Like lawyers and astute politicians, the suffragists put forth many arguments, often in the same speech, to promote their case in hopes that one or two might result in a favorable reception. As Brown notes, they "slipped and slid easily from democratic principles to practical politics to biological determinism."[16] Lathrop's speeches exemplify the multipronged approach. In 1915 at a rally on behalf of women's suffrage in New York she took the equal rights approach, claiming that "when women get the vote, they will win the respect of men, at least of those men who can only respect those who have the same rights they themselves enjoy." In the same speech she also made the point that "the vote will make the woman a more useful mother, it will hold her to work for the welfare of the home and the children."

Lathrop avoided language that specifically referenced women's innate biological traits, and she used her sense of humor to poke fun at gender stereotypes. She often told this story when speaking on behalf of suffrage in Illinois. "I was talking to a man recently about suffrage and giving him reasons for advocating it. He listened politely and then said 'I am convinced Miss Lathrop, that if all women were as intelligent and discriminating as yourself, it would be a very good thing for the country if we had equal suffrage. But the great majority of women are not competent to judge of men and affairs in politics. I might illustrate, perhaps by asking if you think your cook is competent to vote intelligently.' 'Well I do not know about that,' I replied, 'but he does vote.'" Conversely, she once argued that suffrage was the "next step in equalizing the rights and balancing the duties of the two types of individuals who make up the human race. Nature has arranged a great demarcation of daily duties between men and women inside of their embracing circle of their common interests."[17]

Lathrop took seriously the democratic ethos of the call to expand suffrage, rejecting, along with Addams and Kelley, the racism and elitism that characterized large segments of the suffrage movement. At the turn of the twentieth century many white suffragists argued that educated, native-born, and respectable women should be given the vote in order to counterbalance the lower classes of men, including immigrants who enjoyed the franchise. In the South suffragists encountered the racist arguments of opponents who often invoked the possibility of racial equality should women be given the vote. In response, white suffragists frequently responded by reassuring the public that women's suffrage would not challenge white supremacy; passage would not automatically mandate that everywhere all blacks be allowed to vote. Although many black women were outspoken supporters of suffrage, they were barred from white suffrage organizations in the South and were at best ignored in the North.

Lathrop often spoke about the importance of extending suffrage to all women. Working women, she pointed out, in "great organized factories have been having since they began that work, an education for the suffrage, because they know in part what they need to safeguard themselves and their families." Lathrop once pointed out that because higher education for women is now a fact, society needed the votes of college-educated women who have contributed so much to social change and the enactment of better laws. Even more so, she went on to say about the right to vote, "do we anticipate a common gain from women of less privilege, women whose status in the world of industry should not be established or changed without their own participation."[18]

Although Lathrop wanted "women of less privilege" to have a say in the social changes that would affect their lives, this did not mean she expected them to make government policy. Lathrop of course promoted civil service standards in place of political patronage as the important criteria for hiring at the Children's Bureau, but as in Chicago she used her own criteria to ensure that the volunteer and professional networks she trusted vetted the appointments. Rather than relying on written exams, Lathrop proudly noted, "a careful investigation of each candidates' fitness was made and personal elements were weighed." These elements included a candidate's educational training, past experience in social work, and the all-important letters of recommendation. By 1919 Lathrop had assembled the workers she wanted. Of 169 employees, only 14 were male. This achievement alone marks her as a pioneer in terms of opening up the government to gender diversity. Yet her hiring practices also reflected her times. Like most men who hire people like themselves through their own networks, Lathrop hired women like herself. They were "white, middle-class, well-educated and unmarried," Muncy tells us, and many had come through such institutions as the Chicago School of Civics and Philanthropy that Lathrop had developed.[19]

In 1915, with an expanded bureau and a better budget, Lathrop was more confident about the bureau's future; she was ready to join the fight against child labor. The NCL, the NCLC, and state and local women's clubs had campaigned against child labor in the various states for several decades. By now the numbers of young children working in factories had steadily declined. With American production becoming heavily mechanized, employers found that young children could not work on the sophisticated machinery. But young adolescents could easily work in garment factories, glass factories, or in textile work. Small children also worked alongside families in farming and in garment work at home. Child welfare advocates believed that the crisis could no longer be left to the states. Too many states, particularly in the South, had lax or no child labor laws at all. In 1914 the NCLC launched an all-out push for federal legislation to limit child labor.

To publicize the problem, the bureau put out two studies in 1915, one enumerating the various child labor laws in every state and the other an in-depth study of how the state of Connecticut enforced their laws.

Lathrop testified on behalf of the bill as it made its way through Congress, but the NCLC took the lead in pushing the legislation. The law was designed to make use of the federal government's constitutional power to regulate interstate commerce. The Keating-Owen Child Labor Bill, named after the two cosponsors, prohibited the transportation across state lines of materials such as coal that had used the labor of children under sixteen and factory goods that involved the labor of children under fourteen. The Department of Labor, which housed the bureau, was to have the responsibility to enforce the law. By keeping a low profile as the law made its way through Congress, Lathrop avoided potentially troubling suggestions from some that the bureau might now be moving beyond its original role as an agency of investigation and education.

Once the Keating-Owen Child Labor Bill was passed in 1916, the Children's Bureau moved front and center to enforce the law, and Lathrop fought hard to make sure the bureau could do so on its own terms. First, in September 1917 she—with Kelley and Wald—convinced her Chicago friend Grace Abbott to accept the position of head of the Child Labor Division. The men at the NCLC had other ideas; they suggested their own candidate for the job, a male attorney who had been instrumental in drafting the legislation. Lathrop resisted the push, insisting that her candidate met her professional requirements for the job.

Lathrop tangled with the male leadership of the NCLC several times. She "resented the paternalistic attitude of its chief Washington lobbyist, Alexander McAlvey," according to Lindenmeyer.[20] When opponents of the law challenged its constitutionality in court, Lathrop hired Roscoe Pound of the Harvard Law School to defend it on behalf of the government, but McAlvey, on behalf of the NCLC and without consulting Lathrop, hired attorney Thomas L. Parkinson of Columbia. Again Lathrop refused to budge on her choice, insisting, successfully, that Pound take the lead.

When the law went into effect in late 1917 Abbott's Child Labor Division, with few resources, focused on the particularly dismal situation in the South, where the child labor regulations were below the new federal standards. The law authorized the division to enforce sanctions against those employers who knowingly employed underage children. Because the southern states did such a poor job of registering births, the bureau spent much time and money on the difficult task of verifying the ages of working children while continuing to campaign for better birth certification.

During the campaign to root out child labor Lathrop emphasized the importance of working with state and local officials. She wanted to allay the fears of many who objected to the growing powers of the federal government. By relying on local agencies, Lathrop also helped the many women who were playing such important roles at the local level.

The Keating-Owen Child Labor Act, as meager as it was in terms of combating child labor, did not last long. In the spring of 1918 the US Supreme Court declared it unconstitutional. The Constitution's interstate commerce clause, the Court concluded, did not give the federal government the power to regulate child labor in a factory or mine because each enterprise took place in one state, not in between states. The reformers were deeply disappointed, and Lathrop admitted that the decision embarrassed the bureau, but she maintained an air of optimism about future decisions, taking heart in the fact that it was a narrow five-to-four ruling against the law. Lathrop already had another means to get at the problem—the powers given to the president of the United States during wartime.

In April 1917 the United States entered World War I on behalf of Britain and France. Many Americans, including a number of progressives, were unhappy with Wilson's decision to join the conflict. Opponents viewed the war as a fight between imperialist powers caught in the machinations of their own complicated treaty obligations. Addams was one of the most outspoken critics of the war. Lathrop also opposed the war, according to her friend Alice Hamilton, who at the time was a government employee inspecting the health and safety of war munitions plants. "We [Julia and I] were both pacifists but neither of us took a conspicuous anti-war stand, for the same reason—we were deeply attached to our jobs and feared to lose them."[21]

During the war Lathrop not only put her public embrace of pacifism on hold; she also aligned herself with the majority of suffragists in NAWSA who were willing to put their push for the women's vote on hold as well. As the suffrage movement grew in the 1910s some women challenged the NAWSA strategy of pursuing state-by-state campaigns to obtain the vote. Two activists, Alice Paul and Lucy Burns, had spent time in Britain and were energized by the militancy of suffragists who engaged in civil disobedience to bring attention to the cause and to pressure lawmakers into taking action. Paul, Burns, and their allies were convinced that the quickest and most effective approach to obtaining the vote was to once again concentrate on a federal amendment guaranteeing equal suffrage. In 1913 they formed a subcommittee of NAWSA, the Congressional Union (CU), which in 1914 broke with the larger organization. In 1916 Paul organized the National Women's Party (NWP), made up of women already enfranchised by their states who would push for the federal amendment.

In 1916 Paul and her allies publicly opposed President Wilson's reelection, along with the rest of the Democratic Party, because of their unwillingness to support a federal suffrage amendment. The Republican Party also refused to officially endorse an amendment, but its presidential candidate, Charles Evans Hughes, did endorse the cause. In early 1917 Paul and the CU, after an unsuccessful meeting with the newly reelected President Wilson, turned to a new strategy of picketing outside the White House gates; thousands of other women wrote letters of support to Paul.

Lathrop was not one of the supporters. On the contrary, she and some thirty other women signed a petition of protest to the women of the CU, just three days after the picketing began on January 10. "As loyal suffragists, deeply interested in securing the vote for women by all legitimate means and as speedily as possible," they protested the picketing, considering the act a form of "heckling," akin to the former militants of the English suffragists, which they believed would only arouse criticism, if not hostility, from the public and the president. They believed such action was not the "democratic expression of the will of the majority of suffragists," and they worried that those who were hostile to the cause would mischaracterize the movement.

Lathrop's opposition to the new tactic is not surprising. Hers had always been a more moderate approach. Many if not all of her sister petitioners were government employees, and they were comfortable working within traditional structures on behalf of social change. Yet Lathrop, ever the bridge builder, reached out directly to Paul, sending her a copy of the petition along with her personal comments. "My dear Miss Paul," she wrote, "this protest was brought to me yesterday with most of the attached signatures, and I added mine as a matter of conscience." She then went on to assure Paul that she respected their differences. "I know well that you are acting also on conscience," she wrote, "and I am only transmitting this because it seems fair to do so. It is not for publication."[22]

The US entry into World War I in April would not deter the suffrage militants. Taking no official position on the war, they continued the picketing of the White House, pointing out that the US claim as a truly democratic country rang hollow. But during World War I such criticism was considered counter to the war effort. The picketers were arrested. In jail, under horrific conditions, Paul and the other arrestees continued their protest, entering into hunger strikes and enduring the horrors of forced feeding in order to bring attention to their demand that they be treated as political prisoners.

NAWSA women took a much different position. NAWSA's leader, Carrie Catt, agreed that the organization would not push a demand that the issue of suffrage be taken up by Congress during the war because it was not a wartime measure. Moreover, Catt, who had always been a pacifist, agreed to support the war and to urge her members to work on behalf of the war effort at home. Like Lathrop, who would use wartime mobilization to push a long-term child welfare agenda, Catt decided to use the opportunity provided by wartime mobilization to fulfill her goal after the war. Catt believed that by supporting the war, she could extract a promise from President Wilson that he would eventually support and work for the federal amendment.

Pushed by the suffrage militants, indebted to Catt and the NAWSA, and aware that political realities were moving in favor of suffrage, Wilson began actively pushing the federal amendment through Congress. Once through Congress in June 1919, the state-by-state ratification process took another fourteen months. The triumph of women's suffrage, at least for white women and those women of color who could vote in some states, did not end the disagreements between the women of the NWP and the larger group of women, like Lathrop, affiliated with NAWSA. In 1920 the NWP embarked on a national campaign to end discrimination against women through the passage of a federal equal rights amendment to the US Constitution. The social feminists affiliated with NAWSA, including Lathrop, rejected the campaign for equal rights legislation because they feared that it would jeopardize special protective labor legislation for women workers. NAWSA reorganized itself as the League of Women Voters to help women as voters continue the work of addressing social welfare. Fittingly, Lathrop became an active member of the League of Women Voters during her retirement years.

During the war Lathrop, like Catt, was determined to make the war crisis serve her agenda; in her case it meant efforts to promote social welfare and to keep the work of the bureau relevant. Like many progressives,

Lathrop hoped the government's role in a wartime economy would result not only in greater regulation but also more social experimentation. In 1918 Lathrop convinced the War Labor Board to insist that the provisions of the now-defunct Keating-Owen Bill apply to the manufacture of war materials. The federal government also banned child labor in laundries and restaurants at all military bases and Defense Department facilities. The bureau's Child Labor Division took responsibility for enforcing the orders, but, especially in the case of wartime production, violations were rampant.

Lathrop took a multifaceted approach when it came to "exploiting" the war on behalf of children. With an allotment of $150,000 from President Wilson's War Fund, and his personal endorsement, that "there could be . . . no more patriotic duty than that of protecting the children who constitute one-third of our population," the bureau launched the Children's Year in April 1918. To assist in this effort Lathrop turned again to women's organizations—in this case, the Women's Committee of the Council of National Defense, where she was serving as head of the Children's Welfare Division. The Women's Committee in turn activated women in local communities across the country. To learn more about and to publicize the health of America's children, the bureau launched a drive to weigh and measure children under six years of age—close to seven hundred thousand children were measured—and many of the children received full physical examinations. The bureau helped launch recreation programs and a widely publicized back-to-school drive, designed to counteract the growing trend of young adolescents taking jobs to fill the shortage of adult male labor during the war.

Lathrop ended the Children's Year in April 1919, using her tried-and-true method of publicizing social welfare issues—organizing conferences. The bureau organized a series of regional conferences on standards of child welfare. A committee of five then met in Washington to consider the suggestions that came out of the regional sessions and to approve a set of standards of child welfare. In keeping with the bureau agenda, the standards included improved public health clinics for pregnant women and their young children, better birth registration, improved health care for school-age children, an increase in the legal age for factory employment, and improvements in the juvenile justice system. Not stopping there, the committee called for better wages for fathers, better housing conditions, public provisions for "wholesome" recreations, and a commitment to continuing the improvement of child welfare standards throughout the states.

Not all Americans endorsed this ambitious agenda, but Lathrop, in classic fashion, claimed the conferences were a "summing up of national opinion on the standards of child welfare."

Lathrop also turned to military benefits as a way to improve family incomes. In 1917 she and Lee Frankel of the American Association for the Advancement of Labor Law successfully pushed for passage of the Military and Naval Insurance Act. A voluntary program of death or disability benefits available for all veterans, regardless of circumstance, soldiers would receive monthly stipends, along with payments in case of death and disability in the line of duty. The law reflected Lathrop's concern about male unreliability. It specifically insisted that married soldiers and sailors must designate their wives and children as beneficiaries. In boasting about the features of the bill, Lathrop, not surprisingly, emphasized its role in helping American youth: "The Government thus makes good for the soldier's child the educational standard which it tacitly sets up when it extends the allowance for child's support until the age of eighteen. This age limit implies the equivalent of a high-school education and is one of the most noteworthy features of the bill."[23]

When the Great War ended, Lathrop and other progressives hoped to extend government responsibility for promoting educational possibilities. The bureau and the NCL once again turned to the regulation of child labor. This time they focused on the spending clause in the Constitution, giving Congress the right to levy taxes. In 1919 Congress passed an amendment to a revenue bill that would tax goods manufactured in violation of the now-defunct 1916 child labor standards. One provision of the new law, which received strong NCLC endorsement, transferred the powers of enforcement from the bureau's Child Labor Division to the Treasury Department. The timing of the NCLC endorsement seemed suspicious; it approved the transfer while Lathrop and Abbott were traveling in Europe and could not mount opposition. Deeply disappointed, Lathrop dismantled the division in 1919, and Abbott returned to Chicago. The Treasury work did not last long anyway. The US Supreme Court, this time in an eight-to-one decision, struck down the federal law, ruling in 1922 that the tax code could not be used to regulate child labor.

Lathrop may have referred often to the public's strong support for the bureau, but we can see that she faced significant obstacles. The difficulties reinforced her cautious side. She strongly believed that women had important political and professional roles to play in addressing social problems;

however, she was uninterested in joining those feminists who challenged traditional family life, at least not publicly. During Lathrop's tenure the bureau staff studied and publicized on the subjects that had concerned her for decades—the state of juvenile justice law around the country, the mothers' pensions laws in states across the country, and the conditions of child labor. The bureau also published many pamphlets on all aspects of raising healthy children, but almost nothing on sex education, known in those days as "sex hygiene."

Many people wrote to Lathrop, asking that the bureau publish information on sex education. The GFWC, one of her staunchest supporters, requested that the bureau put out information on the subject. She agreed that it was important, and her staff often responded to the inquiries with suggestions about articles and other organizations that might be helpful. During her tenure, however, the bureau did not put out its own information on the subject, claiming that with limited resources and so many other demands, they simply could not. Soon after World War I Lathrop's bureau grew bolder. In 1919 the agency published a report suggesting that teaching sex education in the schools would have cut down on the epidemic of venereal disease during World War I among US soldiers.

Lathrop was even more cautious when it came to birth control. At the time many people argued that access to contraception could improve the health and well-being of mothers and children, but she was determined that the bureau not be associated with the issue. Bureau staff could not distribute information on contraception techniques even if they had wanted to because it was against the law. But to her "regret," Lathrop and her staff agreed that they could not publish anything at all on the question of contraception and its importance, referring those who wanted studies on the subject to other sources. When asked her opinion on birth control by public health experts, Lathrop declined to provide her views because she did not want them associated with the bureau. Among other things she worried that the bureau might lose the support of Catholic congressmen if it in any way became associated with contraception.

Lathrop refused to speak out on behalf of birth control advocates Margaret Sanger and Mary Dennett when they campaigned to legalize contraceptives. Dennett, founder of the National Birth Control League, expressed particular disappointment in 1916, writing to Lathrop that her organization had "naturally assumed that you would be 'with us.' The facts and figures [on children] presented by your Bureau have furnished us with our strongest economic arguments." Lathrop agreed to a private conversation with Mary Dennett, where she apparently was rather forthcoming about her personal support of contraception. But she remained unwilling to go beyond her private support. In 1920 an upset Lathrop wrote to Dennett to ask whether it was true, as she had just learned, that in a recent speech promoting a birth control bill the activist had mentioned it "had the sanction of Miss Julia Lathrop of the Children's Bureau." Dennett immediately wrote back, assuring Lathrop that although her speech had made use of data about children from the bureau, she "never made public what you told me in private conversation. . . . I shall of course be immensely glad when you feel free to speak out. In the meantime I will keep my promise to not quote you."

Lathrop replied to Dennett with thanks. "Of course," she noted, "I can make no objection to the manner in which any of the data furnished by the Bureau is used, that being no part of the business of a scientific bureau." Lathrop may have cared about the "scientific" legitimacy of the bureau, but she always attended to the politics, and in her letter to Dennett she got to the heart of the matter: "I am concerned by the effort on the part of some people to make it appear that the bill for the Protection of Maternity and Infancy has any relation to voluntary motherhood [birth control]."[24]

Lathrop had good reason to worry about her opponents' ongoing efforts to weaken support for the Maternity and Infancy Act. More than anything else in 1920, Lathrop wanted Congress to pass the law, which provided public health care for pregnant women and young children throughout the county. In 1921, at the end of her term as chief of the Children's Bureau, Lathrop succeeded. Chapter 6 sets the stage for understanding why she was so determined to pass the new law, focusing on Lathrop's ongoing work as chief to help struggling families and to rouse the nation about the need for better maternal and infant health-care standards. Chapter 7 tells the story of her monumental achievement.

6

Saving Children, Helping Mothers

"A Federal Bureau for Children, its chief a woman, one of your own; what new and mannish venture does she embark on?? She rouses the nation—or tries to rouse it—to the neglect of the baby. She takes the baby out of the obscure, so often neglected and hidden crib into the full light of publicity. 'Suffer not this little one to be lost sight of. It is a child of the nation!'"

—Lillian Wald[1]

When Lillian Wald made those comments about Lathrop and the Children's Bureau at Vassar's fiftieth anniversary, she was reacting to widespread criticism of the female reformers; they were not behaving as proper women and were threatening the larger social order built around traditional families. In a strategic move Wald emphasized that activist, educated women were not breaking away from their traditional essence but rather fulfilling it. Beyond strategy, Wald's words highlighted Lathrop's own sense of her most important job as chief of the Children's Bureau—to rouse the nation about the health and welfare of babies and their mothers and to do something about it.

For Lathrop the bureau's infant mortality studies highlighted the critical need to improve standards of care for pregnant women and their young children. Lathrop's work over nine years would lead to passage of the Sheppard-Towner Maternal and Infancy Act, America's widest reaching federal social welfare program to date. Women all over the country wrote to the chief seeking advice about pregnancy and childbirth and telling her of various financial challenges they faced in their efforts to be good mothers. Lathrop's correspondence strengthened her conviction that all mothers and children, regardless of class, ethnicity, or race, deserved access to adequate health care.

As early as 1913 the Children's Bureau launched its programs of health education with the publication of its pamphlet, *Pre-natal Care*, followed one year later by *Infant Care*. To write the pamphlets Lathrop hired Mary Mills West, a widow with five children who turned to writing in order to support her family. In giving West the job, Lathrop rejected advice from some who argued that male doctors should write the bulletins. As she said, "There is a real strategic advantage in having them come from a woman who has herself had the experience of bringing up a family."[2] Lathrop turned out to be right. The pamphlets contained the latest science on pregnancy and baby care written in a style that was accessible to literate, middle-class mothers. They became instant best sellers, topping all other government publications. The agency distributed thirty thousand copies of *Pre-natal Care* within the first six months of publication. Lewis Meriam and Fanny Fiske both reported to Lathrop while she was convalescing in Rockford that the bureau could barely keep up with demand.

The pamphlets represented both the strengths and limitations of the progressive approach to child welfare. *Pre-natal Care* covered many important topics in thirty-eight pages, including the best diets for pregnant mothers, how to arrange for the best medical care, what mothers could expect during childbirth, how to prevent infections that could harm mother or baby, and how to nurse the newborn. West reassured mothers that contrary to popular belief, pregnant women need not worry that if they become upset about something they see or some event in their lives that it will mark their babies. She advised pregnant and newborn mothers to take care of themselves, to get plenty of rest, and to exercise. West and her colleagues at the bureau respected the work of mothers. The latest scientific approaches to childcare were meant to keep babies healthy and to lighten women's burdens. "The care of a baby is readily reduced to a system unless he is sick," West told her readers. "Such a system is not only one of the greatest factors in keeping the baby well and in training him in a way which will be of value to him all through life, but reduces the work of the mother to the minimum and provides for her certain assured periods of rest and recreation."[3]

Lathrop knew it would be hard for many mothers to follow the bureau's advice. In 1918, speaking to an audience of public health workers, Lathrop quoted from one of the mothers who had written to her about the many pamphlets on childcare the bureau had published by then. "I like the Bulletins. Some of the things I knew before, some of them my neighbors have told me, but there are things you can't do when 8 people live in two rooms."[4] Lathrop and West asserted that the advice was predicated on an adequate standard of living to which all mothers and their children were entitled.

However, because the pamphlets presupposed access to this standard of living, some of their recommendations were irrelevant to many American mothers. Many immigrant mothers couldn't read the pamphlets, and even if they could, some of the advice, such as securing the services of physicians or personal nurses for childbirth or arranging for a hospital birth was far outside the world these women inhabited.

The bureau staff embraced science and health experts because they understood that modern advancements could improve the lives of millions of American mothers and children. But they could be dismissive of traditional home remedies and childcare practices that fell outside their middle-class experiences and sense of the most "modern" practices. For example, the infant mortality studies assumed that the high rate of infant death from gastrointestinal diseases could be explained by the diets of foreign-born mothers. Like the Hull House women who set up the coffeehouse, the reformers advocated the bland diet of middle-class white Americans that we now know was not necessarily healthier.

The bureau also condemned one of the most important aspects of health care among poor and foreign-born women—the use of midwives, especially when they practiced unsupervised by nurses and doctors. One study of maternal and infant care in rural Mississippi accepted without question the conclusion of the state Board of Health that more African American women than white women died during childbirth because of their reliance on black midwives. In truth the bureau worried about what they viewed as the ignorance and superstitions of all midwives, regardless of color, and they lauded those "more intelligent midwives [who] would be glad to have a county nurse to advise them and to teach them better methods of practice."[5]

By promoting the importance of trained nurses, public health doctors, and trained childcare professionals, the bureau provided opportunities for more women to enjoy professional careers. The staff elevated the task of raising children as work that required scientific knowledge. In doing so, the women honored the job of mothering, labor that the larger society often takes for granted. But raising the standards of childcare also meant that women now had ever more responsibilities that kept them close to home. Lathrop often said that fathers must be important participants in childcare, but she assumed that for most mothers childrearing and homemaking were full-time tasks.

Lathrop fought to improve the wages of working-class fathers, and she promoted state-funded pensions for widows of young children precisely so mothers would not have to do wage work but could care for their children just as more prosperous mothers were able to do. Lathrop's attitude reflected a realistic view of the difficulties most women faced in combining wage work and childcare. The bureau's studies on infant mortality in factory towns, she argued, showed that mothers of young babies did not choose to work; only the mothers of young babies in the poorest families went to work and that the numbers dropped off as husbands' wages increased. But many mothers had to do wage work outside the home and needed better jobs and fairer pay. African American activists understood that black mothers, with fewer resources than even immigrant whites, were likely earning incomes; they did not assume that good motherhood precluded working outside the home.

Even as the pamphlets on maternal and infant care reached a large audience, Lathrop wanted to go bigger. Since her Hull House days, when she urged Jane Addams to publish her ideas on settlement work, Lathrop understood the importance of the press. The bureau supplied information to popular women's magazines such as the *Ladies Home Journal* and *Woman's World*, newspapers across the county, and well-known progressive journals like *The Survey*. The bureau also provided information to religious organizations, which would publish bureau advice in their church newsletters and magazines.

The widespread publicity paid off. Although middle-class women could most easily read the advice pamphlets, historian Molly Ladd-Taylor writes that poor women who had some reading and writing skills read them as well. Women from every "region, social class and educational background" wrote to the bureau about the information contained in the bulletins. The work on behalf of children's health was surely the most popular bureau initiative. Many poor mothers resisted the bureau's efforts to curb child labor, viewing the child labor campaigns as intrusions on parental rights and threats to the family well-being. But mothers across the social spectrum embraced the bureau's efforts to keep babies alive and healthy. Most of the correspondence came from women in small towns and rural communities, and most of the women—but not all—were white, native-born Americans. Women wrote over 125,00 letters a year to the bureau seeking advice about pregnancy and childcare.[6]

Every letter sent to the bureau received a personal response, and Lathrop answered many of the letters herself. Carrying on the Hull House tradition, she added her sympathetic voice and some informal efforts to the latest science in order to help mothers and children. Lathrop could now leverage her position as head of a federal agency when seeking the assistance of welfare workers around the country. Many of the letters contained requests for information about pregnancy and childcare; in addition, they reflected the fears and frustrations of mothers who did not have access to health care.

Sometimes anxious and loving fathers wrote to Lathrop hoping she could tell them how to procure funds to help their children. The bureau did not have access to such funds, but moved by the plight of many letter writers, Lathrop used her knowledge, connections, and important position to help—quickly if possible. James Smith of southern Illinois wrote in August 1918 to ask Lathrop's advice about his six-year-old stepdaughter who was stricken with polio. "I have had her at St. Louis and they say they can cure and make her walk alright but they need $200 and $50.00 a week for her board. So now I would like to see if I could get any assistance from the state to pay the Bill as I have five of a family plus our two selfs [he and his wife] to provide for. . . . I would only be so glad to see her run and Romp about with the other Children. So please let me know what you Can do and anything you can do will be gladly received and very Thankful I remain yours Truly and obedient servant." One week after the bureau received the letter Lathrop wrote back to tell Mr. Smith that she will contact Miss Annie Hinrichin, executive director of the Welfare Commission of Illinois. "I confess that I do not know what you can do for this child," Lathrop wrote Hinrichin, "but I hope very much that either there is some public fund or you can interest some generous spirit if the facts are as stated." Lathrop's personal intervention clearly meant something. Two weeks later Hinrichin wrote back to Lathrop, informing her that the Department of Public Health had taken up the case and a nurse would soon be visiting the Smiths and arranging local care for the child. She also indicated that the department would be making funds available to help the family and suggested that some local resources might also be found.[7]

More letters came not from anxious fathers but from mothers who wrote about neglectful and sometimes abusive husbands. During World War I Mrs. McDermott of Long Island wrote to Lathrop, explaining that she was a mother of three children under the age of twelve, and she was ill herself. "I am trying to earn an honest living for my family by doing washing and ironing from morning till night while my husband running around at large in Jersey without ever giving me any income to support myself or children. I don't want my husband but I need support. I would like to know if you could use him to fight in the draft because he is no earthly use to me or the family. I was told to write to you for information hoping you will kindly help me." In response Lathrop suggested she write to a Mrs. Cherry of the New York State Charity Association.[8]

By staying away from such controversial issues as divorce, however, Lathrop could offer little but sympathy to women who badly needed to escape their marriages. "I am an invalid and kept ill all the time," wrote Mrs. Appleyard from a farm in North Carolina, "because of my husband's treatment and mismanagement. He does not allow me to have one word to say about anything but blames me for anything that happens. . . . He has threatened to kill me but I jumped out of the window and ran to a neighbor. . . . I have three children, a boy 13 but he is so small and nervous and two girls 14 and 16 the health of the eldest is in bad condition. . . . These children are all trying their best to get an education. I know how to take care of my children but my husband won't let me do anything. My husband always thinks he knows it all and is afraid we will forget he is boss. He is scarce ever at home goes to Charlotte both Saturday and Sunday." After explaining that her husband makes the family work on the farm, despite their illnesses, but refuses to provide for them, Mrs. Appleyard ends by asking if there is any way she and her children could be assisted.

Lathrop replied to Mrs. Appleyard that she has contacted the State Board of Charities in North Carolina to see about assistance. She also urged her to report her husband to authorities. "Sometimes it does work miracles if a man who has been all his life accustomed to his own way is suddenly shown that the law and public opinion have another way." Beyond those specifics, she could only offer Mrs. Appleyard her personal concern. "I wish I knew of some way to be of service to you."[9]

Lathrop knew what to do about parents who badly needed decent jobs. She did not hesitate to make use of her position or her personal connections. In 1915 Mrs. Mooney of Washington, DC, had just lost her husband to pneumonia. He was a patrol officer with no pension. Mrs. Mooney wrote to Lathrop, asking her for a job. A widow with three children, ages eight to eleven, she was afraid she would lose them to the "district unless I get some employment of some kind. . . . Work as a caretaker or charwoman would be of great help to us." Although Lathrop had no job at the bureau for the widow, she wrote directly to one of the city commissioners, sending along the relevant passages of Mrs. Mooney's letter and asking whether the office could either provide a job for the mother or some financial assistance. The commissioner's office promised to attend to the situation immediately.[10]

Lathrop could not always obtain such quick responses. One determined girl, Rosie Caporale, likely the daughter of immigrants, wrote to Lathrop in 1915 on behalf of her father, a peddler, who sold vegetables to miners in Colorado. The letter, addressed to Miss Julia Lathrop, Washington, began with "Dearest friend, I am a girl of a very big family and my Father is a very poor man and we are working very hard to make a living." After the 1914 coal miner strike that had put Mr. Caporale out of work was over, he wanted to resume selling vegetables to the mining camps close to his home at the Berwind and Tabasco Mining Company. Officials told him he could only peddle at camps much farther away from the family home in Elmora. Rosie explained, "he cant leave his family alone. . . . my father . . . is kind of old and can not do heavy work we are six girls [the two boys are deaf and mute] and all work very hard raising vegetables and cannot get enough to eat." Rosie asked Lathrop "if you would do me the favor of giving this to the government and tell him if he will kindly give him [her father] a pass that will allow him to peddle" at the Berwind and Tabasco Mine Company camps. "My father's name is mr angelo caporale. Dear miss," Rosie ended her letter, "if I am disturbing you please excuse me I give my best regards to you and the government. I am your Friend Rosie Caporale."

Lathrop wrote back, telling Rosie that she sent the letter along to Colorado congressman Edward Keating to see whether his office could help. In May 1915 a disappointed Rosie wrote again to Lathrop because she had not yet heard from the congressman. "please [*sic*] excuse the trouble but dear friend I did not hear from Honorable Edward Keating of Pueblo up to date I am awfully sorry that you could not help as well. . . . I close as your faithful friend Miss Rosie Caporale." Lathrop replied two weeks later to "My dear Rosie" that she had sent her latest letter on to the congressman. We do not know the outcome, but Lathrop told Rosie that she was sure the congressman would "do whatever he can. Yours with best wishes," she signed off, "Julia Lathrop, Chief."[11]

Other ordinary Americans pushed back when they did not like the responses they received from Lathrop and her staff. Mrs. C. of Illinois wrote to Lathrop in 1914, asking for the *Infant Care* and *Pre-natal Care* pamphlets. After receiving them she wrote again to tell her that she was "using all her spare time studying them. . . . I never had learned anything about it [pregnancy and child care]. I had no idea the government helped at such work. . . . Your mission is something that brings blessings to many who are needy." But, as Emily Abel points out, Mrs. C. did not "surrender control" to the bureau experts. When Lathrop advised that she institutionalize her disabled son who was having trouble in school, Mrs. C responded, "I believe my boy would worry his self sick if sent away to school."[12]

Lathrop focused on the problems of white families, but not exclusively. On May 20, 1914, James C. Waters Jr. of Washington, DC, a prominent black attorney and "special agent" for the NAACP, wrote to Lathrop. He was following up on the suggestion of W. E. B. Dubois, then editor of the organization's famous monthly, *The Crisis*, that he seek Lathrop's help in securing justice for twelve-year-old Sarah Rector. The story of African Americans in Oklahoma, including Sarah, was intertwined with the history of Indian tribes of Oklahoma and the policies of the US government. Sarah was a resident of Taft, Oklahoma, an African American town situated in what had been Indian territory before Oklahoma became a state in 1907.

In 1887 the Dawes Act mandated that Indian common property be broken up and that Indians be provided with individual plots. This was done in part to "civilize" the Indians by transforming them into American farmers. Equally important, the transfer of what the government termed as "surplus" Indian land was a boon to white settlers seeking farmland. African Americans also received land in Oklahoma. After the Civil War Indian tribes had to free their black slaves and grant them rights to land. The distribution of land under the Dawes Act now extended not only to Indians and their former slaves but also to all blacks who had resided in Indian Territory, including some 4,407 children living in Creek Nation.

Sarah Rector was one of the children who received her land in 1906 when she was four. Whereas whites received the rich farmland, Indians as well as African Americans like Sarah were allotted the poor, rocky soil. But it turned out that much of the Oklahoma land was valuable in another way—it gushed oil. One such gusher happened to be on Sarah's land. Since 1911, when the oil was discovered, Sarah's guardian, Mr. B. B. Jones, a white man appointed by the local county to manage her affairs, had been living quite well while Sarah and her family remained in a dirty shanty. Newspapers reported that while Mr. Jones was earning some $15,000 a month from her oil earnings, Sarah was allotted $50 a month.

Seeking Lathrop's help, Waters sent articles from newspapers that described the situation as well as some correspondence he had undertaken already to officials in Oklahoma and the Bureau of Indian Affairs (BIA). "I have the honor," Waters wrote, "of asking if you will look into this case and see what if any truth there is to the various allegations that are being made . . . about the manner in which this colored girl is being neglected out in Oklahoma, while white men have control of her estate and control it NOT for her best interest." Waters went on: "All the more remarkable . . . Taft, Okla. is a community that is made up entirely of members of the Negro race. Yet a white man is said to have been entrusted with the mismanagement of her large inheritance."

Lathrop wrote back to Mr. Waters, promising that she would give the matter her personal attention. Over the next few months they entered into a correspondence. In asking for Lathrop's help, Waters acknowledged the limited power of the bureau, but he also knew that Lathrop could skillfully leverage her reputation, what he called her "moral power." "Your jurisdiction doubtless will not extend beyond an exercise of this same sort of power, but I do hope you will go as far as you can in this manner for that the distinguished head of the Children's Bureau can do things has long since been carried beyond the shadow of any doubt."[13]

Lathrop did look into the matter, writing to the senator from Oklahoma just one week after Waters first contacted her to ask how she might proceed; he suggested she contact the BIA. Lathrop's response to the case over the next few months exemplifies her commitment as a racial liberal to take seriously the plight of African Americans, but only to a point. In late June, while Lathrop was traveling out west, her office notified her that Miss May Childs Nerney of the New York NAACP arrived at the Children's Bureau hoping to see Lathrop to tell her that the civil rights organization was going to undertake their own investigation of the Rector matter. Lathrop asked that the NAACP put off their investigation until she had a chance to return to Washington to speak directly with representatives of the civil rights organization. In early July she wrote to the BIA, asking them whether it was not in their jurisdiction to deal with the case because it had the resources to "better ascertain the facts and secure any action."

The BIA commissioner wrote back, telling Lathrop, as he had already told Waters, that the agency was not authorized to supervise affairs of the Creek freedmen allottee such as Sarah. He did, however, enclose a long communication from a local Oklahoma judge, Thomas Leahy, who was supervising the affairs of the estate. Concurring with the Oklahoma governor, who already denounced the "manufactured, irresponsible declarations" of the civil rights community, the judge explained all that he and others were doing to help Sarah.[14] The family now had a new five-room cottage, thanks to the judge. He had "allowed" Sarah's mother to settle a debt by selling off some of her land and by having the mother take out a loan from her own daughter's estate! The judge also arranged for new furniture. The children had been walking two miles to their school until he convinced Mr. Rector to allow one of his older horses to be used by the children for transportation, along with a saddle and buggy purchased by the guardian. The Rector family, he maintained, "chose" the particular guardian because he was a neighbor. To the criticism that Sarah had received so little money, the judge replied that he was only acting in her best interests, keeping money out of the "irresponsible" hands of the black community. "I do not believe that her money should be spent, and other members of the family and neighbors get the benefits just because she has it. Possibly my judgment is wrong, but I have based this conclusion after thirteen years of . . . Government service . . . among *these people*."

Lathrop thanked the BIA commissioner for sending the judge's letter. She did not express concern about Judge's Leahy's "help," nor did she seem troubled that no member of the black community had any control over Sarah's fortunes. We cannot know for sure why she did not address this issue, but we do know that most whites, including liberals, did not believe that African Americans, particularly from the rural South, could manage their own affairs. Quite remarkably, Lathrop told the BIA commissioner, "It certainly appears to me that the Judge's statement of the case and the approval of the Secretary of the Interior [the BIA is situated in the Interior department], will be satisfactory to our correspondents."[15]

Waters and the NAACP were, of course, not satisfied with the judge's report, which they had already seen. The attorney thanked Lathrop for her continuing interest in the case but went on to detail his concerns, particularly about the sale of Mrs. Rector's land. Most especially he pointed Lathrop to the report of Miss Kate Barnard, chief of the Oklahoma Charities Department. Barnard was at the time fighting hard against what she knew to be a corrupt system that cheated both the Indians and the freedmen of Oklahoma.

During the summer it appears that Lathrop did meet with NAACP representatives. Mr. Waters sent her a long memo outlining exactly why he thought it appropriate for the bureau to investigate even though he knew that authority now rested with local officials. "The legislation under which the U.S. Govt. [The Interior Department] gave over its control of the [Indian] lands, including Sarah Rector's property was fathered by Oklahoma men who stoutly maintained that the *best interests* of ALL the people of Oklahoma demanded that such legislation be passed." To ascertain if the new legislation is serving the best interests of all, he argued, "nothing could be better than to have some representative of the Children's Bureau go to Taft, Okla., and see for herself, or himself as the case may be, just what the state of the case is."[16]

We have no evidence that Lathrop sent any bureau staff member to help in the investigation. Dubois, Waters, and others did not give up, however. According to historian Stacey Patton, the Rector case prompted Dubois to set up a Children's Department in the NAACP. "The relentless Dubois continued to use *The Crisis* as a vehicle to investigate how Oklahoma's greedy oil tycoons, real estate brokers, bankers, judges, attorneys, land speculators, utility corporations, and federal agencies used various mechanisms—including broken treaties, congressional acts, competency laws, guardianships and other extralegal devices to deprive America's wealthiest black children and thousands of other juvenile inheritors of land during the opening decades of the twentieth century." As for Sarah, Waters continually pressed that she be allowed to leave Oklahoma, to be well educated so that she could competently manage her financial affairs as an adult—an education, he noted, "she cannot get even though her wealth equaled the ransom of a thousand kings." Judge Leahy promised in May that he would send Sarah away to school in the fall of 1914, but the NAACP could not obtain any confirmation that he had followed through. In November Waters wrote to Lathrop to ask whether she had received any information as to Rector's whereabouts, and she responded immediately that she had not. Just before Christmas Judge Leahy informed Waters that Sarah and her older sister Rebecca were attending Booker T. Washington Children's School at the Tuskegee Institute and that their mother will be joining them for the Christmas holiday: "I have received excellent reports from the Institute as to these children." On January 13, 1915, Waters wrote to tell Lathrop of the good news, but he could not help commenting on her unsuccessful efforts to gain some information: "it would seem that the [Oklahoma] Department of Corrections and Charities have not accorded your inquiries in this behalf that courtesy which efficient workers would extend to each other everywhere in such cases."[17]

Sarah Rector attended Tuskegee for about one year. The black community could never succeed in having a black guardian appointed to handle her affairs, but its continued agitation helped the family attain a much better standard of living. With better oversight, her estates remained intact. "Sarah Rector was one of the lucky few black children," Patton writes, "whose guardian did not completely swindle her out of her estate before she came of age."

As for the relationship between Waters and Lathrop, the lawyer's last letter to Lathrop suggests his understanding that social norms required he be deferential to the white government official, but he also pushed back. "If I have annoyed you I am sorry," he said, "but . . . I sincerely hope that any estimate you may deign to make or pass upon the humble part that I played in the premises may not be formulated without due regard for the fact that I was profoundly interested and desirous of certain ends which to date have in goodly measure actually been attained." Now that this particular case was resolved, the cautious Lathrop could address her larger concerns about race and, perhaps, be more forthright about her skepticism concerning all the reassurances she had been given. She wrote back to Mr. Waters immediately, thanking him for letting her know about the situation with Sarah Rector: "it does seem, as you point out, *that for the time being*, we have reason to be satisfied with her care. This case is very properly one which should interest us all and I am very gratefully obliged for your communications to the Bureau."[18]

The letters sent to the bureau stirred Lathrop's sympathy for many individual families struggling to raise their children. They also reinforced her conviction that, as she told Mr. Waters, the struggles should interest the larger society. The many letters from mothers who worried about childbirth and the health of their young babies touched Lathrop especially. "I would like to know," an Idaho mother wrote to Lathrop in 1916, "if your people can give me an answer on this. . . . I am living 25 miles away from any Doctor. We have 4 small children, my Husband is only making 1.35 a day. . . . I am looking for the stork about the 19 of april. . . . How am I going to get 35 dollar to have a doctor, for he will not come for less. . . . Talk about better babys, when a mother must be like some cow or mare when a babys come." Lathrop responded, "I have read your letter with a great deal of sympathy and earnestly wish that I knew how to be of service to you." Lathrop understood that the only true way to help this mother from Idaho and so many others was through social policy. She told the mother, "Sometime I hope that our country will be so organized that there will be a doctor and nurse stationed at various points, so that no one can be twenty-five miles from a physician."[19]

Lathrop's relentless efforts on behalf of the first nationwide public health program available to all mothers and infants, regardless of background, is the subject of the next chapter.

7

The Making of the Maternity and Infancy Act, 1921

"Of all the activities in which I shared during more than forty years of striving, none is, I am convinced, of such fundamental importance as the Sheppard-Towner Act."

—Florence Kelley, 1926

Lathrop's success in establishing a national health program for mothers and infants was years in the making. Before working on national policy, the bureau encouraged local communities to launch initiatives that would make available information on healthful baby care. Health organizations in such major cities as Philadelphia, New York, Chicago, and Indianapolis launched their own campaigns, sponsoring Baby Weeks between 1911 and 1914 to highlight the importance of combating infant mortality. The local events during Baby Weeks provided information on healthy baby care for women of various social classes. In 1915 the bureau, building on the best practices in these cities, published a set of instructions for other communities interested in the programs.

That same year the bureau organized rural conferences in Iowa and Wisconsin. One of the most popular features of the local conferences was the better baby contest. Historian Laura Lovell writes that Dr. Lydia De-Vilbiss, a public health doctor in Kansas, convinced Lathrop that the contests were helpful in getting the message across, telling her that "instead of going into the county districts and trying to persuade the farmer folk to do what we want them to do, this plan proposes to put them on their mettle and let them do for themselves what we want them to do and what we should have difficulty in getting them to do in any other way." Lathrop next coordinated with the General Federation of Women's Clubs (GWFC) to launch the first national Baby Week in 1916 and then again in 1917. Lathrop noted that the 1916 event was successful "far beyond our most extravagant anticipation . . . with observances . . . in more than 4,700 communities."[1]

World War I offered Lathrop the best opportunity to highlight the importance of maternal and child health care. When President Wilson provided money to undertake the Children's Year activities, he asked that the organizers come up with "certain irreducible standards for the health, education and work of the American child." With new federal funds Lathrop increased the circulation of the pamphlets on infant and maternity care. The bureau and local women's groups sponsored child health conferences where volunteer doctors and nurses examined babies and taught parents how to care for their children. Lathrop wanted the wartime activity to generate enough support that local governments would move to establish permanent public health services for mothers and babies. The conferences strategy worked, with "six and a half million children receiving medical examinations, twenty-four states permanently employing public health nurses, 143 health centers opened and ten states establishing milk stations."[2]

After the war Lathrop moved to solidify through law the growing cooperation between the federal government and the states on behalf of maternal and infant health. Most of the existing state and local programs targeted America's urban centers. Lathrop knew from the letters she had received and the work of her staff that the women in rural areas faced particular hardships. The early proposals for federal legislation focused specifically on the health-care crisis in rural communities. As the bill made its way through Congress, Lathrop and allies needed the support of urban lawmakers; thus, the final bill extended funds to cities as well. Lathrop herself insisted that the funds be available to help mothers and children regardless of social background; she did not want Americans to view the Maternity and Infancy Act as charity. Lathrop understood then what contemporary supporters of government programs understand: it was important that government initiatives maintain widespread popular support. One good way to gain and maintain support was to make it a universal entitlement rather than based on financial need.

It took four years to move from the first proposals for the Maternal and Infancy Act to the bill that passed in 1921. The final law granted federal assistance to states for instruction on nutrition and hygiene, prenatal and child health clinics, and visiting nurses for pregnant women. Jeanette Rankin, a progressive activist from Montana and the first woman elected to Congress, introduced an early version of the bill in 1918. In 1919 Rankin was no longer in the Congress; Representative Horace Mann Towner of Iowa and Senator Morris Sheppard of Texas sponsored a revised bill. To ensure the passage of the Sheppard-Towner Maternity and Infancy Act, Lathrop used all the political skills in mobilizing, publicizing, and compromising she had honed over a career spanning almost three decades.

Lathrop marshaled her supporters with caution but determination. She reached out to her usual allies such as the GFWC for support. In 1919 she turned to the newly formed League of Women Voters (LWV), which had emerged out of the National American Woman Suffrage Association. The new organization wanted to push for women's political rights and to fight for social reforms that had long interested many women suffragists like Lathrop. She asked the LWV to form a Child Welfare Committee to push for Sheppard-Towner. Taking her by-now familiar approach, she told the LWV that it is "absolutely impossible for a government bureau to push [such] measures within with success. If the matter were one which the League of Women Voters took an interest it would add to the enormous strength of the bureau. We would of course advise and cooperate in any manner you would have us, but Congress always questions bills that are introduced by government bureaus without backing from voluntary public-spirited agencies." In a similar vein Lathrop told the GFWC that the bureau could not openly lobby for a bill "that would seem to increase its power and responsibility." But she needed their support. "I should be, of course, very happy to see the measure urged that it cease to be in any sense a Bureau measure."[3]

The urging and pushing was coordinated by the Women's Joint Congressional Committee (WJCC), a coalition of women's social welfare groups founded in 1920 that included the LWV, Kelley's National Consumers League, the Women's Trade Union League, the Women's Christian Temperance Union, the National Association of Colored Women, and the National Council of Jewish Women, among others. Whenever three or more WJCC member organizations endorsed or opposed a bill, they jointly formed a subcommittee with a professional staff to do their congressional lobbying. The WJCC "formalized the lobbying network that Wald, Addams and finally Lathrop had built."[4]

Women's magazines also played an important role in mobilizing support for Sheppard-Towner. The *Ladies Home Journal, Woman's Home Companion, Good Housekeeping,* and *McCall's* urged their readers to contact their congressmen and published petitions, which their readers could sign and circulate.

In addition to the women's groups, the American Federation of Labor, the Democratic, Socialist, and Farmer-Labor Parties, and the successful Republican candidate for president in 1920, Warren G. Harding, all supported the bill, as did the pediatrics section of the American Medical Association. Many congressmen moved to support the bill when the Nineteenth Amendment, guaranteeing women the right to vote, was ratified in 1920. They believed that women would vote as a bloc on behalf of welfare for mothers and children. Lathrop and her allies had good reason to be hopeful about the bill not only because of the women's vote: even though 1920 saw the resurgence of conservatism in the White House, first with Republican Warren Harding and then Calvin Coolidge, in the early 1920s Congress still contained a formidable bloc of progressive congressmen that voted on behalf of activist government.

Nonetheless, as the bill made its way through the legislature, opposition mounted. The American Medical Association opposed a law that would increase the role of female professionals in the area of health care. Right-wing organizations, including women's groups—indeed, women did not vote as a bloc—opposed what they saw as the growing power of government to regulate the lives of American families. In 1920 the National Association Opposed to Woman Suffrage renamed itself the Woman Patriots, turning their fire on the Children's Bureau and all efforts to expand government social services. Sheppard-Towner, they declared, was an effort to invade the privacy of American families and to replace husbands and fathers as the rightful authorities at home with the government. With fears about spreading Bolshevism still in the air in 1920, the Patriots decried the health plan as the work of the un-American Julia Lathrop out to destroy the traditional family.

Both opponents and supporters of the act used the politics of gender to promote their positions. Twenty years earlier Illinois legislators questioned Lathrop's suitability to address issues surrounding children because she was a single woman; now she faced such attacks again, but on a bigger stage. Missouri senator James Reed was particularly hostile to the Children's Bureau. "It is now proposed to turn the control of the mothers of the land over to a few single ladies holding Government jobs at Washington," he said. "I question whether one out of ten of these delightful reformers could make a bowl of buttermilk gruel that would not give a baby the colic in five minutes. We would better reverse the proposition and provide for a committee of mothers to take charge of the old maids and teach them how to acquire a husband and have babies of their own." On the other side, when Florence Kelley addressed legislators who opposed the bill on the grounds that the federal government could not afford the expense, she called on the widespread sympathy felt for vulnerable children and mothers. "No woman in the United States would begrudge the increase in salaries. . . . Why does Congress wish women and children to die?"[5]

Lathrop ensured the bill's passage by accepting a number of compromises. Her original bill called for medical care to mothers and children in addition to health education; the final law provided only educational programs. Lathrop probably knew in advance that, as it turned out, when the legislation was implemented the line between health education and preventative medical care could be blurred. Early on, the bill called for an annual appropriation of $4 million, but the final act funded the programs for only five years and reduced the appropriation to $1.25 million. The Children's Bureau also had to give up sole authority for approving the state applications for the federal funds.

While making concessions, Lathrop fought very hard to keep as much responsibility as possible in the hands of the bureau. Meeting with the US Surgeon General Rupert Blue in 1919, she told him that as a result of pushback from public health officials, she had agreed to change her original draft bill that gave sole authority to the bureau and to allow for the sharing of authority with representatives from Blue's Department of Public Health and the US Bureau of Education. But she was not willing to concede that child health was a matter of "clinical medicine only." When Blue raised the possibility that a proposed new Department of Health would incorporate the Children's Bureau, Lathrop replied that she actively opposed such a move, arguing that the bureau belonged in the Department of Labor because it is the department "interested in securing the welfare of the masses of the wage earners of this country. . . . The problem of child welfare must in some manner secure the coordination and collaboration of the doctor, the nurse, the teacher and every contribution which science can make."

Nor was Lathrop willing to rely on private charity. Blue suggested that the Red Cross could take charge of maternity and infant care. Lathrop told him that although she thought the organization could help launch the program, she "had no doubt that the public of this country would prefer a plan to protect maternity and infancy . . . supported solely by taxation, giving a service dignified of a country school teacher rather than a service supported by contributions like the Red Cross."[6]

Lathrop proceeded cautiously yet doggedly. We saw her caution in her efforts to disassociate the bureau from any efforts to expand contraception. She also assured legislators wary about the spread of socialist ideas that her interest was maternal health benefits only; she did not endorse European-style programs of cash payments for mothers. Her doggedness is reflected in her determination to delay her retirement until she could be sure the bill would pass. By June Lathrop was sixty-three years old. Entering her ninth year at the bureau, she wanted to return to Rockford. As early as April 1921 she reached out to her protégée Grace Abbott, asking her whether she would take over as the next bureau chief. Harriet Taylor Upton, vice president of the Republican National Committee, persuaded Lathrop to stay for a bit, arguing that her presence in Washington was critical to the bill's passage. Lathrop also waited to resign until she could be assured that Abbott would be appointed as her successor. She feared that Republican Party loyalty rather than experience and professional expertise might dictate the appointment. By August the bill seemed ready for passage, though one main obstacle was the opposition of Congressman Samuel Winslow, a Republican from Massachusetts, who disliked Lathrop. Upton Taylor now told Lathrop that if she would resign, "he [Winslow] could say he was less opposed because he had gained what he wanted."[7] With that and the knowledge that Abbott, backed by Lathrop's powerful network of activists and Upton Taylor, would be appointed as her successor, Lathrop submitted her resignation, which President Harding accepted.

The Maternal and Infancy Act passed in November 1921 and was Lathrop's crowning achievement as bureau chief. "Of all the activities in which I shared during more than forty years of striving," stated her close friend Florence Kelley, "none is . . . of such fundamental importance as the Sheppard-Towner Act."[8] Participation was voluntary; states that set up programs approved in Washington then became eligible for federal funding. Women's groups lobbied their state legislators and governors on behalf of the act. Lathrop herself became one such lobbyist; in retirement she worked hard to convince the Illinois state legislature to accept funding. It was a cruel irony that although forty-five states agreed to accept Sheppard-Towner funds, the enormous power of the American Medical Association in Illinois prevented its passage in Lathrop's home state.

In its seven-year existence hundreds of thousands of women attended child health and prenatal conferences and took part in mothers' classes funded by the Sheppard-Towner Act. Just as Lathrop had hoped, the initiatives stimulated local governments to expand health care. In 1926, for example, over one thousand new, permanent health centers and almost two hundred prenatal clinics were established. In remote areas, where mothers could not get to the conferences and clinics, visiting nurses traveled in difficult conditions to help treat sick children and instruct mothers.

The implementation of Sheppard-Towner provided many jobs for women. The bureau, in charge of administering the act, employed clerical staff, public health doctors, and nurses as well as social workers, all of them women. Using Sheppard-Towner funds, the state programs expanded their hiring of public health nurses and doctors, the majority of them women. The act also funded the hiring of dieticians, home economists, and social workers. And the bureau kept its hand in all aspects of the program. The final authority to approve state programs rested with a new board, drawn from the bureau, the Departments of Public Health, and Education. However, at its first meeting the board elected Abbott, the new bureau chief, as its chair. The board essentially "rubber stamped the Bureau's decisions on [the suitability of] state programs."[9]

The Sheppard-Towner Maternity and Infancy Act contained many weaknesses. First, the original legislation only allowed for five years of funding, ending in 1925. By the mid-1920s a more conservative Congress, backed by a very conservative president, Calvin Coolidge, supported only limited funding for two more years, period.

Both locally and nationally staff workers who administered the programs showed only a limited understanding of minority Americans. The Children's Bureau made serious efforts to address the health needs of mothers and children regardless of race and ethnicity. The bureau encouraged the states to hire staff members from communities of color and hired a black physician to train midwives in the rural South. Indian and Anglo nurses brought care to Indian reservations and attended to Hispanic Americans in New Mexico. Nevertheless, the white professionals in the 1920s, just as in the earlier decades, disdained traditional methods of health care and nutrition. Sheppard-Towner staff took a major role in pushing both the licensing of midwives and their training. These programs had the biggest impact on women of color. Many midwives embraced aspects of the new training while refusing to give up on all of their traditional practices. But others probably left midwifery altogether or were "driven underground," according to Molly Ladd-Taylor, afraid they would face prosecution.[10] In truth the meager resources available in the poor minority communities, along with cultural bias, limited the success of the program. Although infant mortality dropped significantly for whites, particularly in rural areas, it remained high for babies of color.

With all of its problems, however, Sheppard-Towner marked a victory in the decades-old effort to employ the politics of maternalism to grow the social welfare state. For Lathrop the death of babies was not about the individual failings of American parents but about larger social conditions. To make the democratic promise of equal opportunity for all a reality in the twentieth century, the larger society had to address these conditions. "We still cling to the shaken but not shattered belief that this free country gives every man his chance and that an income sufficient to bring up a family decently is attainable by all honest people who are not hopelessly stupid, or incorrigibly lazy," she told an audience of public health officials in 1918. The evidence from the bureau studies of infant mortality, however, showed otherwise, so she concluded her speech with a bit of that wit but also that deep conviction that propelled her forward. "The fathers of 88 per cent of the babies included in the Bureau's studies earned less than $1,250 a year; 27 per cent earned less than $550. As the income doubled the mortality rate was more than halved. Which is the more sage and sane conclusion! [sic] That 88 percent of all these fathers were incorrigibly indolent or below normal mentally, or that sound public economy demands an irreducible living standard to be sustained by a minimum wage and such expedients as may be developed in a determined effort to give every child a fair chance?" If, by 1921, Lathrop could not achieve that decent living standard, she at least obtained some measure of the other "expedients" in the Maternity and Infancy Act.[11]

"To give every child a fair chance," Julia Lathrop had spent eight years educating Americans about the evils of child labor, the value of mothers' pensions, and about new standards for health care and child rearing. She assisted individual families and mobilized support across the country for maternal and infant health services. She was now ready to return to Rockford to live with Anna.

8

Retirement and Keeping On

"The present time is one in which it requires unusual courage to be courageous."

—Julia Lathrop, April 1925

Julia Lathrop returned to Rockford in late 1921 as a private citizen. She filled her so-called retirement years with a hectic schedule just as she had done her entire adult life. At Hull House she often went to bed early but then was up in the middle of the night at her desk, hard at work. During her days at the Children's Bureau she took catnaps in order to keep up the pace. At Vassar's anniversary gathering in 1915, with Lathrop in attendance, one speaker referred to her as the college's "most distinguished alumna," and the audience loudly applauded. To cover up the fact that she had been sound asleep, Lathrop vigorously joined in the enthusiastic clapping. The audience, realizing what happened, "added laughter to their applause."[1]

Lathrop's retirement days were equally busy—she was used to being tired. She campaigned across the country for causes she had long championed such as the Sheppard-Towner bill. She worked hard as president of the Illinois League of Women Voters and a vice president of the national League of Women Voters (LWV), mobilizing women on behalf of social welfare. She addressed the plight of Native Americans and participated in the campaign against capital punishment. As a delegate to the Child Welfare Committee of the League of Nations, she promoted international standards of children's well-being. Lathrop, like Jane Addams, Florence Kelley, and others in her reform network, also contended with a conservative backlash; opponents of social welfare programs tried to limit them by tainting their promoters as allies of Bolshevism and worldwide communism.

Lathrop's many civic activities didn't stop her from enjoying a rich personal life with family—particularly her sister Anna with whom she shared a home—and friends. Lathrop approached the last decade of her life with the same traits that were familiar to all who knew her—her determination, her sense of humor, and her hyper-modesty.

Lathrop spent time in her last years in Washington, New York, at Vassar College, and at Hull House. She traveled to Europe and to South America, but while in Rockford she and her sister delighted in decorating their home. Lathrop worked in her library brimming with books, photographs, graphs, and papers. She and her sister filled the house with furnishings from their many travels. From Paris in 1926 she wrote to her sister that she had "yielded to temptation of some Russian silver and sent home . . . a pair of candlesticks and a small dish. The candle sticks are 18th [century] or early 19th, probably the dish is 17th and is interesting, I hope you will think." In Rockford the year earlier she wrote to Anna, who was away at Vassar for her own college reunion, that "today the new chaise lounge in two parts duly arrived. I uncrated it with much joy." Lathrop went on to detail her efforts to find the right print for their porch awning, suggesting that because she saw nothing at home that she liked, her sister might check out two wholesale places in New York City.

During Anna's time away Lathrop worked in the garden alongside their assistant, John. With the weather "hot and bright, all things [are] alive in the garden and growing."[2] During one European trip in 1929 Lathrop told her sister, "I think and think of the garden. . . . If we could only interest someone in killing the pests that almost killed the perennials . . . last year. At least zinnias, marigolds, and ageratums and our precious mourning brides were strong last year." Of course in the end Lathrop assured her sister, with insistent underlining, "whatever you do or not do in the garden I am sure I will like." Letters to Anna were filled with descriptions of the flora she observed, whether it be the forsythia outside Washington, DC, "billowing like yellow silk dresses on the lawn," or the Luxembourg Gardens in Paris, with its pear trees "just coming into bloom."[3]

Anna shared her sister's interest in clothes. "I advise that black and brown ensemble," Julia wrote to her sister during one stay in Washington. "It would be smart and useful and you deserve it. Do run in and get that or a better color if you prefer." During her travels Julia commented to her sister about the fashions she observed. Reporting from an ocean liner, she once noted, "All kinds and ages of ladies and gentlemen wear sport shoes on the deck. I have been neglectful about getting mine out. Perhaps tomorrow I shall. . . . Not withstanding shawls are said to be 'out' they are worn a good deal on this boat."[4]

Lathrop's devotion to her "Dearest Ann" shines through her letters. She praised Anna for her civic work, which included the League of Women Voters. Lathrop told her often how much she cared for her and how very much she missed her while she was away. En route to Europe in April 1929, she wrote, "You have no idea how much I look forward to the bright day when I see you and Bobbie [Anna's daughter] again." Eleven days later, in the midst of what she termed "inexpressibly tiresome meetings" at the League of Nations in Geneva, she told her sister, "If I didn't have you and Bobbie to look forward to, I'd expire. . . . I cant [*sic*] tell you how much time I squander thinking of Home and Family." Once, in thanking her sister for cheering her up, she wrote, "Yesterday and today as so many times before I have reflected upon your amicability, wisdom and eloquence and have thanked a kind Fate for Such a Sister." She signed it "Most Possible Love, JCL."[5]

Lathrop gardened, decorated her home, dined with family and friends, toured many countries, and shopped along with her work. For a while she contemplated running for office herself, as a candidate for the US Congress. After some consideration, she opted for her customary approach of mobilizing on behalf of causes rather than promoting herself. "The more I think things over" she told Grace Abbott in 1923, "the more I feel sure that I ought not to run for anything. This makes me all the more eager to see what can be done to influence platforms and promote good candidates."[6] That same year she became president of the Illinois League of Women Voters for two years and later served as a vice president and adviser in public welfare for the national LWV.

Founded just after women gained suffrage, the League educated women about politics and government and urged them to participate in politics. The organization endorsed no political party or candidate, but the social feminists' agenda was clearly among its members' highest priorities. Lathrop saw the League's various goals as interrelated. Thus, she argued in her convention address to the Illinois League in 1923 that if women wanted the Illinois Legislature to institute Sheppard-Towner programs, they needed to be educated. "The reason that we do not succeed better . . .

is that we do not inform ourselves better as to the background and history of other legislation which competes with that which we endeavor to secure. . . . We are righteously indignant, of course, but perhaps also rightfully helpless if we cannot prove how state money can be found for a good purpose after we have shown its importance." Lathrop spent many days in Springfield, the Illinois state capital, testifying on bills concerning maternal and infant care, child labor, the shorter working day, and the minimum wage. She talked to legislators frequently about the importance of women on juries, women's participation in political parties, and women's political education.

Lathrop could take pride in the growth of the LWV both in Illinois and nationally. Nevertheless, she faced major setbacks in her efforts to promote the social welfare of children; none was bigger than her home state's unwillingness to participate in the Maternity and Infancy Act. Illinois doctors probably had Lathrop and Grace Abbott in mind when they denounced the legislation as "a menace sponsored by 'endocrine perverts [and] derailed menopausics.'"[7]

In addition to promoting Sheppard-Towner, the LWV devoted considerable attention to the campaign for a child labor amendment to the US Constitution. By 1922 the Supreme Court had twice struck down efforts to regulate child labor through legislation. Led by Florence Kelley and the women of the Children's Bureau, the LWV and the General Federation of Women's Clubs (GFWC), the National Child Labor Committee (NCLC), and the National Consumers League (NCL), which now included Lathrop as one of its vice presidents, quickly launched a campaign for a constitutional amendment banning child labor. Introduced in the US Congress in May 1922, the amendment authorized the federal government to regulate, limit, or prohibit the labor of children under the age of eighteen.

Opponents of Sheppard-Towner criticized the proposed amendment as government overreach, another example of social activists determined to invade the privacy of the home. Historian Kim Nielsen summarized the position of the opponents: "The government bureaucracy created by Sheppard-Towner would control the infancy of all children, and the Child Labor Amendment would render parental control ineffective."[8] Grace Abbott and Kelley, among others, were undaunted by the challenge of passing the amendment, which required not only passage in Congress by a two-thirds majority vote but also ratification by three-quarters of the states. Lathrop, ever the pragmatist, was more pessimistic, especially because of the opposition she was encountering over Sheppard-Towner. In 1922 she told Grace that although she supported efforts to enact state laws, "just this time seemed to me a hard time, to launch a new constitutional amendment and that perhaps a waiting time might be temporarily wise."

The amendment passed both the House and Senate in 1924, but Lathrop's pessimism turned out to be well founded in terms of the campaigns in the states. With the LWV actively engaged on behalf of the amendment, Lathrop became vice chair of a committee, which included the LWV and the NCLC, known as the Organizations Associated for Ratification of the Child Labor Amendment, to coordinate the campaign. The committee organized speaking tours and created pamphlets and posters for the cause. After some initial state successes, the ratification process stalled. Southern cotton mill owners launched a major counteroffensive against the amendment and, along with the hostility of large farming interests, doomed its passage in most of the south. The National Association of Manufacturers (NAM) also mobilized against the initiative, as did newspaper publishers who feared the regulation of newspaper boys selling on the streets.

One of the most pivotal fights took place in Massachusetts. Originally activists assumed that the Bay State, with its progressive history of labor laws, would be an easy sell, but they soon found fierce opposition mounting from the NAM. The Catholic Church was a vocal opponent of the measure, which it saw as an intrusion on parental prerogatives. The Church also feared that once adolescents were prevented from labor, public schooling would expand; during those same years education activists had been calling for greater federal funding of public schools, a measure the Church saw as a threat to parochial schools. Lathrop agreed to go to Massachusetts to campaign for the cause, but she was not enthusiastic. She confided to her friend Kelley in the summer of 1924, "I would rather go to the dentist . . . but I suppose both are necessary."[9]

Throughout the country opponents of the amendment—among them the Woman Patriots—emphasized that its supporters were undermining traditional family values. The amendment addressed factory labor, not daily household chores, but critics often emphasized that the new law would undermine character building that came when parents expected their adolescents to help with ordinary household chores. Lathrop clipped and saved one powerful example of this line of attack. A cartoon published by the *Columbus Dispatch* shows the parents on a family farm, dismayed by their lazy teenage children, clad in stylish clothes of the 1920s, who refuse to obey their parents. As Nielsen points out, the message is that the "Child Labor Amendment subverts everything. Children will disobey and ignore their parents while being transformed into lazy, decadent, but perhaps modern, adults who smoke cigarettes and bob their hair."[10]

The Massachusetts referendum failed that November; Lathrop also campaigned in New York the next year, but the state of New York had to table the amendment in the legislature for fear it would not pass a public referendum. By early 1925 Lathrop was clearly discouraged about the efforts. After returning home from a fruitless effort to lobby the Minnesota legislature, she confided, "This winter my sense of the value of politeness and social attentions has fallen to the lowest possible point. Courtesies really pleasant and warmly meant are offered as a balm for knock-down blows." But, as always, she rallied, declaring in the next sentence to one of her comrades in the fight, "I am cast-down but not dispirited."[11] Despite all efforts, by 1932 only six states had passed the amendment; it did not include Lathrop's Illinois, though she vigorously lobbied the state legislature. It would be left to Franklin Roosevelt's New Deal to attack the problem of child labor through federal legislation.

By the end of the 1920s Lathrop's signature legislation, the Sheppard-Towner Act, came to an end. In 1927 the first bill authorizing the act was set to expire; despite the continued enthusiasm of the women social reformers and the Children's Bureau, they were unable to muster enough votes to renew Sheppard-Towner for more than two years. The opposition from male medical professionals was critical. As Muncy writes, "While public service values were central" to the child welfare women, "the fee paying element was so central to the AMA's conception of the medical profession that its members often referred to the female doctors engaged in Sheppard-Towner activities as social workers."[12]

During the Coolidge years from 1923 to 1929 Lathrop lobbied vigorously against efforts to cut the Children's Bureau's budget and to shrink its responsibilities. Grace Abbott and Lathrop hoped that when Herbert Hoover assumed the presidency in 1929 he would push for the renewal of Sheppard-Towner. He had served in government since the days of Woodrow Wilson, and during World War I he seemed deeply interested in child welfare. Although he initially endorsed an extension of the bill for another two years, he never worked to assure its passage. In keeping with his philosophy, he made clear that his preference was to end the federal grant-in-aid program with one based solely on voluntary and state funding.

Lathrop, Abbott, and their allies soon realized that the Hoover administration was determined to shrink the responsibilities of the Children's Bureau as the agency primarily involved in child welfare, most particularly in the area of health. After 1929, with Sheppard-Towner terminated, many states struggled to maintain their programs, but without federal help it was increasingly difficult to do so, particularly when the country was in the throes of the Great Depression in the early 1930s. The end of Sheppard-Towner, in the words of historian Molly Ladd-Taylor, marked the triumph of the old principle that social feminists had "spent their lives trying to change: that children's welfare was primarily the responsibility of individual mothers, not society."[13]

But Lathrop not only attended to social welfare in the United States during the 1920s; in 1922 the League of Nations appointed her to its Child Welfare Committee. President Wilson fervently believed in the creation of an international body established as part of the Versailles Treaty; indeed, he was one of the principle architects of the League, which was designed to resolve international disputes peacefully. Nevertheless, the US Congress, reflecting opposition to the treaty and the League on both the right and the left, rejected ratification. Many social activists concerned about women's issues, child welfare, and labor rights participated, ex officio, as members and consultants to League committees that addressed these problems on a global basis.

Work on child welfare was originally part of a League advisory committee formed to investigate the problems of traffic in women and children. In 1922 the US State Department appointed Lathrop's successor at the Children's Bureau, Grace Abbott, to represent the United States on the committee in an unofficial capacity. Abbott worked to broaden the focus to larger issues regarding the welfare of children. She and Lathrop strongly believed that although the issue of prostitution garnered the most publicity, for the vast majority of children the issues of poverty, poor health, and education were more important and required a separate committee. Two committees, one on the traffic in women and children and another on child welfare, emerged in 1925. While government representatives served on both committees, each would have a special expert, known as an assessor, on the committee; Lathrop became an assessor for the Child Welfare Committee.

The committee's agenda, which Lathrop worked hard to create, was impressive. It set out to study laws relating to infant health, age of consent at marriage, repatriation of dependent children, child labor, and family allowances. Additionally, the committee included on its agenda one of the long-running concerns of the social reformers, the effect of movies "on the mental and moral well-being of children."[14] Continuing the social reformers' tradition of finding private funds to support public initiatives, Abbott secured a grant from the American Social Hygiene Association to help finance the committee's work.

Work on the League's advisory committee frustrated both Abbott and Lathrop. Lathrop, as we saw, wrote to her family about the impossibly tiresome meetings. The Americans and the Canadians continually complained to Lathrop that the committee allowed appointments of unqualified people to conduct investigations. Abbott also worried that the committee did not have enough financial support for its work. Because the United States was not a member of the League, Abbott and Lathrop had more freedom to decide which proposals they would promote to the General Assembly; however, the power of the US government did not back up their views. Moreover, participating nations were reluctant to cede control over rules and regulations regarding children in their countries.

Nevertheless, Lathrop often spoke publicly about the committee's importance. Reporting on her first meeting in Geneva in 1925, she told the National Conference of Social Workers audience that she "came away with an almost overwhelming sense of the power of the Committee." First, she believed, "A new interest in child welfare exists throughout the world." She pointed out the work of South American countries now spending "lavishly" for education and health care. European countries have now written constitutions, which, different as they might be, all show "in common a new conception of the duty of the state to protect the young."

Lathrop believed in the power of the League advisory committees to "discover and make known facts." Again she reflected the progressive faith in social science: once informed, the public would embrace the cause of social justice. "A fruitful fact needs no compulsory legislation nor military sanction, nothing but a chance to be used," she told the social workers. She of course admitted that "this pursuit and diffusion of knowledge is by no means a primrose path. It is a matter of endless exacting toil." But, she confidently concluded, "The Child Welfare Committee has one obvious advantage—It need make no converts to its cause. They were already made. All the parents of the world are its willing audience if its skill and its gift of tongues enable it to make itself understood."[15]

Lathrop's faith in worldwide cooperation extended beyond child welfare. Like many progressives horrified by World War I, she embraced the postwar efforts to prevent war through mutual disarmament. Many of Lathrop's organizations were part of these efforts, among them the GFWC and the WJCC that had mobilized on behalf of Sheppard-Towner. Lathrop also belonged to the National Council for the Prevention of War. In 1921 the National Council for the Limitation of War distributed a Christmas poster showing shepherds gazing at the star of Bethlehem, shadows of modern-day soldiers, and the words "Before Another Christmas . . . Less of Armament and None of War." Sometime in the 1920s Lathrop sent her Christmas greetings to friends using postcards of this poster.[16]

In 1924 Lathrop entered into the debate surrounding the staging of a national Defense Day. After World War I, much to the War Department's dismay, the US Congress, reflecting American sentiment, reduced the size of the American military and the its budget drastically. In response the War Department, along with conservative patriotic groups such as the National Security League, organized a one-day program for September 12, 1924, to test National Guard and army reserve forces' responsiveness to possible military attacks. New York City, for example, was the site of a mock attack, with airplanes dropping flour bombs. Lathrop and others in the disarmament movement were alarmed. In a paper entitled "Defense Day and Patriots," Lathrop argued that national security meant social security. "The proposed demonstration [Defense Day] is costly in itself but that is not the point. Insofar as it enlists public interest it will serve the requests to Congress for appropriations for military purposes, and that may be presumed to be one advantage in the minds of its promoters. War preparations cost enormously. They cost sums which should be spent for those permanent national defenses—education, the conservation of public welfare and development of natural resources."[17]

Author of the Maternity and Infancy Act, a proponent of the Child Labor Amendment, and a member of the international peace movement, Lathrop was among a group of activist women specifically targeted in the mid-1920s by conservative patriotic groups. The high point of the post–World War I Red Scare came in the wake of anarchist bombings in eight American cities. In 1919 and 1920 thousands of American immigrants, legally in the country but not citizens, were charged as subversives, determined to bring revolution to the United States just as revolution had overtaken Russia in 1917. Of the thousands rounded up, only several hundred, including the famous anarchist Emma Goldman, were deported. By the middle of 1920 most Americans' fears had subsided, and the dramatic efforts of the Justice Department to quell revolution were over. But that did not stop conservative groups, including women's organizations, from exploiting concerns about the Russian Revolution to undermine the progressive women who had been so influential just before and after World War I.

During the ongoing debates over the extension of Sheppard-Towner and the Child Labor Amendment, the Woman Patriots charged Lathrop and her protégée at the Children's Bureau, Grace Abbott, as coconspirators to "use the Children's Bureau for 'despotic power' promotion of revolution by legislation and of 'international control of children.'" The specific charges stemmed from a Children's Bureau publication, issued under Lathrop's name in 1919, about maternity benefit programs around the world. A staff member of the Library of Congress prepared the report, according to historian Lela Costin, for the bureau. The publication noted that a Russian, Madame Alexander Kollantai, had done the most extensive report ever written on maternity benefits and insurance. A member of the Communist Party, Kollantai played a prominent role in the early days of the Bolshevik Revolution as a government official who worked on promoting women's issues. Here was "proof" that Lathrop was spreading Communist propaganda.

Lathrop herself had no idea who Kollantai was. In 1924 she wrote to the head of the Library of Congress, asking him "for any information which is available as to the standing and authority of Madame Kollantai." The chief of documents wrote to Lathrop with sympathy and irritation "on the basis of an utterly inconsequential book note, they have built up a straw man of approval of bolshevick [*sic*] doctrine." He told her that "the book is a diligent summary of existing facts [about maternity benefits] with notations of laws, etc., all supplied to original source." Showing some humor himself, he added, "With some trepidation, I enclose a newspaper picture of Kollantai to let you see the viper you have been nursing."[18]

The patriot organizations focused most especially on Addams and Kelley as dangerous radicals. Kelley had identified herself as a socialist; Addams was a particular target not only because of her fame but also her outspoken pacifism during World War I and her continued association in the 1920s with the Women's International League for Peace and Freedom (WILPF); in 1920 Addams became the international president of the organization.

Prominent men in the antipeace movement, such as Richard Merrill Whitney, charged that the 1923 national WILPF convention "was certainly the most subversive, certainly the most insidiously and cleverly camouflaged anti-American and un-American public meeting that has been held in this country since the United Sates entered the European war."

In April 1923 Brigadier General Amos Frees, who headed the Chemical Services Division of the War Department, directed one of his staff members, Lucia Ramsey Maxwell, to compile a chart, now known as the Spider Web Chart, to link seventeen women's organizations and twenty-nine individual women in order to show the "international socialist-pacifist movement to bring about international socialism." An important aspect of the chart was to link the pacifist organizations to the women's organizations pushing social welfare legislation, such as the WJCC, the LWV, and the NCL. As Lathrop put it to her friend Kelley, depicted as a key link in the web, "Do you understand that the authors of the Spider Web are the persons who led the attack on Sheppard-Towner?"[19] Henry Ford's *Dearborn Independent*, a virulently anti-Semitic publication, reflecting its owner's views, published the Web; the chart and the articles that described the Bolshevik influence on American women's organizations were then picked up and widely distributed elsewhere in the country. The WJCC fought back against the false charges regarding the women and the organizations listed on the Web. The secretary of the War Department apologized for the circulation of the inaccurate charts, stating in the spring of 1924 that all remaining copies of the chart would be destroyed, but it hardly mattered. The attacks against the women's organizations and the prominent leaders increased.

One of the most important women's organizations, the Daughters of the American Revolution (DAR), became a spearhead in the fight against these so-called dangerous women, including Lathrop. Founded in the 1890s, the DAR membership, which stood at 156,000 in 1926, was limited to women who could show they were descendants of Revolutionary War veterans. Excluded from many male patriotic organizations, the DAR allowed women to feel more included in celebrations of the Revolution. Until 1923 the DAR had endorsed a number of progressive initiatives, including the Sheppard-Towner Bill. But the rising tide of conservatism affected the organization soon after that, and the ascension of a leadership team now deeply concerned about radicalism and pacifism set a very new tone for the organization. In 1923 the DAR endorsed the preparedness agenda of the War Department; they also mounted an attack on WILPF as a subservice organization.

The DAR tactic that gained the most national attention surrounded the charge that the national organization kept a blacklist of speakers and organizations that local leagues were instructed to avoid. Massachusetts DAR member Helen Tufts Bailie asserted that the organization had a list of 131 men, 87 women, and 306 organizations. Beside each name on the list were one or more designations indicating why the person was undesirable. Lathrop was listed as a "feminist, internationalist, socialist, and pacifist." As Bailie explained to Lathrop, "your name is on the D.A.R.'s blacklist, and the Children's Bureau also. The D.A.R. have as part of their program the destruction of the Children's Bureau, registering their determination in resolutions passed at [their] Continental Congress." The DAR denied that it had a list; so too did other activists in the antiradical movement, though conservative Mary Robinson of the Massachusetts Public Interest League claimed that her organization "would consider itself at perfect liberty to make lists of pinks, reds, or yellows—if it saw fit." For her efforts to reform the DAR, Bailie was expelled. Many other women resigned in protest over the DAR's national campaign. "I resigned from the D.A.R. last spring," Mrs. Elaine Eastman wrote to Lathrop, "after protesting actively and vainly, for more than a year, against the absurdities of the National Board. My initial rebellion was on the matter of the attack upon you for some imaginary disrespect to the flag." Lathrop thanked Eastman, noting that while she knew she was unpopular and had been included on a long list of "laborers and radicals" she did not know about any attack regarding her respect of the flag. "Perhaps it is well not to know painful things or disagreeable things or silly things; all of which these attacks of the D.A.R. seem not so much applied to me but as applied to anyone."[20]

That Lathrop was targeted for her "feminism" is somewhat ironic, as she and her colleagues in the fight for social welfare did not view themselves in those terms. The social reformers associated the term feminism with those self-avowed feminists who were members of the National Woman's Party (NWP) in the 1920s, which focused on promoting the Equal Rights Amendment (ERA). The women of the LWV were hostile to the ERA and the NWP because of their fear that such an amendment would make women's special protective labor legislation impossible. The NWP, for its part, remained focused on equal rights legislation rather than other social welfare issues. Although its endorsement of the ERA did land the organization on the infamous spider web, the women of the NWP never became the target of the DAR; instead, the conservative women attacked the social reform women as feminists out to disrupt traditional values by invading the privacy of American families. As Nielsen writes, "The gendering of conservatism—the ideological conflation of a noninterventionist government with the preservation of private and social patriarchy profoundly shaped the politics of the 1920s."[21] By the end of the decade, with the defeat of Sheppard-Towner and the Child Labor Amendment and with the power of the Children's Bureau shrinking, the conservative campaign against the progressive women died down.

Lathrop reacted to all of these attacks with her sense of humor and sense of purpose. Perhaps her calm attitude, in contrast to her friend Kelley, was partly due to the fact that she was not vilified with the same ferocity as her good friend. But her approach was also consistent with her personality. At the national convention of the League of Women Voters in 1925, she spoke about the setbacks in getting the Child Labor Amendment passed; she referred to the particularly difficult climate that she and all of the members were facing in the era of conservative backlash. "The present time is one in which it requires unusual courage to be courageous. But that is the short view. In one form or another, as we decree by our interest or its lack the child will win. This is our opportunity to keep up and keep on with our eyes wider open, and our minds better informed and our courage stouter. We shall keep on."[22]

And "keep on" she did until her death in 1932. Among the things that concerned her during her last years was the plight of American Indians. During the 1920s Indian activists and their allies mounted increasing criticism of the Office of Indian Affairs, also known as the Bureau of Indian Affairs (BIA). The office provided services to the Indians and managed the relationship between the federal government and the Indian tribes. The American Indian Defense Association, led by New York social worker John Collier, criticized, among many things, the bureau's lack of sensitivity to Indian religious practices. Critics also pointed to the wretched state of Indian health and the dismal conditions of Indian schools. Other groups in the 1920s, such as the National Conference of Social Workers (NCSW), which Lathrop had headed in 1919–1920, also took up Indian issues.

In response to mounting criticism, the secretary of the Interior, Hubert Work, authorized in the spring of 1926 an investigation of the government administration of American Indians, most specifically the Bureau of Indian Affairs. An independent nonpartisan organization, the Institute for Government Research, the forerunner of the Brookings Institution, undertook the study. Lewis Meriam, Lathrop's former assistant chief from the Children's Bureau and now a permanent staff member at the institute, directed the study, which came to be known as the Meriam Report. Meriam's *The Problem of Indian Administration*, published in 1928, was a model of progressive social science. An 848-page study, it was thorough as thorough could be. Along with policy recommendations it contained detailed investigations of Indian life, including health, education, economic conditions, family life and the activities of women, the status of Indians now living in urban areas, legal issues surrounding Indian policy, and the administrative organization of the BIA.

Lathrop naturally had only high praise for the Meriam Report, which she noted was directed by a "qualified" veteran of "government, private research, and administration." Lathrop's interest in Indians at the time may have been sparked by Meriam's appearance at the NCSW meeting in 1929, where he spoke about his completed report and called on social workers to address the plight of American Indians. In response to the speech, the NCSW formed an Indian Committee, headed by Lathrop, who addressed the annual convention in 1930 on "What the Indian Service [another name for the Bureau] Needs." She based much of her talk on the report's findings, noting the extreme poverty of most Indians, the poor health, and the "grossly inadequate" care of the Indian children in the BIA's boarding schools. Whatever the common wisdom within the dominant society, she noted that the survey found "too much evidence of real suffering and discontent to subscribe to the belief that the Indians are reasonably satisfied with their condition." As always, she appealed to familial feelings that she saw as common to all. "The Indian is like the white man in his affection for his children and he feels keenly the sickness and the loss of his offspring."

To enable the BIA to "deal justly" with American Indians so that they become "actual not nominal citizens, sound in health, educated, self-directing and self-supporting," Lathrop called both for increased appropriations and an increase in a competent staff of both Indians and whites; attracting such a staff required better pay and better benefits. She ended the talk by encouraging social workers to take careers in the Indian service: "The Indians need some of you."[23] One year later, during her commencement address at Knox College, she urged the graduates to consider government service in the BIA.

The same mix of forward thinking and traditional attitudes that characterized her activism throughout her life was reflected in Lathrop's appeal. Her interest in Indian affairs put her in a small minority of whites who cared at all about Native Americans. Meriam and his staff reflected an appreciation for Indian culture not widely shared by white Americans. "Some Indians proud of their race and devoted to their culture and their mode of life have no desire to be as the white man is. . . . In this desire they are supported by intelligent, liberal whites who find real merit in their art, music, religion, form of government and other things which may be covered by the broad term culture."

Certainly Lathrop was among white liberals appreciative of Indian culture. She was contemptuous of the common assumptions about Indians in the dominant society. "I am sure that, as a child," she told the 1931 graduating class at Knox College, "you were brought up with a great dread of people who scalped you and who were awfully anxious to come to your town to call and slip in the back door and so on. That is a childish notion, I am sure. I suppose that great historians aren't going to write a very satisfactory page of which we can be very proud, about that inevitable conflict between the races which comes when one has strength and means of defense and offense, of which the other knows nothing."[24]

Like most white liberals, Lathrop also reflected attitudes that we would see as very paternalistic. The staff writers who contributed to the Meriam Report paid tribute to Indian culture, but most believed in assimilation as a long-term goal and that short-term respect for Indian mores would be the most effective approach to assimilation. Lathrop concluded that "the promptest and most practicable change from the Indian to the white mode of life, is on the whole the path by which the Indian is destined to survive." The report accepted ideas about racial hierarchy that were similar to the attitudes of Lathrop and her friends when it came to ethnic minorities and most especially African Americans. According to Elmer Rusco, "The fundamental conception that Indians were at a lower level of societal development is evident . . . in the final sentence of the summary report," which calls for a new and better Indian Service as a national atonement to the Indians that "could be a model for all governments concerned with the development and advancement of a retarded race."[25]

The Indian perspective might have been more central to the Meriam Report if Native Americans actually participated in conducting and writing the study. The staff consisted of only one Native American educator,

Henry Roe Cloud, who founded the first Native American college in 1915. A member of the Winnebago tribe, Roe Cloud was the first Indian to graduate from Yale University. Lathrop was a friend of Roe Cloud and had entertained him in her Rockford home. She once lauded him in terms that would appeal to her political circles. "Mr. Cloud is an Indian, a Yale graduate, a gentleman and a scholar." However, Roe Cloud did not write any part of the Meriam Report; rather, his job was to facilitate the work of others by acting as a liaison to the Indian tribes. Lathrop put it, "Trusted by the Indians his presence on the staff was a guarantee of the good faith of the survey, opened every door and insured an extraordinary degree of accuracy as to all material which required the statements of the Indians."[26]

Other Indian activists did not share Lathrop's faith in the report. Nor did they share her conviction that increasing appropriations for the BIA and adding more trained social workers would truly address Indian needs. For attorney and Omaha Indian Henry Sloan, who worked tirelessly on behalf of Indian rights, Indians needed not more social service but rather the true rights of citizenship and political power. Despite the fact that in 1924 Congress granted Indians full citizenship, seven states still did not allow them to vote. As historian Frederick Hoxie notes, "Success would not come to activists like Sloan until . . . the concept of general racial equality had gained broad support." Nonetheless, one can also appreciate the importance of the Meriam Report and those few reformers like Lathrop for highlighting the fact that despite all the promises, Indian conditions were not improving. Again, according to Hoxie, American policy makers learned that "at the height of the Coolidge 'prosperity,' two-thirds of all American Indians were earning less than $100 per year."[27]

For Lathrop "keeping on" in the 1920s also meant participating in the campaign against the death penalty. At the height of the Progressive Era the effort to abolish capital punishment enjoyed some success. Between 1907 and 1917 six states completely eliminated executions, and several others limited their use. But during World War I and its aftermath, with the rising fear of communism and the waning of progressivism, five of the six states actually reinstated the death penalty. The decade of the 1920s, which saw an increase in gangster violence, also saw an increase in the use of the death penalty. Lathrop was not daunted by the lack of support for ending the death penalty. Addams believed that for her close friend it was personal. "For Julia Lathrop," Addams wrote, "so long identified with governmental service in the county, state and the nation, official violence such as an execution held almost an element of complicity on her part which must have been well-nigh unendurable."

The execution of minors naturally concerned Lathrop the most. At the time of her death in 1932 she was hard at work attempting to set aside an execution sentence for one seventeen-year-old Rockland boy. In August of 1931 Russell McWilliams robbed passengers on a streetcar, killing the motorman in the process. The court sentenced the boy to be electrocuted in December. Lathrop immediately went to work, writing a public letter against the sentence, arguing, "Such a death sentence pronounced against a boy of that age is against public policy. Condemning to death so young and underdeveloped a person is a profound miscarriage of justice."

Lathrop next launched a nationwide campaign against the execution of minors in general. She also took responsibility for the McWilliams legal defense along with several distinguished attorneys and Jessie Binford, supervisor of the Juvenile Protective Association. The case was widely covered in the press. Lathrop's impact on the Illinois justice system from her days in Chicago was evident when the Illinois Supreme Court sent the case back to the Rockford court, reminding it that the defendant's age entitled him to special consideration. Just before she entered the hospital in 1932 for what would be a fatal goiter operation, she was still at work on behalf of McWilliams. Explaining why she could not attend a meeting on the case, she displayed her usual humor in writing to Binford. "Unless signs fail, I am likely to go to the hospital next week. . . . Of course it is not really serious, but it would be impracticable, even I can see, to be in a hospital and in the presence of the Governor simultaneously. I am sorry it all happened that way."[28] Although she did not live to see it, Lathrop's work paid off; in April 1933 the governor of Illinois commuted McWilliams's sentence to life imprisonment.

Although Lathrop took up a number of unpopular liberal causes in her last years, she did not embrace all. When she left the Children's Bureau Lathrop noted that she now, as a private citizen, could be less cautious. As she told her successor, Grace Abbott, "I have been a most courteous and patient lady and a new *pose* is now mine."[29] Perhaps that is why she was willing to publicly support the campaign to amend the obscenity law that resulted in the conviction of birth control activist Mary Dennett.

However, Lathrop never fully embraced new ideas about the importance of sexual expression. As Linda Gordon writes, "Neither the nineteenth century 'Free Love' tradition brought into the women's rights movement by Elizabeth Cady Stanton and Victoria Woodhall, nor twenti-eth century sexual bohemianism attracted" the pioneers of the Children's Bureau. When Lathrop's friend Judge Benjamin Lindsey of Colorado, an-other pioneer of the juvenile justice system, asked her to publicly support his controversial book *Companionate Marriage*, she told him that although she refused to write against the book, she would not support it. The book advocated that men and women should live together for a year, as a sort of trial marriage, as long as they agreed not to have children, to see if they were compatible. Lathrop embraced the importance of happy marriages and believed in divorce as a "safeguard of civilized marriage." Moreover, she believed that many adults could live decent lives without marriage. Nevertheless, she felt that "the more radical the departure from older social conventions of marriage the more the old virtues are needed." Rather than allowing for easy, trial relationships, she still embraced what she called "not only love but courageous understanding of what contented permanent marriage requires." Lathrop and many other female social reformers of her era worried that the current emphasis on personal sexual fulfillment was too individualistic. Although sexual compatibility may be important, Lath-rop told Lindsey, a more adequate treatment would emphasize the "im-portance of stimulating the powers of self-direction and self-control. . . . I think it is unfortunately true that 'The Companionate Marriage' may seem to justify 'the self expression' which tends toward percipiency and egotism though I am not sure that is your intent."[30]

Moreover, Lathrop never abandoned her support for Prohibition. She had vivid memories of her days inspecting Cook County charities where she saw how drink had destroyed many families. According to Addams, Lathrop also "disliked a certain self-righteousness in the good citizen when he voted for laws which he himself had no intention of obeying." Southern whites wanted to keep drink away from blacks, northern manufacturers wanted to do the same for immigrant labor.[31] Regardless of whether she shared Addams's conviction that such laws were fundamentally undemo-cratic, in the end Lathrop concluded that the problem was not so much Prohibition but the fact that Congress had been unwilling to put the ad-ministration in the hands of civil servants who, she was sure, would fairly administer the law.

Lathrop continued to push against expectations about how women should comport themselves, but she also conformed to some traditional norms about appropriate womanly behavior. In her last years she embraced her career as a lecturer, but she was also uncomfortable about it. Lathrop gave many speeches to various organizations, such as women's clubs. Her standard charge per lecture in 1923 was $100.00, which in today's money would be around $1,300. In Illinois she spoke for a smaller fee. For women to earn such fees for lectures was quite unusual in the 1920s. Given her very busy schedule of speeches—between October 1923 and January 1924, her personal calendar listed some fifteen speaking engagements, of which approximately half would have been paid—Lathrop was earning a significant amount of money. She was careful to state her fee each time she responded to a speaking invitation. At least once she objected to a request that she thought was an effort to solicit two different talks in two venues for one fee. Yet almost every time Lathrop stated her fee of $100 she would do so in an apologetic manner. To the request that she speak at the Stephens Junior College she told the college president Wood, "If you wish me to speak I must confess that my fee is $100. I really doubt my being worth it." Words to that effect—"I really doubt that I am worth it"—appear over and over in her letters. Lathrop's approach certainly was in keeping with her own modesty, but it also reflected a wider norm about how proper women should behave.

Lathrop lectured on the basis of notes but mostly without a completely prepared speech in front of her. Her appearance on a program drew large audiences because of her captivating style, which combined, as one of her colleagues in the Illinois LWV told it, "wit, and charm, and drollery." Yet when she once wrote home to her sister, Anna, and brother Bill, reporting about a successful lecture she had recently completed, she did so with her trademark self-deprecating humor. "Would you believe it," she told her siblings about a speech she made in Quincy, Illinois, in 1927, "I had so much applause for stopping that I had to rise and bow. But I thought it prudent not to take it as an encore."[32]

Lectures, Vassar functions, travel, family, and friends kept Lathrop busy during her last years. She participated a bit in partisan politics as well, though rather half-heartedly. Lathrop supported Herbert Hoover's presidential campaign in 1928, despite the fact that Eleanor Roosevelt and other reform Democratic women approached her about supporting the party nominee, Al Smith of New York. But when Mabel Walker Willebrandt, an assistant attorney general under Harding and Coolidge, asked Lathrop to sign a letter of endorsement for Hoover, she refused. "The last paragraph of your proposed statement [about Hoover, which praised his abilities] I could sign with hearty accord," she wrote to Willebrandt. "I am a nominal Republican." But when it came to the sentence, "We have been fortunate in President Coolidge," she balked. "I have not so agreed with his views that I could assent" and sign the endorsement.

Lathrop died in 1932 six months before the 1932 election between then-governor Franklin D. Roosevelt and Hoover. We don't know whether she would have voted for FDR, but we know she paid attention to the programs he enacted as governor of New York in the early years of the Great Depression, programs that his New Deal government would later revise and implement on a national level when he became president. She circled an article on the front page of the *New York Times* from the April 28, 1930, with instructions to "cut, preserve for file." The headline: "Governor Demands State Set Up Plan to Insure Jobless." The article outlined Roosevelt's plan to provide unemployment insurance, with the State of New York, employers, and employees all paying into the system. Observing "the unemployment situation is more serious than at any time since 1893," FDR argued that "the example of other countries in undertaking a government program to alleviate the distress of fluctuating employment" must be followed. Lathrop certainly would have embraced the idea that one should look to other countries to see what approaches to social welfare would work—that was her approach throughout her career. The governor also noted that although a few major American corporations had already started programs of unemployment insurance, some financial journalists would "call him a Bolshevik" for wanting a statewide program. Lathrop certainly could identify with Roosevelt on that score.[33]

The winter of 1932 was particularly hard for Lathrop; she was ailing from thyroid disease, and she lost her friend of forty years, Florence Kelley. Although she knew Kelley was ill, as she told Florence's son Nicholas "Ko" Kelley, "I confess I was ill-prepared for your telegram telling me that she had gone."[34] Two months after Kelley's death Julia Lathrop's remarkable life came to an end as well, the result of complications from a goiter operation. Tributes to her accomplishments came pouring in, and Lathrop could no longer, in her diffident way, protest against them.

Conclusion

"Miss Lathrop is proverbially reticent about herself. She will talk enthusiastically on the latest details of her work—but her personal experiences are withheld. She explains this logically enough, by declaring that she and her work are one."

—Laura Hillyer, reporter for the *Boston Traveler*, 1915

Surgery to remove a goiter was common in the 1930s, but it was not without risk; Lathrop left funeral instructions, just in case, for a simple ceremony to be held at her home and a burial at a nearby cemetery. Three days after the surgery, on April 16, 1932, Lathrop died at Rockford Hospital. Although she was not a churchgoer, the Reverend John Gordon of the Second Congregational Church in Rockford officiated the service, conducted at her home on April 17. Attendees included most of her friends from her Hull House days, among them Jane Addams, Sophinisba Breckinridge, and Edith Abbott; Grace Abbott, still chief of the Children's Bureau, was too ill to travel. Many of Lathrop's friends and colleagues around the country could not get to Rockford on such short notice; they celebrated her life with special memorial events.

Lathrop's close friend Alice Hamilton, at the time on the Harvard University medical school faculty, did make the long trip to the funeral. A month later Hamilton wrote to one of Lathrop's sisters-in-law, Molly Lathrop, asking whether she could stop by to visit when she came to Illinois on business. "I would very much like to see you Lathrops, especially Mrs. Case." Hamilton did not want to ask Anna directly for fear that Lathrop's sister would hesitate to say no, even if she might "feel it an added strain to see someone she associates so much with Julia. . . . It is well nigh impossible," her old friend wrote, "for me to believe in Julia's death. Even as I write it I shrink from the words. My own personal loss is very great, but I do know what it has meant to that close-knit family." Molly wrote back to say that not only would the whole family be delighted to see her but that Anna would be "especially glad if she would stay with her."[1]

Newspapers all over the country carried the news of Lathrop's death. The articles usually quoted Jane Addams, who stated that Lathrop was "one of America's most useful women." The newspaper articles listed Lathrop's work at Hull House, the Illinois Board Charities, her work on behalf of juvenile justice, her job as chief of the Children's Bureau, and her work at the League of Nations.

In the months and years that followed her death, friends and allies weighed in with more detailed tributes highlighting Lathrop's particular contributions and talents. Her former colleague Graham Taylor, with whom she founded the Chicago School of Civics and Philanthropy, saluted her as the pioneer who brought "the point of view and the technique of social work into the practical operation of government." She was also a great politician who could "rally the support of the general public; and her courage in meeting powerful opposition was matched by keen strategy in making the issue definite." Edith Abbott emphasized Lathrop's promotion of social science that led to social reform. "She supported us in rejecting the academic theory that social work could only be 'scientific' if it had no regard to the finding of socially useful results and no interest in the human beings whose lives were being studied." In her tribute, Lillian Wald noted Lathrop's pragmatism and caution in picking her battles: "Precipitation at the importunate time was never her mistake"; nevertheless, once she decided action was needed, "her courage carried her through." Like her friend Florence Kelley, Wald continued, Lathrop was a woman of action: "Both of them gave a lesson that should never be forgotten; namely, that dissatisfaction with social conditions is only an emotional indulgence unless the protest and indignation are translated into constructive measures." Jane Addams wrote that despite all her "strenuous efforts, Julia Lathrop's wit never failed." She also noted Lathrop's confidence in young people, "in their ability to right the old wrongs of the world, each in his own way." W. E. B. Dubois saluted her as "a fine woman and a great social worker . . . who is especially to be remembered by us [the black community] as a woman without prejudice, who recognized that Negroes, and particularly Negro children have a right to life and education and opportunity." Grace

Abbott summed it all up, saluting Lathrop's "challenging mind, her gay courage, and her shrewd understanding of social forces and social needs."[2]

Many of the tributes noted Lathrop's modesty. The AP story on her death stated pointedly that "Miss Lathrop's activities in the field of welfare work had been incessant and the fruits of her efforts she considered a greater reward than widespread recognition."[3] Unlike her friends Addams, Hamilton, Kelley, and Wald, Lathrop left no memoir. Perhaps this is why Jane Addams wrote her biography of Lathrop, published just after her own death in 1935. Lathrop's personal characteristics, disinterestness, selflessness, and modesty can be seen as very positive attributes for both men and women—so too her desire "to see all sides of an issue."[4] The constant praise of her selflessness and modesty also conforms to norms about proper women; they are not associated with achieving men. But Lathrop's traditional female traits coexisted with some attributes that pushed against the constraints of her day. In her thirties Lathrop lived in a community of single women, when the vast majority lived either as wives or with family members. She was willing to take on a fight and was tenacious in pursuit of her goals; she traveled the country and the world speaking forcefully on causes she supported.

The causes Lathrop embraced also reflected a woman ahead of her time. Ten years out of college, she joined with others who pushed Americans to move away from deeply held beliefs about the virtues of unregulated industrial capitalism. In Chicago she challenged the status quo when it came to staffing public institutions, relentlessly pushing to have professionally trained personnel at hospitals and mental institutions. At a time when no special courts for youth existed, she fought for a juvenile justice system that would recognize the unique problems and needs of children subject to arrest. In an era like our own, rife with hostility toward immigrants, she defended their rights; she also pushed to end political and legal discrimination against African Americans and to provide more opportunities for black children.

As head of the Children's Bureau Lathrop fought for natal and prenatal care for all mothers and infants as a matter of right. She, along with her allies in progressive social reform, rejected the commonplace biological explanations for poverty and crime. At the bureau she worked to show that poor families suffered high infant mortality rates not because of inferior genes but because of intolerable social conditions.

Lathrop also advanced women's political and professional opportunities. During the Progressive Era, with its focus on social problems, Lathrop and her allies emphasized the special contributions women could make in tackling these issues. She was an ardent suffragist, and as head of the bureau she provided hundreds of jobs for women. She helped develop social work as a profession; she promoted the work of women as social scientists as well as social reformers.

During the 1920s, with progressive social reformers on the defensive, Lathrop maintained her commitment to providing health care for children and mothers and to ending child labor. She spoke out against military preparedness as a distraction from what she saw as the important job of government: "education, the conservation of public welfare and the development of natural resources." In an era of isolationism she continued to work across national boundaries on the social welfare needs of children. For her efforts she was subject to vilification as a Bolshevik intent on a government takeover of family life.

Ahead of their time, Lathrop and Kelley did not live to see a vindication of their ideas during FDR's New Deal. Addressing a Depression even greater than the Panic of 1893, the New Deal implemented national labor legislation to regulate hours and wages and to eliminate many forms of child labor. The New Deal also combined state and national programs to provide income supports for American families and aid to poor children and their mothers. At a celebration of the Children's Bureau's twenty-fifth anniversary in 1937, President Roosevelt praised the foresight of Julia Lathrop and Grace Abbott. Referring to his newly instituted programs for maternal and infant health under the newly enacted Social Security Act, he noted, "I am grateful, [for their] vision and statesmanship . . . with their co-workers and their successors now responsible for the administration of the Children's Bureau [they] have developed so fine an instrument for us all to use in our efforts to advance the day when all children shall have a fair chance in the world."[5]

Although Lathrop's work reflected new ideas about the role of government in providing for the common good as well as about the needs of mothers and children, she and her colleagues often reflected traditional middle-class ideals concerning what constituted proper family life. She was adamant that poor mothers could not adequately care for their children if they worked outside the home. She was certainly not wrong about the difficulties working mothers faced in combining work and family; however, she did not fully appreciate the resources poor parents could bring to bear in rearing their children. Although she promoted the rights of immigrants, African Americans, and Indians, she, like many of the progressive reformers, believed in the superiority of European cultures.

Lathrop and the other women social reformers emphasized women's special ability to address the problems of women and children as one way to carve out new professional opportunities and new places in the political arena. Lathrop argued forcefully for a new education at Vassar College that would offer its students more job opportunities after college and a chance to contribute to the well-being of their society. The politics of maternalism practiced by Lathrop and her sister reformers had its costs, however. Although it pushed women into new areas, to some extent it also reinforced stereotypes about women as uniquely suited to be domestic caretakers who ought to be confined to certain jobs associated with domesticity.

By appealing to a widespread sympathy for children, Lathrop and her allies helped build support for a social welfare state in a country that feared the growth of big government. When so many Americans privileged individual rights and responsibility, Lathrop and her allies thought a focus on children would encourage a more collective vision, leading to more social welfare programs for all Americans, young and old. Lathrop believed that the Maternity and Infancy Act of 1921, for example, would lead to a national health-care program for all American adults. It took almost ninety years, before the United States implemented a broad national health insurance program; however, the Affordable Care Act of 2010 still did not represent a universal program. "Putting children first," as Linda Gordon has termed Lathrop's strategy, does not necessarily lead to broader programs because the "very identification of children as uniquely deserving tended to undercut the claims of adults to public help, which then made it more difficult to help children."[6]

Julia Lathrop anticipated that years later her work would be critiqued just as she and her friends were critical of earlier reformers. She hoped that when historians and, perhaps, history students looked back, they would do so with appreciation for those who struggled to make a better world and to rise above the prejudices of their times, even if they did not always succeed. She wrote about this in 1908 while still in Chicago in a paper about how the new social service improved on older charity approaches. J. Lathrop gets the last word:

It is not so bad for us to know that inevitably posterity will look on our best achievements with the same condescension which we look back, and yet will in turn do full justice to the spirit of those who . . . did all [they] could to see and compass in [their] day. We do not know what questions will present themselves to our successors—we can ask no better of posterity than to be put down as among those who, in their day and by their glimmer, strove to discern the still veiled ideal of social justice.[7]

PRIMARY SOURCES

PRIMARY SOURCE 1

"JULIA LATHROP QUESTIONNAIRE, FILLED OUT IN ADVANCE OF
HER VASSAR COLLEGE 50TH ANNIVERSARY REUNION"*

Biographical Records Questionnaire

As this sheet will be placed in the permanent files of the Biographical Records at the Alumnae
Office, please fill it out carefully and completely and legibly.

NAME AND FAMILY RECORD
Maiden name (in full) _Julia Clifford Lathrop._ Class _____

Place of birth _Rockford, Illinois_ Date of birth _1858_

Father's name _William Lathrop_ Nationality _USA_ His college _Rockford Semn_

Mother's name _Sarah Adeline Potter_ Nationality _USA_ Her college _now Rockford Col_

Other nationalities in your ancestry _____

Check ☑ single ☐ married ☐ widowed ☐ divorced ☐ married more than once

Husband's name _____ Nationality _____

Husband's college _____ Degree _____ Occupation _____

Children: name   sex   date of birth   date of death   college attended

EDUCATIONAL RECORD
Prepared for college in _by tutor Rockford. (also attended from childhood the public sc._
and was for two years a student at Rockford College.
       give name of school and place

Years in college _1877-80_ Home address while in college _Rockford Ill_
   as 1901-04

Graduate study; professional and technical training
     dates   course   institution   degree

OCCUPATIONAL RECORD

Chronological list of occupations since graduation, beginning with the first

For many years, at intervals a resident Hull-House

Present occupation

if business, give { name of firm or institution
                   nature of firm's business
                   your position

(*Alumnae who wish new positions or advancement may write to the Director of the Vocational Bureau, Vassar College.*)

PUBLIC RECORD

Public offices held, social, business, philanthropic, etc., civic, county, state, national, both elective and appointive

For about 13 years, with intervals of years off — was a member Illinois State Board Charities, a voluntary position; for nine years Chief US Children Bureau in dept. of Labor, a presidential appointment.

CHURCH AFFILIATION *reared in congregational family,*

MEMBERSHIP IN ORGANIZATIONS AND CLUBS

LITERARY RECORD

Books written or edited; articles or papers contributed to press or periodicals   (*Copies are requested for the College Library if not already presented*)

No literary record. I have of course in connection with work indicated above written many brief articles. Few are preserved and few deserved to be preserved —

OTHER CREATIVE OR PRODUCTIVE WORK

I have spoken much on the subjects in the social with which I have been concerned,

INTERESTS AND ACTIVITIES NOT ALREADY MENTIONED

SUPPLEMENTARY DATA

ADDRESS

Please give name and address as you wish them to appear in the 1930 Address Register

Name *Julia C. Lathrop*

Address *1204 National Ave*

Rockford Illinois

If the address to which you wish your mail from Alumnae Office sent differs from the above, please add it at address below

SIGNATURE *Julia C. Lathrop*

DATE *December 19, 1929*

PRIMARY SOURCE 2

WHAT THE SETTLEMENT WORK STANDS FOR
BY JULIA C. LATHROP, HULL HOUSE, CHICAGO*

Before this great audience, composed of people of different views, different activities, representing the most distant parts of our country, and yet drawn together, animated by a common impulse, to consult about our common social welfare, I realize the importance and at
the same time the difficulty of stating briefly, or at all, what the settlement stands for. Some
of those who will speak at this meeting and those who will speak at the succeeding sessions
of our committee will give what is far better than abstract explanation: they will state what
settlements are doing in various fields.

— — — — — — — — —

Thirteen years ago, when Arnold Toynbee died, his friends sought how to best perpetuate
his memory. This young Oxonian was a student of history and economics, but his studies
did not withdraw his interest from the life outside his academic halls. Rather did history and
economics, interpreted by his passion for humanity, irresistibly thrust him out into the thick
of life—into that life whose unregarded misery in many a town besides London has finally
made the whole world shudder at the cheerful *laissez faire* of the old political economy. He
lived for a time in East London, going there first as a charity organization visitor. He made
a wide acquaintance among workingmen, and knew Whitechapel [neighborhood] by actual
contact. He lectured much in London and the great English manufacturing towns. A book
of fragments, "The Industrial Revolution," is all that is left in print of his work. After his
untimely death his friends determined to build a house in East London where university
men might live, as has been said, "face to face with the actual conditions of crowded city life,
study on the spot the evils and their remedies, and, if possible, ennoble the lives and improve
the material conditions of the people." The opening of Toynbee Hall was a natural and intimate sequence of the labors of a whole circle of social students and reformers. Toynbee was
the first so-called Settlement, and the forces which initiated it show that union of brotherly
zeal for humanity and scientific ardor for truth which should characterize every settlement.
Thus the settlement recognizes, as this Conference recognizes, that goodness of individual
sentiment, unguided by science and exact knowledge, is belated. It is outgrown. The laboratory of the biologist, the researches of statisticians, do so much to alleviate the material ills of
life that poor rule-of-thumb good will must cease her fumbling, and submit to be the willing
handmaid of the new philanthropy and the new education.

Following Toynbee Hall since 1885 have come about seventy-five small groups of people, some perhaps far afield from the ideal suggested above, all independent of each other,
and varying in almost every respect save that of residence in the district it is desired to influence. They have made their homes in the most arid and crowded parts of various English and
American cities, to lend a hand toward improving their neighborhoods and toward gaining
a little exact knowledge of social conditions. Forty-four settlements are in the United States,
some details of whose scope and work will be found in the report which our committee has

* Julia C. Lathrop, "What the Settlement Work Stands For," *Proceedings of the National Conference of Charities and Corrections of the 23rd Annual Sessions*, Grand Rapids, MI, June 4–10,
1896, 106–110, Public Domain.

filed with the Secretary of the Conference. It will be shown here, as I have just suggested, that the movement is loose and unorganized, without any centre or head, that there is between some of the settlements little in common save the name and the fact of residence, so that what I may say cannot describe accurately all, but is only offered as, in my opinion, describing those which are representatives and wisest.

Living in such a neighborhood as the University Settlement at Delancy Street, New York, or the College Settlement, St. Mary's Street, Philadelphia, residents usually establish kindergartens, clubs, and classes for children as a beginning, because these means of training children too young for public school and giving social pleasure to older children are usually lacking in such neighborhoods. As an acquaintance between the residents and the settlement and the neighborhood grows, and the character of its need becomes more evident, the sort of work undertaken depends upon the ability of the settlement to furnish from its residents or its friends people to undertake the work; for the settlement, having once become established in the good will of its neighborhood, is able to exercise its most gracious function and extend a double hospitality, so that people can know each other whose different lives within the same city, strangely enough, preclude personal acquaintance. I sometimes think that the usefulness of a settlement to its city is best measured by the number of non-residents whose personal help it can obtain.

A club of women from one of the Chicago settlements chances to be first on a printed list of Illinois Federated Women's Clubs; yet the suggestion of the possibility of such a club's existence in the east end of the Nineteenth Ward not only would have been thought absurd, but the club could not have existed without the effort and common meeting ground of the settlement. One settlement may develop an evening academy, with nominal fees, with great classes of young men and women, supplying a sort of instruction not given by the public school or any night school. Another may do most in more purely social lines, supplementing the crowded loneliness of the tenement house by all sorts of gayeties and merry makings. Another may put its chief strength into co-operation with city authorities—upon urging better tenements to the public and to wealthy investors, better sanitary inspection, better public schools, pure water, proper sewerage, clean streets, small parks, an indefinite variety of things. Another settlement may do charity work, although, when the word "charity" is mentioned, the settlement usually shivers as though its mantle were a wet blanket; but really what a travesty upon neighborliness it would be to open your door to a neighbor hungry for learning and close it to a neighbor hungry for bread! In most settlements some or all of the residents are people who have had the best that our schools and universities can give. They are trained to look for causes. Eager as they are to meet the immediate wants of a meagre life, they are not satisfied with that, and are earnest to find the roots of the matter—to learn the conditions which have made that meagerness. They are inevitably drawn to try to learn the conditions of industrial life, upon which the conditions of social life so largely hinge. They become acquainted so far as they can with those who from the standpoint of the working-man are giving the same problems the intensest thought. Necessarily, they welcome opportunity for the discussion of those problems from every point of view. The settlement stands for a free platform. It offers its best hospitality to every man's honest thought.

Lecky [William Edward] has pointed out in a little essay on the "Political Value of History" that there was a time when the best patriotism, all the most heroic self-sacrifice, was thrown into the defence of such causes as the free expression of religious beliefs, a free press, a free platform, and an independent jury box, that these are now secure, and that a kind of language which at one period of history implied the noblest heroism is now the idlest and cheapest of clap-trap, that men are called upon to consider new issues in each generation. If this be true, then the settlement asks earnestly, What are the crucial questions of this day?

Nor does it hesitate to answer that on the material side they are the industrial and economic questions upon which social questions so largely hinge. On the moral side it is the question of an enlargement of our notion of personal responsibility, a quickening of the sense of social interdependence. If individual good will is outdated because it is unscientific, it is again outworn because its scope is inadequate.

At the time of the American Revolution there were men who had a clear and beautiful ideal of social democracy, and there can be no doubt that in the simpler conditions of that day it seemed to be secured by the personal and political freedom which they had gained. Does not, however, the complexity of life in which each household is changed from a self-sustained producer to a purchaser, with all the ramifying interchanges so familiar to us, so absolutely unknown to them, compel a readjustment, a new understanding, of our social interdependence? May not our morality be too small for our relationships? Everything grows great. Interests interlace. Tremendous physical forces, set at work, have compelled tremendous combinations of money and men. Greatness begets greatness; and great combinations of wealth will be met by great combinations of men. The cost of misunderstanding between these great combinations has become so alarming and so well understood that we see already more and more exemplified between them that armed peace which exists between European powers. But is this enough? War is better than piracy, and an armed peace is better than war; but does it satisfy the ethical sense of civilization that these great interests should be left merely resting upon their defences?

Finally and briefly, then, I would venture to say that, considered upon American soil, the settlement may be regarded as a humble but sincere effort toward a realization of that ideal of social democracy in whose image this country was founded, but adapted and translated into the life of to-day.

PRIMARY SOURCE 3

"BABYOLOGY" IDEA UNCLE SAM'S LATEST; PET IDEA OF HIS
$5,000 A YEAR WOMAN "CHIEF": NOT YET REALITY, BUT 'TWILL
BE SOON IF JULIA C. LATHROP HAS HER WAY—SHE'S DELEGATED
ESPECIALLY TO STUDY BABIES

BY LAURIE HILLYER*

A circular, chute-like arrangement for escape in case of fire was installed some years ago at a
state insane asylum in Illinois. The management was tremendously proud of it and exhibited
it to a dark, slim young woman who appeared one morning, announcing she was Julia C.
Lathrop of the state board of charities on tour of inspection.

"Fine," commended Miss Lathrop, "does it work?"

"Why-ee," admitted the management, "it would empty the building instantly in case
of fire. But we haven't had any fires, so it hasn't been tried."

Miss Lathrop immediately gathered her skirts about her, stepped into the chute, and
spiraled to the ground, four stories below. Not because of this incident, but on account of
the spirit that prompted it, Miss Lathrop was later appointed head of the United States
children's bureau. Uncle Sam adopted her as one of his nieces. She was the first woman
appointed chief of a federal bureau. The man with the long beard and red-white-and-blue
suspenders allowed her $5000 a year, the largest salary paid any woman in government em-
ploy, told her to select nine assistants, and study babyology, the newest and most important
science in the world.

---

* Laurie Hillyer, "Babyology" College Uncle Sam's Latest; Pet Idea of His $5,000 a Year Woman
"Chief," *The Boston Traveler*, March 13, 1915, found in the AAVC Files, Box 4, Vassar College
Special Collections

KNOWS A LOT ABOUT BABIES

Miss Lathrop probably knows more about babies than any unmarried woman in the country. She also knows a bit about colleges, for she is a Vassar graduate and member of its board of trustees.

So the statement made by her during an interview at the Tremont Temple is of some importance.

She thinks American colleges for women—the phraseology isn't hers—aren't "hitting the nail on the head." They teach culture and omit the study of the child. They admit woman's the preserver of the race, but neglect to teach the most advanced and approved methods of raising children. If the woman's college doesn't reform, it's a failure.

During an interim in the suffrage meeting Sunday afternoon in Tremont Temple, Miss Lathrop, who had not yet spoken, strolled behind the scenes, seated herself on a stool, and outlined the idea that is interesting her beyond others.

Miss Lathrop has a disarming friendliness. You wouldn't suspect she is a trustee of a college, government official, linguist, globe-trotter—all sorts of things. She has a keen sense of humor, and confesses, in a whisper, that one of her relaxations is "reading trash—after midnight."

Miss Lathrop is proverbially reticent about herself. She will talk enthusiastically on the latest details of her work–but her personal experiences are withheld. She explains this, logically enough, by declaring she and her work are one.

So it was quite characteristic that she plunged into her latest idea for the betterment of America's choicest crop, America's babies.

"WE ARE STILL ANTEDILUVIAN"

"We are still in the antediluvian age," she declared, "regarding arts of the household. We have countless woman's colleges, but the national problem—the care of the child—is a science taught not by experts, but amateurs; not in college but at home.

"The woman's college teaches only culture. It does not touch upon the science of the world, which is the science of the child."

"You mean all colleges should teach prenatal care, domestic science, mothercraft, and so forth?"

Miss Lathrop shook her head.

"Sporadic efforts have been made in that direction. I mean psychology of the child's mine, mental history, and the great principles of motherhood.

"Originally men's colleges taught only culture. Then they broadened out. Institutes of technology resulted. Men learned engineering, architecture, the practical sciences to which they expected to devote their lives. We should have a woman's college where the most important thing in the world—the child—is studied."

"Do you mean each woman's college should include such a course?"

"A particular college should be devoted to it. No definite steps have been taken. The idea's in its infancy. You can tell the world about it," she laughed.

Mrs. Maud Wood Park began her introduction, and Miss Lathrop skipped to the stage.

PRIMARY SOURCE 4

INCOME AND INFANT MORTALITY

Miss Julia C. Lathrop,*

Chief of Children's Bureau, Washington, D. C.

Read before Sociological Section, American Public Health Association at Chicago, Ill., December 9, 1918.

> Miss Lathrop, who is a leader in the country-wide movement to save the babies, tells us in this article how an insufficient wage, a mother who is obliged to labor, and a community that is careless about its housing, constitute three very important factors to the infant mortality.

THIS paper attempts no more than to indicate from facts gathered in the United States the immediate practical bearing of the subject upon the great interest of this association. It refers chiefly to the material secured by the infant mortality inquiry of the Children's Bureau and I shall quote from the series of reports prepared by members of the Bureau staff, mentioning only a few outstanding coincidences between varying incomes and varying infant mortality rates as shown with marked uniformity in the studies.

Infant mortality is the first subject mentioned in the law creating the Children's Bureau which directs it to investigate and report upon all matters pertaining to the welfare of the children, and it was the first subject of field study undertaken when the Bureau went into operation in 1912. For the last six years, a series of studies of infant mortality has been carried on. To this writing, intensive field studies have been made, with a substantially identical schedule, in eight cities, ranging in population from about 50,000 to more than half a million inhabitants, and differing widely in characteristics. They include a "steel city," Johnstown, Pa.; two textile cities, Manchester, N. H., and New Bedford, Mass.; Brockton, Mass., a center for the manufacture of high-grade shoes; Saginaw, Mich., a manufacturing city with no one predominating industry; Waterbury, Conn., chiefly given over to the manufacture of brass; Akron, Ohio, a rubber manufacturing center, and Baltimore, Md., a large cosmopolitan city. In addition, rural studies of maternal and infant welfare have been made, with especial reference to showing the amount and quality of care obtainable for mothers and babies in the remoter and newer country areas.

None of the studies made by the Bureau attempt to approach infant mortality as a medical question; they merely set down the co-existence of certain conditions of life with varying infant mortality rates. They are concerned with the economic, social, civic, and family conditions surrounding young babies. So far as the Bureau was aware, the method employed was new. Instead of basing the inquiry on the children who died, the criterion was really the children born in a given calendar year. The surroundings of each child were traced through his first year of life, or such shorter period as he survived, by women agents of the Bureau who called upon each mother and obtained the information through direct personal interviews.

For obvious reasons, only the urban studies undertake to state income in terms of cash receipts, and it is with these studies we are now concerned.

Although in each city studied the

* Julia C. Lathrop, "Income and Infant Mortality," *American Journal of Public Health* 9, no. 4 (April 1919): 270–274.

Income and Infant Mortality 271

earnings of the mother and other income facts were secured, the earnings of the father were selected as the standard of income, not only because in most cases such earnings constitute the family income, but because of the conviction that the earnings of a man should be sufficient to support his wife and young children in safe comfort. Great pains were taken to make the income figures as accurate as possible. While it was plainly necessary to accept the mother's statement with reference to matters directly pertaining to the daily life of the baby, it was thought that she might not always know about her husband's earnings and that other sources of information might be more important. Hence, in one of the earliest studies a test was made of the accuracy of the mother's answers to the income questions by comparing them with facts about the father's earnings collected from as many sources as possible; payrolls were consulted and employers and the fathers themselves were interviewed. A comparison of the results of this test with the mothers' answers was fully satisfying as to the substantial accuracy of their statements, and they have been accepted for all the studies made.

All of the studies included in this discussion were made before the United States entered the war; so the figures given cannot be taken to represent wages or prices as affected by war conditions. During the past year a study has been in progress in Gary, Indiana, a war industries town. The findings of this study have not yet been analyzed.

The infant mortality rates have been tabulated in each city in connection with the earnings of the fathers up to a maximum of $1,250. Beyond this sum it became difficult to secure the facts. Except in the largest city studied, moreover, the number of instances of higher income was so small that they could not be divided into groups representing enough cases upon which to base percentages. Data were secured about the fathers of 23,-780 babies, including stillborn children. More than one-fourth (26.9 per cent) of these fathers earned less than $550 during the year following the baby's birth. Only one in eight (11.9 per cent) earned as much as $1,250.

City	Total Births	Father's Earnings			
		Under $550		$1250 and Over	
		Number	Per Cent of Total	Number	Per Cent of Total
All cities......	23,780	6,404	26.9	2,839	11.9
Johnstown, Pa....	1,499	243	16.2	524	35.0*
Manchester, N. H.	1,643	499	30.4	105	6.4
Brockton, Mass....	1,247	156	12.5	137	11.0
Saginaw, Mich....	1,015	182	17.9	143	14.1
New Bedford, Mass.	2,662	1,004	37.7	173	6.5
Waterbury, Conn. .	2,197	808	36.8	192	8.7
Akron, Ohio	2,322	374	16.1	307	13.2
Baltimore, Md....	11,195	3,138	28.0	1,258	11.2

* In the study of Johnstown many incomes were returned as "ample," and such incomes have been included in the $1,250 and over group in this table with a result that the proportion of such incomes is perhaps exaggerated.

In general the lowest income groups are the highest infant mortality groups in all of the cities studied.

INFANT MORTALITY RATES BY FATHER'S EARNINGS.

City	Deaths of Infants Under One Year of Age Per 1,000 Live Births, by Specified Annual Earnings of Father		
	All Earnings	$1250 and Over	Under $550
All cities..........	111.2	64.3	151.4
Johnstown..........	130.7	87.6	260.9
Manchester.........	165.0	58.3	204.2
Brockton...........	96.7	73.5	67.1*
Saginaw............	84.6	22.2	142.0
New Bedford........	130.3	59.9	168.7
Waterbury..........	122.7	68.4	151.1
Akron..............	85.7	40.0	117.5
Baltimore..........	103.5	64.7	138.0

* Contrary to the findings for other cities, the mortality rates for the earnings groups under $550 and $550 to $849 were considerably lower than for the group $650 to $849. Two explanations for this peculiar showing may be advanced: First, the groups are comparatively small, having but ten deaths in each class, and consequently they may have been considerably influenced by exceptionally favorable conditions in the year selected; second, the earnings as reported in the lowest earnings group do not always reflect the family's standard of living.

It is impossible to state a normal infant mortality rate. Perhaps the best statement, because the most stimulating to continuous effort, is that of the authority who has said that if all children were well born and well cared for the infant mortality rate would be negligible. Emphasis upon being well born is justified by the fact that in the birth registration area of the United States more than 46 per cent of the infant deaths occur during the first month of life. Many of these children fail to survive because of conditions antedating birth.

It may well be noted here that while the figures of the Bureau's studies and of other investigations clearly indicate the coincidence of the mother's exhausting toil and poor living conditions with the inability of the child to survive the first month of life, there is included within this 46 per cent a field which calls for the concentrated effort and study of physicians, social students and biologists.

The contrast between the most favorable and the least favorable rates in the cities studied indicates the favoring result of income which permits proper housing, proper surroundings and care, and which connotes a fair degree of education.

Income is important for what it buys. Its adequacy may be tested, for example, by housing. A comparison of rent paid with infant mortality rates in Manchester, N. H., shows the general tendency of infant mortality rates to fall as housing conditions improve. According to the report of the Children's Bureau on infant mortality in that city, there were 175 homes of live-born babies where the rental paid was less than $7.50 per month and the infant mortality rate among babies in these homes was 211.4 or more than double the census figure for the registration area in 1915 of 100 per 1,000 living births. The largest number of babies, 703, was found in homes where the rent paid was from $7.50 up to $12.49. The rate for this group was 172.1. There

were 300 babies in the next class, where the rentals were from $12.50 to $17.49, and the infant mortality rate among them was 156.7. Only 62 babies belonged to homes with a rental of $17.50 and over, and six deaths occurred among them. Here the rate was about 1 in 10 or the equivalent of the census figure for 1915. The parents of 186 babies owned their homes, and the infant death-rate was still lower, 86 per 1,000. The Johnstown Report says: "In homes of 496 live-born babies where bathtubs were found, the infant mortality rate was 72.6, while it was more than double, or 164.8 where there were no bathtubs. . . . In a city of Johnstown's housing standards, the tub is an index of a good home, a suitable house from a sanitary standpoint, a fairly comfortable income, and all the favorable conditions that go with such an income."

Income plays a chief part in determining the location of the home as well as the kind of home. The report for Waterbury, Conn., shows that the infant mortality rate for children born in houses located on the street was 120.6, while that for children born in houses placed on the rear of a lot or on an alley was 172.0.

Overcrowding is another housing condition that accompanies low income. The report on Manchester, N. H., says: "The infant mortality rate showed a steady increase according to the number of persons per room. It was 123.3, where the average was less than one; 177.8 where the average was one but under two; and 261.7 where the average was two but less than three." It is significant that in Brockton, where wages, taken by and large were better than in any other city studied, and where the infant mortality rate was markedly low, there is no acute housing problem. Yet in Brockton, as in the other cities, the infant mortality rate was highest in the most crowded homes.

In houses where there was less than one person to a room, infant deaths occurred at a rate of 86.5 per thousand births; where there was more than one person to a room, that rate rose to 110.2. Only 32 out of 1,210 Brockton babies were born into homes where there were more than two persons to a room. There is available much foreign material which confirms the impression conveyed by the Children's Bureau studies of the fundamental importance of decent sanitary housing.

A woman, who was the mother of six children and whose husband earned $2 a day, after reading certain of the Children's Bureau bulletins on the care of children wrote to the Bureau: "I like the Bulletins. Some of the things I knew before, some of them my neighbors have told me, but there are things you can't do when 8 people must live in two rooms."

Another test of the adequacy of income is the employment of the mother. The Johnstown report says: "It is impossible to judge from statistics alone whether or not the work done by an individual woman, either her own housework or work for money is so excessive as to affect her during pregnancy or while nursing to the extent of reacting on the health of the baby, but the fact is that the infant mortality rate is higher among the babies of wage-earning mothers than among the others, being 188, as compared with a rate of 117.6 among the babies of non-wage-earning mothers. Wage-earning mothers and low-wage fathers are in practically the same groups, and it is difficult to secure an exact measurement of the comparative weight of the two factors in the production of a high infant mortality rate." In Johnstown, no woman-employing industries were found, but many of the poorest foreign mothers kept lodgers and boarders, the percentage of mothers contributing to the family income varying from 47.6 per cent in the lowest wage group to 2.0 per cent in families where the father earned $1,200 or more. In the case of this type of working mothers, although there is severe toil, the baby profits because there is not the necessity for artificial feeding which exists when the mother is away from the child during working hours. In Manchester, N. H., where there is a great demand for women workers in the textile trades, 679 mothers of babies were employed during the year following their baby's birth, 353 in the home, 326 outside, and 885 were not employed. While the rate for the babies of mothers at home and with no employment save that of caring for their households was 122.0, that for mothers employed outside the home was 312.9.

That mothers apparently do not choose to go out to work leaving young babies at home is shown by the lessening proportion of mothers employed as the husband's wages increase. In Manchester, 65.7 per cent of the mothers whose husbands earned less than $550 were gainfully employed during the year following the baby's birth, while only 9.5 per cent of the mothers whose husbands earned more than $1,250 were so employed. When it is realized that the infant mortality rate greatly increases when the mothers go out leaving young babies at home and that the number of mothers so employed rapidly decreases as the father's wages increase, the connection between income and infant mortality becomes more impressive than if viewed from any other approach.

Poverty may be accompanied by ignorance. Although it is not possible to gauge the relative ignorance of the care of children according to income, it is clear that poverty takes away the defenses by which the effects of ignorance may be evaded. Sir Arthur Newsholme, Medical Officer of the English Local Government Board, offers a spirited defense of the working-class mother in this connection. He says:

"Maternal ignorance is sometimes regarded as a chief factor in the causation of excessive child mortality. It is a comfortable doctrine for the well-to-do person to adopt; and it goes far to relieve his conscience in the contemplation of excessive suffering and mortality among the poor. . . . There is little reason to believe that the average ignorance in matters of health of the working-class mother is much greater than that of mothers in other classes of society. . . . But the ignorance of the working-class mother is dangerous, because it is associated with relative social helplessness. To remedy this, what is needed is that the environment of the infant of the poor should be levelled up toward that of the infant of the well-to-do, and that medical advice and nursing assistance should be made available for the poor as promptly as it is for persons of higher social status."

Among the essentials of a lowered infant mortality rate are:

1. Medical and nursing care at the service of all mothers and infants in this country, a policy which has been discussed in the Fifth Annual Report of the Children's Bureau with reference to foreign experience and the setting forth of a plan for rural provision in the United States.

2. Adequate teaching in the normal hygiene of maternity and infancy made available for all girls and women.

3. Community responsibility for decent housing and sanitation.

But finally, and fundamentally, a general recognition throughout the country that a decent income, self-respectingly earned by the father is the beginning of wisdom, the only fair division of labor between the father and the mother of young children, and the strongest safeguard against a high infant mortality rate.

We still cling to the shaken but not shattered belief that this free country gives every man his chance and that an income sufficient to bring up a family decently is attainable by all honest people who are not hopelessly stupid, or incorrigibly lazy. The fathers of 88 per cent of the babies included in the Bureau's studies earned less than $1,250 a year; 27 per cent earned less than $550. As the income doubled the mortality rate was more than halved. Which is the more safe and sane conclusion! That 88 per cent of all these fathers were incorrigibly indolent or below normal mentally, or that sound public economy demands an irreducible minimum living standard to be sustained by a minimum wage and such other expedients as may be developed in a determined effort to give every child a fair chance?

PRIMARY SOURCE 5

"Under the Twentieth Amendment," cartoon, Columbus Dispatch, found in the Julia Lathrop Papers, folder—Papers, Child Labor, 1925, Microfilm, Reel 4, Julia Lathrop Papers, Archives, Rockford University, Rockford, IL.

PRIMARY SOURCE 6

Julia Lathrop to Edith Abbott, Christmas card, circa 1921, Box 57, Folder 5,
Grace and Edith Abbott Papers, University of Chicago Research Center,
University of Chicago Library, Chicago, IL.

PRIMARY SOURCE 7

ADDRESS OF MISS JULIA LATHROP, VICE-PRESIDENT OF THE NATIONAL LEAGUE OF WOMEN VOTERS, ON "WHAT NEXT," GIVEN THURSDAY AFTERNOON, APRIL 16, AT THE CHILD WELFARE COMMITTEE CONFERENCE OF THE NATIONAL LEAGUE OF WOMEN VOTERS CONVENTION IN RICHMOND, VA.

JULIA LATHROP*

What next? Keep on. Democracy moves slowly and painfully, but it moves forward. Remember the movement which culminates in the Twentieth [Child Labor] Amendment has, conservatively speaking, been actively urged for 107 years, first by one man, by small groups of individuals, by societies and associations, then by legislators and Congressmen and Senators, Governors and Presidents. Ever since 1818 when the Governor of Rhode Island called the attention of the legislature to the fact that children were working in the mills and were growing up without schooling.

Remember that an effort lasting 107 years to give the children of this nation that fair chance to which our romantic Declaration of Independence states they are entitled is a brief snatch of time in the long work of making that great Dream of Democracy come true. There is an effort to make it appear that the Constitutional Amendment is a novel freakish proposal, in truth, the last resort.

It is a fact that Congress passed the resolution with enthusiasm that the popular support was hearty and unforced. The public is still of the opinion that children should have—every one—a fair chance for the nurture and education which launches them as adults with a fair chance for an active and happy life. But the public has suddenly changed and declines in a series of states to satisfy the amendment so that the opposition announces that it is beaten and that the government will never again venture to try to [illegible] uniform standard for the work of children.

The public has been deceived by a whirlwind campaign of misrepresentation which swept the country like a sirocco. It knew neither East nor West. North or South. The four ratifying states—California, Arkansas, Wisconsin and Arizona—represent wide variety in geography and population. . . .

- - - - - - - - -

We now realize that the quick attack of last winter was to have been anticipated. The clash of reactionary and progressive opinion never ceases. Just as old as the efforts to treat all children fairly and open opportunity to them are the efforts to maintain the status quo, to restrict rather than widen their path of education and training. The growth of state child labor laws, schools and compulsory education has been slow and unequal always with the same opposition to be overcome. The opposition today is rich, powerful, ingenious, able to command the printing press, the newspapers, to some degree the clergy and the learned, to fill the very air now so costly, with its arguments.

---

* Julia Lathrop, "What Next," Speech at the Sixth Annual Convention of the National League of Women Voters, Richmond, VA, April 16–22, 1925, Papers of the League of Women Voters, 1918–1974, Part II, Series A: Transcripts and Records of National Conventions, 1919–1944, and of General Councils, 1927–1943, Folder 002634–006–0557 W. 23, 2–4.

Why should we have thought it would leave the children in undisputed possession of their victory? No, we who would be friends of children were too confiding, too confident, a little dull. . . .

The question is can we save for the children the Twentieth Amendment—There is only one answer. Make the truth prevail. To this end what methods. First some of us believe in the old plan of petitions. To gain volunteers for house to house canvass the best and most devoted persons must enlist in each community. They must train themselves to present the facts clearly and without color or exaggeration or resentment—undue resentment let us say. A large amount of material is available and can be obtained through the league. To learn to be a good canvasser for signature to a petition, such as will be presented, is in itself a fine educational opportunity—to canvass is a fine civic service.

But all this cannot be a scattering fire. The time, the conditions must be decided carefully. . . . Every legislator should hear from his constituents by petition, by call, by letter, by deputation, by whichever means promises the best understanding of the facts. Not all will have open minds, perhaps, but with calm second thought the majority will give honest consideration.

Can we hold a citizenship school in each senatorial district in states where work is needed, in such schools the consideration of the rights of children and the Child Labor Amendment would be prime features. Such a school with a session devoted to this subject, could obtain aid in the way of literature and speakers from the National League and would have the advantage of placing the Child Labor Amendment in its true relation to other problems of social progress, and political significance.

Nothing gave us more courage the latter part of this winter than the cooperation of the women's missionary societies. . . .

The present time is one in which is requires unusual courage to be courageous. A weary acceptance of apparent defeat is easier. But that is the short view. . . . In one form, sooner or later as we decree by our interest or its lack, the child will win. This is out opportunity to keep up and keep on with our eyes wider open, and our minds better informed, and our courage stouter. We shall keep on.

STUDY QUESTIONS

1. Whether it was through their work at social settlements, training women for new professions, working in government, or securing the vote, Julia Lathrop and her colleagues saw themselves as providing new opportunities for women. Do you think this was true? Elaborate. To what extent did their approaches reinforce older traditions?

2. Lathrop and her allies fought to expand the role of government in providing health care and regulating child labor. Many activists and officials opposed these initiatives. According to the author, both sides made use of the politics of gender to promote their positions. Provide some examples.

3. Were Lathrop and her close friends ahead of their time regarding attitudes about racial and ethnic minorities? Could you also argue that they were very much a reflection of their time? Provide examples.

4. Lathrop was among a group of progressive reformers at the turn of the twentieth century who prioritized the problems of poverty. How did she explain the causes of poverty? How did it differ from the more widely accepted views about poor people at the time?

5. As a politician Lathrop was both cautious and determined in pursuing her goals. She made many compromises in order to obtain reforms, such as the establishment of the juvenile court or the Maternity and Infancy Act. What do you think about Lathrop's approach?

6. Many people who knew Lathrop noted her wit but also her great modesty—her unwillingness to promote her own achievements. In the early twenty-first century many feminists point out that more so than men, women still find it difficult to acknowledge and promote their achievements. Do you agree? Why might women still find it hard to promote their successes?

7. In reforming Illinois public charities early in her career Lathrop fought against the patronage system, favoring the appointment of trained professionals to staff the institutions. She also relied on club women and other volunteers, believing that because they were not motivated by monetary concerns, they could be more objective about the public charities. Do you think that prominent citizens, whether female or male, because they serve without pay, are disinterested representatives of the larger good?

NOTES

INTRODUCTION

1. "Julia Lathrop, Child Welfare Leader, Dies," *Chicago Herald and Examiner*, April 16, 1932; "Julia Lathrop Dies, Aged 74," *Youngstown Ohio Vindicator*, April 16, 1932; Julia Lathrop Papers (JLP), Rockford University, Folder—1932, Her Death, News Clippings, Tributes, Memorials, Rockford College Library, Rockford, Illinois, Reel 5, microfilm copy in the Vassar College Special Collections (VCSC), Vassar College Library, Poughkeepsie, NY.

2. William Chenery, "A Great Public Servant," typescript taken from *The Survey*, September 1, 1921, JLP, Folder-Correspondence 1921, Reel 3; Jane Addams, "A Great Public Servant, Julia C. Lathrop," *Social Service Review* 1, no. 2 (June 1932): 280.

3. Molly Ladd-Taylor, "Toward Defining Maternalism in U.S. History," *Journal of Women's History* 5, no. 2 (Fall 1993): 110, 111; Sonya Michel, "Maternalism and Beyond," in *Maternalism Reconsidered: Motherhood, Welfare and Social Policy in the Twentieth Century*, ed. Marian van der Klein, Rebecca Jo Plant, Nichole Sanders, and Lori R. Weintrob (New York, Oxford: Berghahn Books, 2014), 27; Kathryn Kish Sklar, Anja Schüler, and Susan Strasser, "Introduction: A Transatlantic Dialogue," in *Social Justice Feminists in the United States and Germany*, ed. Kathryn Kish Sklar, Anja Schüler, and Susan Strasser (Ithaca: Cornell University Press, 1998), 5; Linda Gordon, *Pitied but Not Entitled: Single Women and the History of Welfare* (New York: The Free Press, 1994), 31, 106. An early and important study of social feminism is J. Stanley Lemons, *The Woman Citizen: Social Feminism in the 1920s* (Urbana: University of Illinois Press, 1973).

4. Robyn Muncy, *Creating a Female Dominion in American Reform, 1890–1935* (New York: Oxford University Press, 1991), 49.

5. Chenery, "A Great Public Servant," 3.

6. Alice Hamilton, *Exploring the Dangerous Trades: The Autobiography of Alice Hamilton, M.D.* (Boston: Little Brown and Company, 1943), 63.

7. Biographical Records Questionnaire of the Alumnae Office, filled out and signed by Julia C. Lathrop, December 19, 1929, AAVC Files, Box 4, VCSC. See also Primary Source 1.

1: CHILDHOOD AND EDUCATION AT VASSAR:
OLD TRADITIONS AND NEW PATHS

1. "Lathrop Ancestors and Family," 1, Box 57, Folder 2, Grace and Edith Abbott Papers, Special Collections Research Center, University of Chicago Library, Chicago, IL (hereafter

cited as Abbott Papers), retold in Jane Addams, *My Friend, Julia Lathrop* (1935; repr., Urbana: University of Illinois Press, 2004), 5.

2. Mary O'Connor Newell, "America's First Official Mother," *Chicago Sunday-Record Herald*, May 19, 1912, Julia Lathrop Bio File, VCSC.

3. Addams, *My Friend, Julia Lathrop*, 17, 18, 27, 119.

4. Ibid., 20.

5. Lathrop's transcript listing her courses can be found in the Julia Lathrop Biography File, VCSC; Matthew Vassar's address to the Board of Trustees, February 26, 1861, Matthew Vassar Papers, Folder 1.204, VCSC.

6. "Reveal Julia Lathrop as Retiring Girl in Her College Days," *Chicago Daily Tribune* (1923–1963), May 7, 1932, Proust Historical Newspapers Chicago Tribune (1849–1989).

7. Julia Lathrop to Anna Case, November 29, 1919, Box 58, Folder 6, Abbott Papers, University of Chicago Library.

8. Newell, "America's First Official Mother."

9. Lynn D. Gordon, *Gender and Higher Education in the Progressive Era* (New Haven, CT: Yale University Press, 1990), 121, John Raymond quoted; Helen Horowitz, *Alma Mater, Design and Experience in the Women's Colleges from Their Nineteenth Century Beginnings to the 1930s* (1984; repr., Boston: Beacon Press, 1985). Some of the material on Vassar College for this section of the chapter comes from the Vassar College Encyclopedia, http://vcencyclopedia .vassar.edu. See also *Prospectus of the Vassar Female College, Poughkeepsie N.Y.* (New York: C. A. Alvord, 1865), http://bit.ly/2f1uLDA.

10. John Raymond, "A College for Women in Poughkeepsie, N.Y." A report on the college's first seven years to the US Commissioner of Education, http://vcencyclopedia.vassar .edu/interviews-reflections/a-college-for-women.html.

11. Class Prophecy for Julia Lathrop, Julia Lathrop Bio File, VCSC.

2: "J. LATHROP'S HERE!"
SINGLE WOMANHOOD AND A NEW LIFE AT HULL HOUSE

1. Jane Addams, *My Friend, Julia Lathrop* (1935; repr., Urbana: University of Illinois Press, 2004), 33, 34.

2. Ibid., 34.

3. Ibid., 28.

4. Daniel T. Rodgers, "In Search of Progressivism," *Reviews in American History* 10, no. 4 (December 1982): 123.

5. Jane Addams, "Outgrowths of Toynbee Hall," written for the Chicago Women's Club, December 3, 1890, Jane Addams Papers, Reel 3.

6. Alice Hamilton, *Exploring the Dangerous Trades: The Autobiography of Alice Hamilton, M.D.* (Boston: Little Brown and Company, 1943), 68.

7. Kathryn Kish Sklar, *Florence Kelley and the Nation's Work: The Rise of Women's Political Culture, 1830–1890* (New Haven, CT: Yale University Press, 1995), 187.

8. Nancy Pottishman Weiss, "Save the Children: A History of the Children's Bureau, 1903–1918" (PhD diss., UCLA, 1974), 143; Sklar, *Florence Kelley and the Nation's Work*, 202, 203.

9. Sklar, *Florence Kelley and the Nation's Work*, 202, 203, 373n.

10. Estelle B. Freedman, *Maternal Justice: Miriam Van Waters and the Female Reform Tradition* (Chicago: University of Chicago Press, 2003), 280.

11. Julia Lathrop to Jane Addams, n.d., JLP File—Correspondence with Jane Addams, Reel 1.

12. Sklar, *Florence Kelley and the Nation's Work*, 193.

13. James Weber Linn, *Jane Addams: A Biography* (New York: D Appleton-Century Company, 1935), 140.

14. Francis Hackett: "Hull House—A Souvenir," *The Survey* 54, no. 5 (June 1, 1925), reprint, http://tigger.uic.edu/depts/hist/hull-maxwell/vicinity/nws1/documents/hackett.PDF, 9. See also Hamilton, *Exploring the Dangerous Trades*, 64.

15. Addams, *My Friend, Julia Lathrop*, 41, for the parrot story. On Lathrop's favorite reading, Mary O' Connor Newell, "America's First Official Mother," *Chicago Sunday-Record Herald*, May 19, 1912.

16. Linn, *Jane Addams*, 136.

17. Charlene Haddock Seigfried, "The Courage of One's Convictions or the Conviction of One's Courage? Jane Addams's Principled Compromises," in *Jane Addams and the Practice of Democracy*, ed. Marilyn Fischer, Carol Nackenoff, and Wendy Chmielewski (Urbana: University of Illinois Press, 2009), 46.

18. Julia C. Lathrop, "What the Settlement Work Stands For," Twenty-Third National Conference of Charities, 1896, http://quod.lib.umich.edu/n/ncosw/ACH8650 .1896.001?rgn=main;view=fulltext, 109. See Primary Source 2.

19. Shannon Jackson, "Toward a Queer Social Welfare Studies: Unsettling Jane Addams," in Fischer, Nackenoff, and Chmielewski, *Jane Addams and the Practice of Democracy*, 156.

20. Shannon Jackson, *Lines of Activity: Performance, Historiography and Hull House Domesticity* (Ann Arbor: University of Michigan Press, 2003), 130, Jane Addams quoted.

21. Jane Addams, *Twenty Years at Hull House with Autobiographical Notes* (New York: Penguin Books, 1981 [c. 1910]), 98, 103; Lathrop, "What the Settlement Work Stands For," 108.

22. Addams, *My Friend, Julia Lathrop*, 38, 40, 41.

23. Julia Lathrop to George Derby, March 15, 1930, JLP, Folder—Correspondence 1930, Reel 5.

24. Robyn Muncy, *Creating a Female Dominion in American Reform, 1890–1935* (New York: Oxford University Press, 1991), 22.

25. Julia C. Lathrop, "Report for the State of New York," National Conference of Charities, Proceedings 1894, Twenty-First Annual Meeting, 306, http://quod.lib.umich.edu/n /ncosw/ACH8650.1894.001?view=toc.

3: SOCIAL RESEARCH AND PROGRESSIVE GOVERNMENT

1. Julia C. Lathrop, "Hull House as a Sociological Laboratory," National Conference of Charities, Proceedings 1894, Twenty-First Annual Meeting, 317, http://quod.lib.umich .edu/n/ncosw/ACH8650.1894.001? view=toc.

2. Julia C. Lathrop, "The Cook County Charities," in *Hull House Maps and Papers: A Presentation of Nationalities and Wages in a Congested District of Chicago, Together with Comments and Essays on Problems Growing Out of the Social Conditions by the Residents of Hull House, a Social Settlement* (1895; repr., Urbana and Chicago: University of Illinois Press, 2007), 128, 122, 123.

3. Jane Addams, *My Friend, Julia Lathrop* (1935: repr., Urbana: University of Illinois Press, 2004), 66; Laurie Hillyer, "'Babyology': College Uncle Sam's Latest Pet Idea of This $5,000 a Year Woman 'Chief,'" *Boston Traveler*, March 13, 1915; Alice Hamilton, *Exploring the Dangerous Trades: The Autobiography of Alice Hamilton, M.D.* (Boston: Little Brown and Company, 1943), 64.

4. Julia C. Lathrop, *Suggestions for Visitors to County Poorhouses and to Other Charitable Institutions* (Public Charities Committee of the Illinois Federation of Women's Clubs, 1905), 6.

5. Leon Fink, *Progressive Intellectuals and the Dilemmas of Democratic Commitment* (Cambridge, MA: Harvard University Press, 1997), 18; Kathryn Kish Sklar, "Hull House Maps and Papers: Social Science as Women's Work in the 1890s," in *Gender and American Social Science: The Formative Years*, ed. Helene Silverberg (Princeton: Princeton University Press, 1998), 127.

6. Lathrop, "The Cook County Charities," 120, 121, 125, 129, 123, 121–122, italics mine.

7. On the contradictions in Lathrop's views of the poor, see Rima Lunin Schultz, "Introduction," *Hull House Maps and Papers*, 25, 26; Julia Lathrop, "The Responsibilities of the New Philanthropy," 1908, 1, 3, Typescript, JLP, Folder—Correspondence, January–June 1908, Reel 2.

8. Julia C. Lathrop, *Village Care for the Insane*, reprinted from the Report of the Twenty-Ninth National Conference of Charities and Corrections (Boston: Geo. H. Ellis Co., 1902), 10.

9. Sklar, "Hull Maps and Papers,"143.

10. Lathrop, "The Cook County Charities," 129, 125–126.

11. Addams, *My Friend, Julia Lathrop*, 77, 80, Lathrop resignation letter quoted.

12. Committee on Civil Service Reform, Illinois Federation of Women's Clubs, letter to presidents of affiliate clubs, 1902, JLP, Folder—Correspondence 1902–1906, Reel 1.

13. Addams, *My Friend, Julia Lathrop*, 58, Taylor quoted.

14. Julia C. Lathrop, Report for the State of Illinois, National Conference of Charities, Proceedings 1894, Twenty-First Annual Meeting, 306.

15. Julia C. Lathrop, "The District Nurse," National Conference of Charities, Proceedings 1894, Twenty-First Annual Meeting, 341.

16. Robyn Muncy, *Creating a Female Dominion in American Reform, 1890–1935* (New York: Oxford University Press, 1991), 67.

17. Julia Lathrop to Edith Abbott, March 25, 1908, Box 57, Folder 5, Abbott Papers, University of Chicago Library.

18. See Primary Source 3.

19. All quotes from Lathrop's 1915 speech are found in Julia Clifford Lathrop, "The Highest Education for Women," in *The Fiftieth Anniversary of the Opening of Vassar College, October 10 to 13, 1915: A Record* (Poughkeepsie, NY, 1916), 81–95; Laurie Hillyer, "Babyology"; Minute Upon the Death of Julia Lathrop, "Minutes of the Board of Trustees of Vassar College, 1931–32," VCSC.

20. Muncy, *Creating a Female Dominion*, 77, 78, Breckinridge quoted; Julia Lathrop to Edith Abbott, August 10, 1920, Box 57, Folder 5, Abbott Papers, University of Chicago Library; Julia Lathrop to Dr. V. H. Podesta, June 12, 1908, JLP, Reel 2—Correspondence, January–June 1908, Reel 2; Mary O'Connor Newell, "America's First Official Mother," *Chicago Sunday-Record Herald*, May 19, 1912.

21. Mrs. DeSisla to Julia Lathrop, February 24, 1908; Mrs. DeSisla to Julia Lathrop, March 2, 1908, JLP Papers, Folder—Correspondence, January–June 1908, Reel 2. The spelling of the name "DeSisla" is approximate.

22. Molly Ladd-Taylor, *Mother-Work, Women, Child Welfare, and the State, 1890–1930* (Urbana: University of Illinois Press, 1994), 79. Julia Lathrop quoted.

4: JUVENILE JUSTICE, IMMIGRANT AID

1. Julia C. Lathrop, "Introduction," in *The Delinquent Child and the Home*, by Sophonisba Preston Breckinridge and Edith Abbott (New York: Survey Associates, 1912), 8.

2. Julia C. Lathrop, "The Cook County Charities," *Hull House Maps and Papers: A Presentation of Nationalities and Wages in a Congested District of Chicago, Together with Comments and Essays on Problems Growing Out of the Social Conditions by the Residents of Hull House, a Social Settlement* (1895 repr., Urbana and Chicago: University of Illinois Press, 2007), 122.

3. Jane Addams, *My Friend, Julia Lathrop* (1935 repr., Urbana: University of Illinois Press, 2004), 100.

4. Linda Gordon, *Pitied but Not Entitled: Single Women Mothers and the History of Welfare* (New York: The Free Press, 1994), 76.

5. Julia C. Lathrop, "The Background of the Juvenile Court in Illinois," in *The Child, the Clinic and the Court*, by Jane Addams, C. Judson Herrick, A. L. Jacoby, et al. (New York: The New Republic, 1925), 292, 293, Report to the Chicago Woman's Club quoted.

6. Victoria Getis, *The Juvenile Court and the Progressives* (Urbana: University of Illinois Press, 2000), 35, Frederic H. Wines quoted, 37, Julia Lathrop quoted.

7. Lathrop, "The Background of the Juvenile Court," 294.

8. Getis, *The Juvenile Court*, 45.

9. Anne Meis Knupfer, *Reform and Rebellion: Gender, Delinquency, and America's First Juvenile Court* (New York: Routledge, 2000), 48, Lathrop quoted.

10. Mrs. Joseph T. Bowen, "The Early Days of the Juvenile Court," in Addams et al., *The Child, the Clinic and the Court*, 299.

11. "Articles of Incorporation of the Juvenile Court Committee," March 26, 1904, Jane Addams Papers, Reel 52.

12. Addams, *My Friend, Julia Lathrop*, 96, 121, Julia Lathrop quoted, 96, Julian Mack quoted.

13. Lathrop, "Introduction," in Breckinridge and Abbott, *The Delinquent Child and the Home*, 9,10.

14. Getis, *The Juvenile Court*, 66, Ethel Sturges Dummer quoted.

15. Breckinridge and Abbott, *The Delinquent Child and the Home*, 28.

16. Annual Report of the General Superintendent and Attorney to the Juvenile Protective Association, 1908–1909, October 1909, 25, Jane Addams Papers, Hull House Association Records, Hull House Activities and Events, Hull House as Meeting Place and Headquarters, Juvenile Court Committee and Juvenile Protective Association, Annual Reports, 1905–1930, Reel 52; Instructions found in Jane Addams Papers, 3, 4, Hull House Association Records, Hull House Activities and Events, Hull House as Meeting Place and Headquarters, Juvenile Court, 1906, Reel 52.

17. Molly Ladd-Taylor, "Toward Defining Maternalism in U.S. History," *Journal of Women's History* 5, no. 2 (Fall 1993): 110; Gordon, *Pitied but Not Entitled*, 135, 136.

18. Mary E. Odem, *Delinquent Daughters: Protecting and Policing Adolescent Female Sexuality in the United States, 1885–1920* (Chapel Hill: University of North Carolina Press, 1995), 5.

19. Annual Report of the General Superintendent and Attorney to the Juvenile Protective Association, 1908-1909, October 1909, 27–31. On maternalists and the efforts to regulate the content of movies, see Leigh Ann Wheeler, *Against Obscenity: Reform and the Politics of Womanhood in America 1873–1935* (Baltimore, MD: Johns Hopkins University Press, 2004.)

20. Lathrop, "Introduction," *The Delinquent Child and the Home*, 8; Odem, *Delinquent Daughters*, 115.

21. Addams, *My Friend, Julia Lathrop*, 37; "The Cook County Charities," *Hull House Maps and Papers*, 120.

22. Grace Abbott to Julia Lathrop, January 13, 1921, JLP, Folder—Correspondence 1921, Reel 3; Julia Lathrop to Grace Abbott, January 22, 1921, Box 57, Folder 7, Abbott

Papers, University of Chicago Library; Florence Kelley to Julia Lathrop, July 21, 1927, JLP, Folder—Correspondence, July–December 1927, Reel 4.

23. Addams, *My Friend, Julia Lathrop*, 57.

24. Khalil Gibran Muhammad, *The Condemnation of Blackness: Race, Crime, and the Making of Modern Urban America* (Cambridge, MA: Harvard University Press, 2011), 101.

25. Marcia Chatelain, *Southside Girls: Growing Up in the Great Migration* (Durham, NC: Duke University Press, 2015), 29.

26. Joanne L. Goodwin, *Gender and the Politics of Welfare Reform: Mothers' Pensions in Chicago, 1911–1929* (Chicago: University of Chicago Press, 1997), 123; "Probation Investigation to Be Made," *Chicago Examiner*, clipping found in JLP, Folder-Correspondence, July 1911, Reel 2.; Joanna Snowden to Julia Lathrop, July 25, 1911; Joanna Snowden to Julia Lathrop, August 2, 1911, JLP Folder Correspondence July 1911, Reel 2.

27. Louise deKoven Bowen, *The Colored People of Chicago: An Investigation Made for the Juvenile Protection Association* (Chicago: Juvenile Protective Association, 1913), 1, 28.

28. Julia Lathrop to Grace Abbott (probably January 1924), Box 57, Folder 10; Florence Kelley to Julia Lathrop, May 1, 1914, Box 59, Folder 2, Abbott Papers, University of Chicago Library.

29. Chatelain, *South Side Girls*, 55.

30. Lathrop, "Introduction," *The Delinquent Child and the Home*, 10, italics hers.

5: "CHIEF"

1. Robyn Muncy, *Creating a Female Dominion in American Reform, 1890–1935* (New York: Oxford University Press, 1991) 19, Lillian Wald story quoted.

2. Ibid., 42.

3. Kriste Lindenmeyer, *"A Right to Childhood": The U.S. Children's Bureau and Child Welfare, 1912–1946* (Urbana: University of Illinois Press, 1970), 21.

4. Julia Lathrop to Lillian Wald, telegram, April 19, 1912, Box 59, Folder 1, Abbott Papers, University of Chicago Library; Jacqueline K. Parker and Edward M. Carpenter, "Julia Lathrop and the Children's Bureau: The Emergence of an Institution," *Social Service Review* 55, no. 1 (March 1981): 62.

5. Lillian Wald, "Julia Lathrop," typescript tribute for the memorial meeting in Washington after Lathrop's death, possibly May 5, 1932, Box 57, Folder 3; Julia Lathrop to Anna Case, November 7, 1921, Box 58, Folder 7, Abbott Papers, University of Chicago Library; Lathrop's dictums about dress can be found in "Grace Abbott of Nebraska," *New Republic*, July 18, 1923.

6. Julia Lathrop to Lillian Wald, January 20, 1913, Box 59, Folder 1, Abbott Papers.

7. Fanny Fiske to Anna Case, October 13, 1913; Anna Case to Fanny Fiske, October 15, 1913, Box 59, Folder 1, Abbott Papers, University of Chicago Library.

8. Fanny Fiske to Julia Lathrop, October 19, 1913, Box 59, Folder 1, Abbott Papers, University of Chicago Library.

9. Emily Lundberg, "Julia Lathrop," *Bulletin* (Child Welfare League of America) 11, no. 4 (May 1932): n.p.; "To J.L. and G. A. on Leaving Home," (n.d. but most likely this took place in the early winter, 1919), Box 58, Folder 11, Abbott Papers, University of Chicago Library.

10. Memorandum for employees of the Children's Bureau, November 19, 1913, file 3–4-1 Central File, 1914–1920; To the Staff of the Bureau from J.C.L., December 3, 1914, file 3–4-2, Central File, 1914–1920, Children's Bureau Records (hereafter CBR), National Archives, College Park, Maryland.

11. Julia C. Lathrop, "The Children's Bureau," Address to the Biannual Meeting of the General Federation of Women's Clubs, *American Journal of Sociology* 18, no. 3 (November 1912): 319–320.

12. Molly Ladd-Taylor, *Mother-Work: Women, Child-Welfare and the State, 1890–1930* (Urbana: University of Illinois Press, 1994), 86, instructions to bureau investigators quoted, 87, Lathrop quoted.

13. "Can You Prove Your Right to Vote?" for Release in Morning and Afternoon Papers of August 9, 1920, US Department of Labor, Children's Bureau, Central Files 1914–1950 (2) Record Group, 102, CBR.

14. Julia Lathrop to Florence Kelley, April 28, 1923, quoted in Jane Addams, *My Friend, Julia Lathrop* (1935; repr., Urbana: University of Illinois Press, 2004), 88; Muncy, *Creating the Female Dominion*, 63.

15. Julia C. Lathrop, "Pass on the Torch," *Woman's Journal* 48, no. 51 (December 21, 1912): 402.

16. Lathrop, "Pass on the Torch," 402; Victoria Bissell Brown, "Jane Addams, Progressivism and Woman Suffrage," in *One Woman, One Vote: Rediscovering the Woman Suffrage Movement*, ed. Marjorie Spruill Wheeler (Troutdale, OR: New Sage Press, 1995), 187, 183, 188.

17. "Big Crowd Attends Suffrage Mass Meeting," *Evening Star*, October 12, 2015; "Child Bureau Her Care," *New York Evening Post*, January 18, 1913; Lathrop, "Pass on the Torch," 402.

18. Lathrop, "Pass on the Torch," 403.

19. Muncy, *Creating the Female Dominion*, 49, Lathrop quoted, 51.

20. Lindenmeyer, *"A Right to Childhood,"* 119.

21. Alice Hamilton, *Exploring the Dangerous Trades: The Autobiography of Alice Hamilton, M.D.* (Boston: Little Brown and Company, 1943), 191.

22. "Not for Publication a Protest," January 13, 1917, Folder 2, Box 59, Abbott Papers, University of Chicago Library.

23. Julia C. Lathrop, "Standards of Child Welfare," *Annals of the American Academy of Political and Social Science* 98 (November 1921): 1, Woodrow Wilson quoted, 3, http//jstor .org/stable1015037; Julia Lathrop, "The Military and Naval Insurance Act," *The Nation* 106 (February 7, 1918): 158.

24. Mary Ware Dennett to Julia Lathrop, January 21, 1916; Julia Lathrop to Mary Ware Dennett, October 28, 1920; Mary Ware Dennett to Julia Lathrop, October 30, 1920; Julia Lathrop to Mary Dennett, November 1, 1920, File 4-0-2, CBR.

6: SAVING CHILDREN, HELPING MOTHERS

1. Lillian Wald, "New Aspects of Social Responsibilities," *The Fiftieth Anniversary of the Opening of Vassar College, October 10 to 13, 1915: A Record* (Poughkeepsie, NY, 1916), 106.

2. Robyn Muncy, *Creating a Female Dominion in American Reform, 1890–1935* (New York: Oxford University Press, 1991), 100, 55, Lathrop quoted.

3. Molly Ladd-Taylor, *Mother-Work: Women, Child Welfare, and the State, 1890–1930* (Urbana: University of Illinois Press, 1994), 83, *Infant Care* quoted.

4. Julia C. Lathrop, "Income and Infant Mortality," *American Journal Public Health* 9, no. 4 (April 1919): 273.

5. Helen M. Dart, *Maternity and Infant Care in Selected Rural Areas of Mississippi*, Rural Child Welfare Series No. 5, Children's Bureau Publication No. 88 (Washington, DC: Government Printing Office, 1921), 23.

6. Molly Ladd-Taylor, *Raising a Baby the Government Way: Mothers' Letters to the Children's Bureau, 1915–1932* (New Brunswick, NJ: Rutgers University Press, 1986), 2.

7. James Smith to Julia Lathrop, received August 22, 1918; Julia Lathrop to James Smith, August 29, 1918; Julia Lathrop to Annie Hinrichin, August 29, 1918; Annie Hinrichin to Julia Lathrop, September 10, 1918; Julia Lathrop to Annie Hinrichin, September 13, 1918, Subject Files, 1914–1920, 9–4–4–1, CBR.

8. Mrs. Hughie McDermott to unknown, June 29, 1918; Julia Lathrop to Mrs. Hughie McDermott, July 8, 1918, Subject Files 1914–1920, 9–4–4–1, CBR.

9. Mrs. Hall (pseudonym) to US Children's Bureau, October 8, 1917; Julia Lathrop to Mrs. Appleyard, July 31, 1917, Subject Files 1914–1920, 9–4–4–1, CBR.

10. Julia Lathrop to Commissioner Newman, July 20, 1918; Thomas H. Claffy, private secretary to Commissioner Newman, July 26, 1915, Subject Files, 1914–1920, 9–4–4–1, CBR.

11. Rosie Caporale to Julia Lathrop (date unknown); Rosie Caporale to Julia Lathrop, May 15, 1915; Julia Lathrop to Rosie Caporale, June 1, 1915, Subject Files, 1914–1920, 9–4–4–1, CBR.

12. Emily K. Abel, "Correspondence Between Julia C. Lathrop, Chief of the Children's Bureau and a Working-Class Woman, 1914–1915," *Journal of Women's History* 5, no.1 (Spring 1993): 85, 83.

13. James C. Waters Jr. to Julia Lathrop, May 20, 1914, James C. Waters Jr. to Julia Lathrop, May 26, 1914; James C. Waters to Julia Lathrop, May 29, 1914, Subject File 1914–1920, 9–4–4–1, CBR.

14. Governor Lee Cruce to James C. Waters Jr., June 2, 1914, Subject File, 1914–1920, 9–4–4–1, CBR, italics mine.

15. Thomas Leahy to the Secretary of the Interior, May 27, 1914; Julia Lathrop to Honorable Cato Stella, Commissioner of Indian Affairs, July 20, 1914, Subject File, 1914–1920, 9–4–4–1, CBR.

16. James C. Waters Jr., memorandum for Julia Lathrop, July 9, 1914, Subject File 9–4–4–1, CBR, italics his.

17. Stacey Patton, "The Richest Colored Girl in the World," *The Crisis* (Spring 2010): 31–34, http://bit.ly/2golFn4; James C. Waters Jr. to Julia Lathrop, November 12, 1914; James C. Waters Jr. to Julia Lathrop, January 13, 1915, Subject File 1914–1920, 9–4–4–1, CBR.

18. Patton, "The Richest Colored Girl," 2; James C. Waters Jr. to Julia Lathrop, January 13, 1915; Julia Lathrop to James C. Waters Jr., January 15, 1915, Subject File 1914–1920, 9–4–4–1, CBR, italics mine.

19. Mrs. M. R. to Julia Lathrop, January 4, 1916, and Lathrop's response, quoted in Molly Ladd-Taylor, *Raising a Baby*, 1.

7: THE MAKING OF THE MATERNITY AND INFANCY ACT, 1921

1. Laura Lovett, *Conceiving the Future: Pronatalism, Reproduction, and the Family in the United States, 1890–1938* (Chapel Hill: University of North Carolina Press, 2007), 137, Lydia DeVilbiss quoted; Kriste Lindenmeyer, *The Right to Childhood: The US Children's Bureau and Child Welfare, 1912–1946* (Urbana: University of Illinois Press, 1997), 71, Lathrop quoted.

2. Robyn Muncy, *Creating a Female Dominion in American Reform, 1890–1935* (New York: Oxford, 1991), 99. See also Jan Dolittle Wilson, *The Women's Joint Congressional Committee and the Politics of Maternalism 1920–1930* (Urbana: University of Illinois: Press, 2007), 30.

3. Julia Lathrop to Mrs. Charles H. Brooks, April 28, 1919, Box 62, Folder 5, Abbott Papers, University of Chicago Library; Muncy, *Creating a Female Dominion*, 104, Lathrop quoted.

4. Muncy, *Creating a Female Dominion*, 103.

5. Theda Skocpol, *Protecting Soldiers and Mothers: The Political Origins of Social Policy in the United States* (Cambridge, MA: Belknap of Harvard University Press, 1992), 501, James Reed quoted; Molly Ladd-Taylor, *Mother-Work: Women, Child Welfare, and the State, 1890–1930* (Urbana: University of Illinois Press, 1994), 171, Florence Kelley quoted.

6. Memorandum Interview with Dr. Rupert Blue, Maternity and Infancy Bill, May 24, 1919, Box 62, Folder 5, Abbott Papers, University of Chicago Library.

7. Lela B. Costin, *Two Sisters for Social Justice: A Biography of Grace and Edith Abbott* (Urbana: University of Illinois Press, 1983), 123, Harriet Taylor Upton quoted.

8. Molly Ladd-Taylor, "Federal Help for Mothers: The Rise and Fall of the Sheppard-Towner Bill in the 1920s," in *Gendered Domains: Rethinking Public and Private in Women's History*, ed. Dorothy O. Helly and Susan M. Reverby (Ithaca, NY: Cornell University Press, 1992), 218, Florence Kelley quoted.

9. Muncy, *Creating a Female Dominion*, 107.

10. Ladd-Taylor, *Mother-Work*, 182.

11. Julia C. Lathrop, "Income and Infant Mortality," *American Journal Public Health* 9, no. 4 (April 1919): 274. Also see Primary Source 4.

8: RETIREMENT AND KEEPING ON

1. Jane Addams, *My Friend, Julia Lathrop* (1935; repr., Urbana: University of Illinois Press, 2004), 31.

2. Julia Lathrop to Anna Case, n.d. 1926; Julia Lathrop to Anna Case, March (?), 1925, Folder 9, Box 58; Julia Lathrop to Anna Case, June 5, 1925, Box 58, Folder 8, Abbott Papers, University of Chicago Library.

3. Julia Lathrop to Anna Case, April 5, 1929, Box 58, Folder 10; Julia Lathrop to Anna Case, April 9, 1925, Box 58, Folder 8; Julia Lathrop to Anna Case, March 30, 1926, Box 58, Folder 9, Abbott Papers, University of Chicago Library.

4. Julia Lathrop to Anna Case, April 9, 1925, Box 58, Folder 8; Julia Lathrop to Anna Case, March 30, 1926, Box 58, Folder 9; Julia Lathrop to Anna Case, April 5, 1929, Box 58, Folder 10, Abbott Papers, University of Chicago Library.

5. Julia Lathrop to Anna Case, April 5, 1929, Box 58, Folder 10; Julia Lathrop to Anna Case, April 16, 1929, Box 58, Folder 10; Julia Lathrop to Anna Case, May 1924, Box 58, Folder 8, Abbott Papers, University of Chicago Library.

6. Robyn Muncy, *Creating a Female Dominion in American Reform, 1890–1935* (New York: Oxford University Press, 1991), 127, Julia Lathrop quoted.

7. Julia Lathrop, "Convention Address of Miss Julia C. Lathrop," president, Illinois League of Women Voters, November 20, 1923, Bulletin, *Illinois League of Women Voters* 3, no. 11 (December 1923): 5, 6; Lela B. Costin, *Two Sisters for Social Justice: A Biography of Grace and Edith Abbott* (Urbana and Chicago: University of Illinois Press, 1983), 142.

8. Kim E. Nielsen, *Un-American Womanhood: Antiradicalism, Antifeminism, and the First Red Scare* (Columbus: Ohio State University Press), 92.

9. Julia Lathrop to Grace Abbott, 1922 (?), Box 57, Folder 8, Abbott Papers, University of Chicago Library; Julia Lathrop to Florence Kelly, July 2, 1924, JLP, File—Papers, 1922–1924, National Consumers League, Reel 3.

10. Nielsen, *Un-American Womanhood*, 98, 99. See also Primary Source 5.

11. Julia Lathrop to Mrs. Webster, February 12, 1925, JLP, File—Correspondence, 1925, Child Labor, Reel 4.

12. Muncy, *Creating a Female Dominion*, 139.

13. Molly Ladd-Taylor, *Mother-Work, Women, Child Welfare, and the State, 1890–1930* (Urbana: University of Illinois Press, 1994), 190.

14. Costin, *Two Sisters for Social Justice*, 95.

15. Julia Lathrop, "Participation in International Child Welfare Work," American National Conference of Social Workers, June 2, 1926, Box 60, Folder 10, Abbott Papers, University of Chicago Library.

16. Julia Lathrop to Edith Abbott, "Merry Christmas and a Happy New Year to Dear Edith Abbott," on postcard of the Christmas poster distributed by the National Council to Limit War, December 20, 1921, Box 57, Folder 5, Abbott Papers, University of Chicago Library. See Primary Source 6.

17. Julia Lathrop, "Defense Day and Patriots," Jane Addams Papers, Reel 30.

18. Costin, *Two Sisters for Social Justice*, 144, *The Woman Patriot* quoted; Julia Lathrop to the Librarian of the Congress, September 27, 1924; Henry J. Harris to Julia Lathrop, August 6, 1924, JLP, File—Correspondence, 1924, July–September, Reel 3.

19. Nielsen, *Un-American Womanhood*, 79, Robert Merrill Whitney quoted, 76; Julia Lathrop to Florence Kelley, June 6, 1924, Box 58, Folder 11, Abbott Papers, University of Chicago Library.

20. Nielsen, *Un-American Womanhood*, 126, Marion Robinson quoted; for Lathrop's listing, see Nielsen, *Un-American Womanhood*, Appendix B, Speaker Blacklist, 148; Helen Tufts Bailey to Julia Lathrop, June 27, 1928, JLP, File—Correspondence 1928, January–June; Mrs. Elaine Goodale Eastman to Julia Lathrop, January 13, 1930; Julia Lathrop to Elaine Eastman, January 25, 1930, File—Correspondence, 1930, Reel 5.

21. Nielsen, *Un-American Womanhood*, 136.

22. Julia Lathrop, "What Next?" Speech at Sixth Annual Convention of the National League of Women Voters, Richmond Virginia, April 16–22, 1925, Papers of the League of Women Voters, 1918–1974, Part II, Series A: Transcripts and Records of National Conventions, 1919–1944, and of General Councils, 1927–1943, Folder: 002634–006–0557 W 23, 4. See also Primary Source 7.

23. Julia C. Lathrop, "What the Indian Service Needs," Official Proceedings of the Annual Meeting, 1930, National Conference of Social Workers, 95, 641–650, http://quod.lib.umich.edu/n/ncosw/ach8650.1930.001/658?view=text.

24. Brookings Institution, Institute for Government Research, *The Problem of Indian Administration: Report of a Survey Made at the Request of the Honorable Hubert Work, Secretary of the Interior, and Submitted to Him, February 21, 1928* (Baltimore, MD: Johns Hopkins University Press, 1928), 6, 86, 87; Julia Lathrop, "Knox College Commencement," June 10, 1931, Address by Julia Clifford Lathrop, "Youth and Politics," 5, 6, JLP, File—Correspondence, 1931, Reel 5.

25. Lathrop, "What the Indian Service Needs, 650; Elmer R. Rusco, *A Fateful Time: The Background and Legislative History of the Indian Reorganization Act* (Reno: University of Nevada Press, 2000), 82, Meriam Report quoted.

26. Lathrop, "What the Indian Service Needs," 642.

27. Frederick E. Hoxie, *This Indian Country* (New York: Penguin Books, 2013), 275; Frederick E. Hoxie, "The Curious Story of Reformers and American Indians," in *Indians in American History: An Introduction*, ed. Frederick Hoxie and Peter Iverson (Arlington Heights, IL: Harlan Davidson, 1988), 221.

28. Jane Addams, *My Friend, Julia Lathrop* (1935; repr., Urbana: University of Illinois Press, 2004), 150, 151.

29. Julia Lathrop to Grace Abbott, 1921, Box 57, Folder 7, Abbott Papers, University of Chicago Library, emphasis hers.

30. Linda Gordon, *Pitied but Not Entitled: Single Women and the History of Welfare* (New York: The Free Press, 1994), 107; Julia Lathrop to Judge Lindsey, December 7, 1927, JLP, File—Correspondence, 1927, July–December, Reel 4.

31. Addams, *My Friend, Julia Lathrop*, 149.

32. Julia Lathrop to President Wood, JLP, File—Papers 1923 Speaking Engagements Refused, Reel 3; "Miss Lathrop and the Illinois League," *Illinois Voter* 7 (June 1932): part 2, 11; Julia Lathrop to Ann and Bill, 1927, Box 58, Folder 10, Abbott Papers, University of Chicago Library.

33. Julia Lathrop to Mrs. Willebrandt, April 4, 1928, JLP, Papers 1927–1928 Child Labor, File—Correspondence, January–June 1928, Reel 5; "Governor Demands State Set Up Plan to Insure Jobless," *New York Times*, August 28, 1930, 1, found in JLP, File—Correspondence, 1930, Reel 5.

34. Julia Lathrop to Nicholas Kelley, February 27, 1932, JLP, File—Correspondence, 1932 and Death of Florence Kelley, Reel 5.

CONCLUSION

1. Alice Hamilton to Molly Lathrop, May 8, 1932; draft of telegram from Molly Lathrop to Alice Hamilton, May 12, 1932, JLP, File—1932 Her death, clippings, Reel 5.

2. Graham Romeyn Taylor, "Julia C. Lathrop: 1858–1932," *The Compass* (April 1932), 6; Edith Abbott, "Julia Lathrop and Professional Education for Social Work," *Illinois Voter* 12 (June 1932, 2 parts): part 2, 8; Lillian Wald, typescript of her address at the Memorial for Julia Lathrop, Washington, DC, May 22, 1932, Box 57, Folder 3, Abbott Papers, University of Chicago Library; Jane Addams, *My Friend, Julia Lathrop* (1935; repr., Urbana: University of Illinois Press, 2004), 41; Jane Addams, "A Great Public Servant, Julia Lathrop," *Social Service Review* 6, no. 2 (June 1932): 284; W. E. B. Dubois, "Julia Lathrop," Postscripts, *The Crisis* 39 (June 1932): 190; Grace Abbott, speech at conference dinner, *Proceedings of the National Conference of Social Work*, 1932, 50, 51, http://indiamond6.ulib.iupui.edu/cdm/ref/collection/PRO/id/105884.

3. "Julia Lathrop Taken by Death," *News Courier* (Elton, Illinois), April 16, 1932, n. p., JLP, File—1932, Her Death, news clipping, tributes, memorials, Reel 5.

4. Anne Firor Scott, "Introduction," in Addams, *My Friend, Julia Lathrop*, x, xvii.

5. Julia Lathrop, "Defense Day and Patriots," Jane Addams Papers, Reel 30; "Washington Honors Julia C. Lathrop," *Vassar Alumnae Magazine*, April 1937, 10.

6. Linda Gordon, "Putting Children First: Women, Maternalism, and Welfare in the Early Twentieth Century," in *U.S. History as Women's History: New Feminist Essays*, ed. Linda Kerber, Alice Kessler-Harris, and Kathryn Kish Sklar (Chapel Hill: University of North Carolina Press, 1995), 85.

7. Julia Lathrop, "The Responsibilities of the New Philanthropy," JLP, File—Correspondence 1908, January–June, Reel 2.

BIBLIOGRAPHY

MANUSCRIPT COLLECTIONS

The author used the following manuscript sources in writing the history of Julia Lathrop's life.

Grace and Edith Abbott Papers, Special Collections Research Center, University of Chicago Library, Chicago, IL.

Children's Bureau Records, Central Files and Subject Files, National Archives, College Park, MD.

Jane Addams Papers, Ann Arbor, MI, University Microfilms International, 1984; Editor, Mary Lynn Bryan.

Julia Lathrop Papers, Rockford University, Rockford, IL, Microfilm edition.

Vassar College Special Collections, Vassar College Library, Poughkeepsie, NY.

SELECTED: CONTEMPORARY SOURCES

Beyond the manuscript collections, the following is a selected list of other sources of the era that the author used to write this book. Many are published and available in libraries or online. They include newspaper articles, memoirs, speeches, and articles written by Lathrop and about Lathrop. They also tell you about various reforms that occupied Lathrop's life's work. Some provide information about the work of other women reformers discussed in the book. For students particularly interested in the US Children's Bureau programs, there are many more government publications, including bureau pamphlets, available in libraries or online.

Addams, Jane. "A Great Public Servant, Julia C. Lathrop." *Social Service Review* 1, no. 2 (June 1932): 280–285.

———. *My Friend, Julia Lathrop.* Introduction by Anne Firor Scott. 1935: repr., Urbana: University of Illinois Press, 2004.

———. *Twenty Years at Hull House with Autobiographical Notes.* New York: Penguin Books, 1981 (c. 1910).

"Big Crowd Attends Suffrage Mass Meeting." *Evening Star,* October 12, 2015.

Bowen, Mrs. Joseph T. "The Early Days of the Juvenile Court." In *The Child, the Clinic and the Court.* By Jane Addams, C. Judson Herrick, A. L. Jacoby et al., 298–309. New York: The New Republic, 1925.

Bowen, Louise deKoven. *The Colored People of Chicago: An Investigation Made for the Juvenile Protection Association.* Juvenile Protective Association, 1913.

Breckinridge, Sophonisba Preston, and Edith Abbott. *The Delinquent Child and the Home*. Introduction by Julia C. Lathrop. New York: Survey Associates, 1912.

Brookings Institution, Institute for Government Research. *The Problem of Indian Administration: Report of a Survey Made at the Request of the Honorable Hubert Work, Secretary of the Interior, and Submitted to Him, February 21, 1928*. Baltimore, MD: Johns Hopkins University Press, 1928.

"Child Bureau Her Care." *New York Evening Post*, January 18, 1913.

Dart, Helen M. *Maternity and Infant Care in Selected Rural Areas of Mississippi*. Rural Child Welfare Series No. 5, Children's Bureau Publication No. 88. Washington, DC: US Government Printing Office, 1921.

Dubois, W. E. B. "Julia Lathrop." Postscripts, *The Crisis* 39 (June 1932): 190.

The Fiftieth Anniversary of the Opening of Vassar College, October 10 to 13, 1915: A Record. Poughkeepsie, New York. 1916.

Hackett, Francis. "Hull House—A Souvenir." *The Survey* 54 no. 5 (June 1, 1925): 275–280.

Hamilton, Alice. *Exploring the Dangerous Trades: The Autobiography of Alice Hamilton, M.D.* Boston: Little Brown and Company, 1943.

Kelley, Florence. *Notes of Sixty Years: The Autobiography of Florence Kelley*. Edited and introduced by Kathryn Kish Sklar. Chicago: Published for the Illinois Labor History Society by the C. H. Kerr Publishing Company, 1986.

Lathrop, Julia C. "The Background of the Juvenile Court in Illinois." In *The Child, the Clinic and the Court*. By Jane Addams, C. Judson Herrick, A. L. Jacoby et al., 290–297. New York: The New Republic, 1925.

———. "The Children's Bureau." Address to the Biannual Meeting of the General Federation of Women's Clubs. *American Journal of Sociology* 18, no. 3 (November 1912): 318–330.

———. "The Cook County Charities." *Hull House Maps and Papers: A Presentation of Nationalities and Wages in a Congested District of Chicago, Together with Comments and Essays on Problems Growing Out of the Social Conditions by the Residents of Hull House, a Social Settlement*. Introduction by Rima Lunin Schultz, 120–129. 1895; repr., Urbana and Chicago: University of Illinois Press, 2007.

———. "Hull House as a Sociological Laboratory." National Conference of Charities, Proceedings 1894, Twenty-First Annual Meeting. http://quod.lib.umich.edu/n/ncosw /ACH8650.1894.001? view=toc.

———. "Income and Infant Mortality." *American Journal Public Health* 9, no. 4, 270–274.

———. "The Military and Naval Insurance Act." *The Nation* 106 (February 7, 1918): 157–158.

———"Pass on the Torch." *Woman's Journal* 48, no. 51 (December 21, 1912): 402–403.

———. "Standards of Child Welfare." *Annals of the American Academy of Political and Social Science* 98 (November 1921): 1–8. http//jstor.org/stable1015037.

———. *Suggestions for Visitors to County Poorhouses and to Other Charitable Institutions*. Public Charities Committee of the Illinois Federation of Women's Clubs, 1905.

———. *Village Care for the Insane*. Reprinted from the Report of the Twenty-Ninth National Conference of Charities and Corrections. Boston: Geo. H. Ellis Co., 1902.

———. "What Next?" Speech at Sixth Annual Convention of the National League of Women Voters, Richmond, VA, April 16–22, 1925. Papers of the League of Women Voters, 1918–1974, Part II, Series A: Transcripts and Records of National Conventions, 1919–1944, and of General Councils, 1927–1943, Folder: 002634–006–0557 W 23, 2–4.

———. "What the Indian Service Needs." Official Proceedings of the Annual Meeting, 1930, National Conference of Social Workers, 95, 641–650. http://quod.lib.umich.edu/n/ncosw/ach8650.1930.001/658?view=text.

———. "What the Settlement Work Stands For." Twenty-Third National Conference of Charities, 1896. http://quod.lib.umich.edu/n/ncosw/ACH8650.1896.001?rgn=main;view=fulltext.

Linn, James Weber. *Jane Addams: A Biography.* New York: D. Appleton-Century Company, 1935.

Newell, Mary Connor. "America's First Official Mother." *Chicago Sunday-Record Herald,* May 19, 1912.

Sicherman, Barbara. *Alice Hamilton: A Life in Letters.* Cambridge, MA: Harvard University Press, 1984.

Wald, Lillian D. *The House on Henry Street.* New York: H. Holt and Company, 1915.

SELECTED SECONDARY SOURCES

The following books and articles, written by scholars, include work on Julia Lathrop and the women of Hull House and the Children's Bureau. There are also materials on activist women throughout Chicago. Additional sources are helpful for anyone interested in the Progressive Era more generally, the history of the juvenile court, the Children's Bureau, women's suffrage, women and higher education, women and the League of Nations, and the work of social feminists throughout the United States in the early twentieth century. This list includes studies that focus on gender, race, and ethnicity within progressive reform. There are also sources that deal with the conservative backlash against Lathrop and her colleagues.

Abel, Emily K. "Correspondence Between Julia C. Lathrop, Chief of the Children's Bureau and a Working-Class Woman, 1914–1915." *Journal of Women's History* 5, no. 1 (Spring 1993): 79–88.

Boris, Eileen. "The Power of Motherhood: Black and White Activist Women Redefine the 'Political.'" In *Mothers of a New World: Maternalist Politics and the Origins of Welfare States,* edited by Sonya Michel and Seth Koven, 213–245. New York: Routledge, 1993.

Brown, Victoria Bissell. "Jane Addams, Progressivism, and Woman Suffrage." In *One Woman, One Vote: Rediscovering the Woman Suffrage Movement,* edited by Marjorie Spruill Wheeler, 178–195. Troutdale, OR: New Sage Press, 1995.

Brown, Victoria Bissell. *The Education of Jane Addams.* Philadelphia: University of Pennsylvania Press, 2007.

Carson, Mina. *Settlement Folk: Social Thought and the American Settlement Movement, 1885–1930.* Chicago: University of Chicago Press, 1990.

Chatelain, Marcia. *South Side Girls: Growing Up in the Great Migration.* Durham, NC: Duke University Press, 2015.

Clapp, Elizabeth J. *Mothers of All Children: Women Reformers and the Rise of Juvenile Courts in Progressive Era America.* University Park: Pennsylvania State University Press, 1998.

Cohen, Miriam. "Women and the Progressive Movement." *History Now* 30 (Winter 2011). www.gilderlehrman.org/history-by-era/essays/women-and-progressive-movement.

Costin, Lela B. *Two Sisters for Social Justice: A Biography of Grace and Edith Abbott.* Urbana: University of Illinois Press, 1983.

Cott, Nancy F. *The Grounding of Modern Feminism.* New Haven, CT: Yale University Press, 1987.

Cronon, William. *Nature's Metropolis: Chicago and the Great West*. New York: W. W. Norton, 1991.

Dubois, Ellen Carol. "The IWSA/IAWSEC in the Age of the League of Nations." In *Women and Social Movements International, 1840–Present*, edited by Kathryn Kish Sklar and Thomas Dublin. http://wasi.alexanderstreet.com/help/view/the_iwsaiawsec _in_the_age_of_the_league_of_nations.

Edwards, Rebecca. *New Spirits: Americans in the Gilded Age 1865–1903*. New York: Oxford University Press, 2006.

Elsthain, Jean Betkhe. *Jane Addams and the Dream of American Democracy*. New York: Basic Books, 2002.

Fink, Leon. *Progressive Intellectuals and the Dilemmas of Democratic Commitment*. Cambridge, MA: Harvard University Press, 1997.

Fitzpatrick, Ellen. *Endless Crusade: Women Social Scientists and Progressive Reform*. New York: Oxford University Press, 1994.

Flanagan, Maureen A. *America Reformed: Progressives and Progressivisms, 1890s–1920s*. New York: Oxford University Press, 2007.

———. *Seeing with Their Hearts: Chicago Women and the Vision of the Good City, 1877–1933*. Princeton, NJ: Princeton University Press, 2002.

Fowler, Robert Booth. "Carrie Chapman Catt: Strategist." In *One Woman, One Vote: Rediscovering the Woman Suffrage Movement*, edited by Marjorie Spruill Wheeler, 295–314. Troutdale, OR: New Sage Press, 1995.

Frankel, Noralee, and Nancy S. Dye, eds. *Gender, Class, Race, and Reform in the Progressive Era*. Lexington: University Press of Kentucky, 1991.

Freedman, Estelle B. *Maternal Justice: Miriam Van Waters and the Female Reform Tradition*. Chicago: University of Chicago Press, 2003.

Getis, Victoria. *The Juvenile Court and the Progressives*. Urbana: University of Illinois Press, 2000.

Giddings, Paula. *Ida: A Sword Among Lions: Ida B. Wells and the Campaign Against Lynching*. New York: Amistad, 2008.

Goodwin, Joanne L. *Gender and the Politics of Welfare Reform: Mothers' Pensions in Chicago, 1911–1929*. Chicago: University of Chicago Press, 1997.

Gordon, Linda. *Pitied but Not Entitled: Single Women and the History of Welfare*. New York: The Free Press, 1994.

———. "Putting Children First: Women, Maternalism, and Welfare in the Early Twentieth Century." In *U.S. History as Women's History: New Feminist Essays*, edited by Linda Kerber, Alice Kessler-Harris, and Kathryn Kish Sklar, 63–86. Chapel Hill: University of North Carolina Press, 1995.

Gordon, Lynn D. *Gender and Higher Education in the Progressive Era*. New Haven, CT: Yale University Press, 1990.

Hicks, Cheryl D. *Talk with You Like a Woman: African American Women, Justice, and Reform in New York, 1890–1935*. Chapel Hill: University of North Carolina Press, 2010.

Horowitz, Helen Lefkowitz. *Alma Mater, Design and Experience in the Women's Colleges from Their Nineteenth Century Beginnings to the 1930s*. 1984; repr., Boston: Beacon Press, 1985.

Hoxie, Frederick E. "The Curious Story of Reformers and American Indians." In *Indians in American History: An Introduction*, edited by Frederick Hoxie and Peter Iverson, 205–228. Arlington Heights, IL: Harlan Davidson, 1988.

———. *This Indian Country*. New York: Penguin Books, 2013.

Jackson, Shannon. *Lines of Activity: Performance, Historiography, and Hull House Domesticity*. Ann Arbor: University of Michigan Press, 2003.

Jane Addams and the Practice of Democracy. Edited by Marilyn Fischer, Carol Nackenoff, and Wendy Chmielewski. Urbana: University of Illinois Press, 2009.

Johnson, Robert D. *The Radical Middle Class: Populist Democracy and the Question of Class in Portland, Oregon.* Princeton, NJ: Princeton University Press, 2003.

Knight, Louise W. *Citizen: Jane Addams and the Struggle for Democracy.* Chicago: University of Chicago Press, 2005.

Knupfer, Anne Meis. *Reform and Rebellion: Gender, Delinquency, and America's First Juvenile Court.* New York: Routledge, 2000.

———. *The Chicago Black Renaissance and Women's Activism.* University of Illinois Press, 2006.

Ladd-Taylor, Molly. *Mother-Work, Women, Child Welfare, and the State, 1890–1930.* Urbana: University of Illinois Press, 1994.

———. *Raising a Baby the Government Way, Mothers' Letters to the Children's Bureau, 1915–1932.* New Brunswick, NJ: Rutgers University Press, 1986.

Lasch-Quinn, Elisabeth. *Black Neighbors: Race and the Limits of Reform in the American Settlement House Movement.* Chapel Hill: University of North Carolina Press, 1993.

Lemons, J. Stanley. *The Woman Citizen: Social Feminism in the 1920s.* Urbana: University of Illinois Press, 1973.

Levenstein, Harvey A. *Revolution at the Table: The Transformation of the American Diet.* New York: Oxford University Press, 1988.

Lindenmeyer, Kristie. *"A Right to Childhood": The U.S. Children's Bureau and Child Welfare, 1912–1946.* Urbana: University of Illinois Press, 1997.

Lovett, Laura L. *Conceiving the Future: Pronatalism, Reproduction, and the Family in the United States, 1890–1938.* Chapel Hill: University of North Carolina Press, 2007.

Lunardini, Christine A. *Alice Paul: Equality for Women.* Boulder, CO: Westview Press, 2013.

McGerr, Michael E. *A Fierce Discontent: The Rise and Fall of the Progressive Movement in America 1870–1920.* New York: Free Press, 2003.

Michel, Sonya. "Maternalism and Beyond." In *Maternalism Reconsidered: Motherhood, Welfare and Social Policy in the Twentieth Century,* edited by Marian van der Klein et al., 22–37. New York, Oxford: Berghahn Books, 2014.

Muhammad, Khalil Gibran. *The Condemnation of Blackness: Race, Crime, and the Making of Modern Urban America.* Cambridge, MA: Harvard University Press, 2011.

Muncy, Robyn. *Creating a Female Dominion in American Reform, 1890–1935.* New York: Oxford University Press, 1991.

Nackenoff, Carol, and Kathleen S. Sullivan. "The House That Julia (and Friends) Built: Networking Chicago's Juvenile Court." In *Statebuilding from the Margins: Between Reconstruction and the New Deal,* edited by Carol Nackenoff and Julie Novkov, 171–202. Philadelphia: University of Pennsylvania Press, 2014.

Nielsen, Kim E. *Un-American Womanhood: Antiradicalism, Antifeminism, and the First Red Scare.* Columbus: Ohio State University Press, 2001.

Odem, Mary E. *Delinquent Daughters: Protecting and Policing Adolescent Female Sexuality in the United States, 1885–1920.* Chapel Hill: University of North Carolina Press, 1995.

Parker, Jacqueline K., and Edward M. Carpenter. "Julia Lathrop and the Children's Bureau: The Emergence of an Institution." *Social Service Review* 55, no. 1 (March 1981): 60–77.

Patton, Stacey. "The Richest Little Colored Girl in the World." *The Crisis* (Spring 2010): 31–34. http://bit.ly/2goIFn4.

Philpott, Thomas Lee. *The Slum and the Ghetto: Neighborhood Deterioration and Middle Class Reform in Chicago.* New York: Oxford University Press, 1978.

Rodgers, Daniel T. *Atlantic Crossings: Social Politics in a Progressive Age*. Cambridge, MA: Belknap Press of Harvard University Press, 1998.

Rodgers, Daniel T. "In Search of Progressivism." *Reviews in American History* 10, no. 4 (December 1982): 113–132.

Rusco, Elmer R. *A Fateful Time: The Background and Legislative History of the Indian Reorganization Act*. Reno: University of Nevada Press, 2000.

Sklar, Kathryn Kish. *Florence Kelley and the Nation's Work: The Rise of Women's Political Culture, 1830–1890*. New Haven, CT: Yale University Press, 1995.

———. "Hull House Maps and Papers: Social Science as Women's Work in the 1890s." In *Gender and American Social Science: The Formative Years*, edited by Helene Silverberg, 127–155. Princeton: Princeton University Press, 1998.

Sklar, Kathryn Kish, Anja Schüler, and Susan Strasser. "Introduction: A Transatlantic Dialogue." In *Social Justice Feminists in the United States and Germany*, edited by Kathryn Kish Sklar, Anja Schüler, and Susan Strasser, 1–75. Ithaca, NY: Cornell University Press, 1998.

Skocpol, Theda. *Protecting Soldiers and Mothers: The Political Origins of Social Policy in the United States*. Cambridge, MA: Belknap of Harvard University Press, 1992.

Stage, Sarah. "Ellen Richards and the Social Significance of the Home Economics Movement." In *Rethinking Home Economics: Women and the History of a Profession*, edited by Sarah Stage and Virginia B. Vincenti, 17–33. Ithaca, NY: Cornell University Press, 1997.

Stebner, Eleanor J. *The Women of Hull House: A Study in Spirituality, Vocation, and Friendship*. Albany: State University of New York Press, 1997.

Steinson, Barbara J. *American Women's Activism in World War I*. New York and London: Garland Publishing, 1982.

Stromquist, Shelton. *Reinventing "The People": The Progressive Movement, the Class Problem, and the Origins of Modern Liberalism*. Urbana: University of Illinois Press, 2006.

Tichi, Cecelia. *Civic Passions: Seven Who Launched Progressive America*. Chapel Hill: University of North Carolina Press, 2009.

Ward, Robert. "Against the Tide: The Preparedness Movement of 1923–1924." *Military Affairs* 38, no. 2 (April 1974): 59–61.

Weiss, Nancy Pottishman. "Save the Children: A History of the Children's Bureau, 1903–1918." PhD diss., University of California, Los Angeles, 1974.

Wheeler, Leigh Ann. *Against Obscenity: Reform and the Politics of Womanhood in America, 1873–1975*. Baltimore, MD: Johns Hopkins University, 2007.

Willrich, Michael. *City of Courts: Socializing Justice in Progressive Era Chicago*. New York: Cambridge University Press, 2003.

Wilson, Jan Doolittle. *The Women's Joint Congressional Committee and the Politics of Merternalism*. Urbana: University of Illinois Press, 2007.

INDEX

CPSIA information can be obtained
at www.ICGtesting.com
Printed in the USA
LVOW01s0620100217

523603LV00004B/4/P